FASHION POWER
THE MEANING OF FASHION IN AMERICAN SOCIETY

Jeanette C. Lauer
Robert H. Lauer

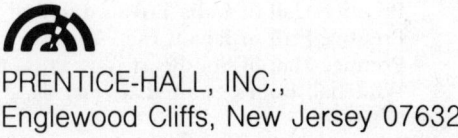

PRENTICE-HALL, INC.,
Englewood Cliffs, New Jersey 07632

Library of Congress Cataloging in Publication Data

Lauer, Jeanette C
 Fashion power.

(A Spectrum Book)
Includes bibliographical references and index.
 1. Fashion—Social aspects—United States.
 2. Fashion—United States—History.   I. Lauer, Robert H., joint author.   II. Title.
GT605.L38   391'.00973   80-27660
ISBN 0-13-306712-2
ISBN 0-13-306704-1 (pbk.)

To

Jon, Julie, and Jeff

© 1981 by Prentice-Hall, Inc., Englewood Cliffs, New Jersey 07632

A SPECTRUM BOOK

All rights reserved.
No part of this book may be reproduced
in any form or by any means
without permission in writing from the publisher.

10 9 8 7 6 5 4 3 2 1

Printed in the United States of America

Prentice-Hall International, Inc., *London*
Prentice-Hall of Australia Pty. Limited, *Sydney*
Prentice-Hall of Canada, Ltd., *Toronto*
Prentice-Hall of India Private Limited, *New Delhi*
Prentice-Hall of Japan, Inc., *Tokyo*
Prentice-Hall of Southeast Asia Pte. Ltd., *Singapore*
Whitehall Books Limited, *Wellington, New Zealand*

Table of Contents

Preface vii

Introduction: The Analysis of Fashion 1
  Functional Explanations of Fashion 3
    Fashion as the Search for Meaning and/or Identity . . . 3
    Fashion and the Struggle for Status 9
    The Economics of Fashion 15
  Dynamic Explanations of Fashion 18
    Fashion as Diffusion 19
    Cycles of Fashion 22
    Fashion as Erotic 24
    Fashion and the Zeitgeist 27
  Critique of Existing Theories 31
  Scope and Method of This Book 36

PART I   THE NATURE OF CLOTHES AND FASHION ... 47

CHAPTER 1   What Mean These Clothes? ... 48
Clothing as Nonverbal Communication ... 49
Clothing and Personality ... 53
Clothing and Moral Character ... 60
    Clothes and Immorality ... 63
    Immoral Women's Fashions ... 67
    Clothing and Morality ... 72
Clothing and Conformity ... 75
Clothing and Social Desirability ... 78
Clothes as an Indicator of Status ... 86
Clothing and Group Membership ... 91
Clothes and the State of the Nation ... 94
Conclusions ... 98

CHAPTER 2   What Is Fashion? ... 113
Meaning and Metaphor ... 114
Metaphors of Power ... 116
    Force ... 116
    Tyranny ... 120
    Royalty ... 127
    Divinity ... 128
Metaphors of Nonrationality ... 132
    Irrationality ... 132
    Mystery ... 141
    Deviousness ... 143
Patterns of Usage ... 145
Conclusion ... 149

PART II   FASHION AND SOCIAL LIFE ... 225

CHAPTER 3   Fashion and Human Nature ... 226
The Nature of Males and Females ... 226
    Gender or Role? ... 227
    The Traditional Female Role ... 229
    Fashion and Sex Roles ... 234

Fashion as Revelation: Qualities of the Sexes 235
   The Life of Reason 235
   The Life of Submissiveness 242
   The Ornamental Sex 246
   The Superior Sex 249
Fashion and the Maintenance of Sex Roles 265
   Harmonizing Nature and Appearance 266
   Clothes as Masculine and Feminine 273
Conclusion 279

CHAPTER 4 Fashion and the Nature of Society 289
Fashion and Social Norms 290
Society Versus the Individual 307
   Fashion as a Coercive Social Fact 309
   Fashion as a Human Enterprise 313
Society as a Zero-Sum Game 324
   In Her Place 328
   "Making It" Through Fashion 335
Conclusion 345

CHAPTER 5 Fashion and National Identity 355
The Meaning of America's National Identity 356
   The Struggle for Identity 357
   Identity as Shared Beliefs 358
Distinctive Fashions for a Unique People 363
   The Need for American Fashions 365
   Dressing the Strong and Virtuous 368
The War for Independence Á La Mode 378
   Let Lovers of Liberty Join Hands 378
   The Virtues of Rebellion 381
   The Fitful Course of War 389
Conclusion 400

CHAPTER 6 The Social Consequences of Fashion 408
Fashion and Physical and Mental Well-Being 409
   Protection Versus Exposure: A Dilemma 410
   The Hazards of Hats 414
   Can You Be Both Fashionable and Healthy? 431
The Economic Consequences of Fashion 431

Fashion and Personal Growth and Fulfillment 447
   The Older View—Fashion as an Impediment 448
   May I Present—Me! 450
   I Am Beautiful 453
   I Can Lick the World 456
Conclusion 462

PART III   A THEORY OF FASHION 473

CHAPTER 7   Fashion, Ideology, and Change 474
Fashion and Change 474
   The Seal of Fashion 475
   Fashion as a Tool of Change 479
Fashion and Ideology 483
A Case Study: The Bloomer Costume 485
The Function of Ideologies in Fashion Change 507
A Theory of Fashion 511
Conclusion 515
Index 569

Preface

William James has said somewhere that humans are composed of three parts—body, soul, and clothes. Although his observation may have been made with tongue in cheek, it underscores a fact of social life, namely, that mode of dress is of central importance. Our interest in the topic was stimulated by our study of the controversy over the Bloomer costume in the 1850s. We were intrigued by the fact that a proposed new fashion could be front page news throughout the nation and generate such intense emotion and conflict. (The story of that conflict will be found in the last chapter.) It led us to investigate further the phenomenon of fashion in American life. We found that descriptions of fashion abound, but that analyses are rare. We offer, therefore, our own analysis of a fascinating facet of social life. It is the result of our reading roughly one thousand professional and popular accounts in books, articles, and newspapers. We believe it provides a comprehensive analysis of the meaning of fashion in American life over the past two centuries.

We are grateful to Lynne Lumsden, of Prentice-Hall, for her support of this project. Finally, we are grateful to our children, to whom this book is dedicated, who always support our endeavors by their pride in our work. They help us understand why, through all the convulsive history of mankind, children have never been out of fashion.

Introduction: The Analysis of Fashion

Fashion has been called, among other things, a tyrant, a despot, a god, and a mystery. As the symbols suggest, observers have been impressed with the impact of fashion on social life. The influence of fashion continues through both the calamities and the prosperities. Neither wars nor depressions have stayed people's interest in what is new in the world of fashion. For example, a study of Muncie, Indiana during the Great Depression, found that the adverse economic conditions did not quell the concern for proper attire:

> The same crowds of wilted people wearing shoes half-soled for thirty-nine cents were thrilling in 1935 to the parade of Grecian sandals from a local "classy boot shop" and to crisp white mess jackets for men's evening wear. . . . The detailed newspaper descriptions of gowns worn at the sorority dances throughout the

depression might have been lifted verbatim, save for certain fashion changes, from the papers of 1925.[1]

Similarly, a writer in *The New Republic* in 1932 remarked that the corset industry was "flourishing at a rate to make the presidents of cordtire companies, steel mills, and cement works bilious with envy."[2] In other words, the concern with fashion remains high throughout the vicissitudes of social life. As van Loon put it.:

> Empires may come and go. Kingdoms may arise and may perish again. Dynasties may reach the highest pinnacle of fame and may sink again into oblivion and cities may be built, grow rich and prosperous and then be wiped out without so much as leaving a trace of their existence, but Fashion will carry on as if nothing more serious had happened than a fire in a small shoe store on some mean side street or a flood which had perhaps inundated a couple of cellars in one of the outlying suburbs.[3]

Popular commentators and social scientists alike have found the topic of fashion to be significant but perplexing, challenging but frustrating. Fashion has been analyzed and explained in diverse ways. It has been lauded and denounced. It has been proclaimed the tyrant of humanity and shrugged off as inconsequential. Some observers have written about the laws of fashion, while others have insisted that the Dame follows no laws but her own whims. We shall begin our own quest for understanding by examining the various explanations of fashion which have been set forth by social scientists. Interestingly, most of these explanations also appear in the popular literature (though not necessarily in the fully developed form of the social scientists), and typically they appeared in the popular media before they were propounded by social scientists. These explanations fall into two broad categories—functional and dynamic.

FUNCTIONAL EXPLANATIONS OF FASHION

Functional explanations of fashion focus on its social consequences. Functionalists argue that a phenomenon such as fashion can be understood in terms of what it does in a society rather than in terms of its origins or causes. The essential question is not how fashions begin and spread, but what functions they serve, what purposes they fulfill, and what consequences they have. The consequences identified by various observers may be primarily individual, institutional, or societal. The consequences are not confined to one level of social reality, of course, but theorists tend to emphasize the functions of fashion at a particular level.

Fashion as the Search for Meaning and/or Identity

One way to look at fashion is in terms of its functions for the individual who is searching for meaning in his or her existence, or who is striving to establish his or her identity. According to Klapp, both fad and fashion "symptomatize a restlessness about identity which is becoming characteristic of much of the modern world"; even in fashion's "most frivolous and desperate searches for novelty" we encounter "not mere sensationalism but a search for meaning."[4] People pursue fashion because they are attempting to construct a more fulfilling life. People strive to discover who they really are, and to express their real selves in various ways, including the expression of self through the selection of fashion. Underlying such a use of fashion is the problematic nature of individual identity in mass society. Because we live in a mass society, the function of fashion has shifted "from class maintenance by status symbols to identity seeking by ego symbols."[5]

The functional significance of fashion for the individual was emphasized earlier by Simmel and Sapir. Simmel, who is normally associated with the "trickle-down" theory of fashion, based his discussion on the assumption of two opposing tendencies in human life—our need to conform to the group and our need to express ourselves as individuals.[6] The need to conform is maintained by imitation. Since fashion always involves imitation, it satisfies our need to conform. At the same time, it satisfies our need for individualization. It marks us as conventional members of a particular group while it simultaneously differentiates us from those who are outside that group (that is, those who do not adopt the fashion).

There are a number of historical instances where the two opposing tendencies may not be present. In such cases, Simmel notes, there will be no fashion. For instance, in isolated, preindustrial societies, there is a "deep-rooted distrust" of the novel, and little or no interest in individualization. Such societies lack fashion. On the other hand, the nature of modern society increases the need for fashion and facilitates the continual change of fashion.

In contrast to Simmel, Sapir focused essentially on one function of fashion for the individual—its "symbolic significance for the expression of the ego."[7] Fashion, according to Sapir, functions as a symbol either of "personal distinction" or of membership in a group that has distinction. Thus, individuals use fashion to enhance themselves and their attractiveness to others. Whether the particular fashion in question refers to clothing, art, recreation, morals, or something else, there is a close, intimate linkage with the ego.

The most recent theorist to stress the role of fashion in the meaning of the individual's life is König.[8] He argues that there are a number of aspects of human nature that underlie the potency of fashion as a social phenomenon. These basic aspects of human nature, however, can be seen in terms of the individual's search for identity and meaning. For König views humans as creatures who are disposed to display their bodies in order to be attractive to others, to present themselves in a way that will gain them recognition, and to secure the awareness and approval of their individuality by others. Fashion is used by individuals in the ongoing effort to establish their own identity, delineate their own distinctiveness, and enhance the meaning of their lives.

There is some empirical evidence to support the arguments of those who view fashion as functional for individual identity and meaning. In his study of clothing, Stone found that people use their mode of dress to establish a particular identity and to give indications of their value and mood.[9] In many cases, the identity is related to the individual's occupation. For example, Stone reported a real estate operator's response to the question of whether he preferred more or less variety in the clothes he wore while working: "A small variety so you will look the same everyday. So people will identify you. They look for the same old landmark."[10]

Individuals may also manipulate their style of dress in order to stress the point that they are not committed wholly to one particular identity. Goffman noted this in his discussion of "role distance," which is the gap between the obligations of a role and the individual's actual performance. The individual is not denying the role, but "the virtual self that is implied in the role for all accepting performers."[11] He gives the examples of the young psychiatrist in a state mental hospital who wears an open shirt in order to express sympathy for patients and distance from an administrative medical role; and the housemaid who will wear a uniform but not confine her hair under a cap, in order to partially reject the occupation and affirm her femininity.[12]

An extensive study was made of the relationship between clothing styles and identity by Julia Reed.[13] She developed a measure which could be used to divide individuals into four groups: high-fashion, low-fashion, nonfashion, and counter-fashion. A total of 221 respondents, all female university students, were placed into these four groups and compared in terms of forty-nine dependent variables. The dependent variables were combined into four groups: identity, attitudes, values, and moods or personality. In general, she found that there were differences in the dependent variables between all four types of fashion groups. For example, if we compare the high-fashion group with the others, we find that the high-fashions differ in various ways from each of the other groups. Compared to the low-fashions, the high-fashions see themselves to be more formal; have a greater preference for social climbing, for conservatism, and for being sophisticated; and are more self-assured. Compared to the nonfashions, the high-fashions see themselves to be more sophisticated and individualistic; have a greater preference for being leaders; give more importance to religious activities; and are lower in Machiavellian tactics. Compared to the counter-fashions, finally, the high-fashions see themselves to be more formal, sophisticated, and expedient; have a greater preference to be attractive and self-assured; and are more dogmatic but lower in Machiavellian cynicism.[14]

The above differences are illustrative of the large number found by Reed. They show how fashion expresses something about individual identity and meaning. Of course, a particular clothing style is only a part of the total means of expression used by an individual, but in some cases it may be critically important. A chief of the Lakota Indians noted how mode of dress can be crucial to an individual's identity and meaning when he recalled the days he spent in a white man's school:

> The clothing of the white man, adopted by the Lakota, had much to do with the physical welfare of the tribe, and at Carlisle School where the change from tribal to white man's clothing was sudden and direct, the effect on the health and comfort of the children was considerable. . . . According to the white man, the Indian, choosing to return to his tribal manners and dress, "goes back to the blanket." True, but "going back to the blanket" is the factor that has saved him from, or at least stayed, his final destruction. . . . To clothe a man falsely is only to distress his spirit and to make him incongruous and ridiculous, and my entreaty to the American Indian is to retain his tribal dress.[15]

An individual may select a particular style, or may be coerced into wearing a particular style. In either case, the mode of dress will have an impact upon that individual's identity and the meaning of his or her existence.

Fashion and the Struggle for Status

A second way in which fashion is functional, both for the individual and for groups, relates to social and sexual competition—the struggle to enhance one's status. A number of theorists have analyzed fashion as a tool that is used to gain advantages over others in the competition. As J. C. Flugel put it, "there can be little doubt that the ultimate and essential cause of fashion lies in competition." That competition is both social and sexual, with the social elements being "more obvious and manifest" while the sexual elements are "more indirect, concealed and unavowed, hiding themselves, as it were, behind the social ones."[16]

Like Flugel, a number of observers have pointed out that people use fashion to indicate their rank, their wealth, and their power, and also to enhance their sexual appeal. These functions apply to all aspects of fashion, that is, to all those methods and accouterments that go into the process of making the individual ready for a public appearance, including the competitive use of cosmetics and other kinds of grooming:

> A woman grooms herself to appear as a desirable sexual object, not necessarily as an attainable one. In grooming herself, she is

preparing to play the part of the *beauty,* not the part of the erotically passionate woman. In this sense, cosmetics and grooming serve to transmute the attraction between the sexes from a raw physical relationship into a civilized *game.*[17]

In discussing fashion as a competitive phenomenon, Flugel also noted the way in which fashion becomes involved in the struggle between social classes. He argued that it is a fundamental human trait to imitate those we admire or envy. Normally, that means we imitate those who are above us in the class hierarchy. And what is "more natural, and at the same time, more symbolic, than to start the process of imitation by copying their clothes, the very insignia of the admired and envied qualities?"[18] But those in the higher classes are not willing to have their symbols of superiority appropriated by those beneath them. They can maintain their insignia of superiority in two ways: through sumptuary laws or by abandoning the styles which are being copied by the lower classes. Sumptuary laws are no longer a viable option. The uppers therefore adopt new styles in order to maintain the distinction between themselves and those beneath them. "And thus fashion is born."[19]

This, of course, is the familiar "trickle-down" theory of fashion. The theory can be traced back to Spencer, Veblen, and Simmel. Spencer argued that fashion is "intrinsically imitative," and that imitation can arise from two different motives: "It may be prompted by reverence for one imitated, or it may be prompted by the desire to assert equality with him."[20] Spencer believed the net effect of fashion was to enhance equalitarianism in the society. "Serving to obscure, and eventually to obliterate, the marks of class distinction, it has favoured the growth of individuality; and by so doing has aided in weakening the Ceremonial, which implies subordination of the individual."[21]

Veblen, on the other hand, saw clothing styles as maintaining rather than diminishing class distinctions. He tied in dress with his ideas about conspicuous consumption among the leisure class. In a magazine article, he wrote that in the most advanced societies

> it has (ideally) become the great, peculiar, and almost the sole function of woman in the social system to put in evidence her economic unit's ability to pay. That is to say, woman's place . . .

has come to be that of a means of conspicuously unproductive expenditure. . . . "Dress," therefore, from the economic point of view, comes pretty near being synonymous with "display of wasteful expenditure."[22]

Furthermore, the display of wasteful expenditure can be achieved not simply by expensive clothes, but by the continual adoption of new styles of expensive clothes (in other words, by fashion changes). Fashion, therefore, is built upon the principle of conspicuous waste. The upper-class individual uses fashion to maintain class distinctions. The lower-class individual tries to emulate the life style of the uppers, but is inevitably thwarted by the lack of resources and by the constantly changing styles.

More recently, Bernard Barber combined the notions of Spencer and Veblen and argued that fashion helps both to maintain class distinctions and also to support America's ideological equalitarianism.[23] The basic features of women's clothes, he wrote, are similar for all classes. Hem length, general form, and colors may be quite similar among all classes, thereby giving the appearance of equality, but there are also subtle differences that symbolize varying social class positions. These differences may involve material or workmanship or timing. Timing is particularly important. New fashions are adopted first by those in the upper class. Gradually, the fashions trickle down to those in the lower classes. By the time the fashion has reached the bottom, those at the top have adopted a new fashion, the symbol of their superior position. "And thus is the social fact of social class difference manifested, as well as the ideology of equalitarianism."[24]

Again, those who analyze fashion as competitive behavior in general, or a trickle-down phenomenon in particular, have some empirical support for their position. People do use clothing to compete with each other socially and sexually. In a 1950 study of a group of college females, Cobliner reported that the young women dressed against each other. That is, they were striving to achieve status and prestige within their peer groups.[25]

People of a lower status can also use clothing in an effort to enhance their status or to challenge the existing status structure. Schwartz reported that black males spent more for clothes than did white males at all income levels in 1950. He examined clothing ads in black and white magazines, and also studied some haberdasheries

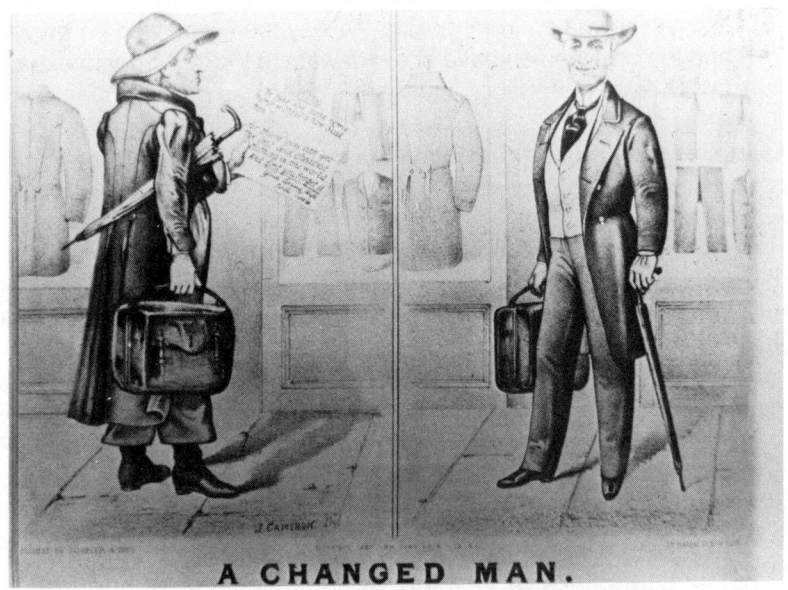

A CHANGED MAN.

FIG. 1. An 1880 Currier & Ives print shows how clothes can enhance a man's status. (*Source: Claudia B. Kidwell and Margaret C. Cristman,* Suiting Everyone.)

in Chicago, to find clues on the spending differences. The ads suggested that blacks are more likely than whites to be concerned with the social advantages of particular clothes rather than with such physical qualities as comfort or durability. Furthermore, many of the items sold to blacks (both in the ads and in the stores) were higher in price than those offered to whites. As a result of these findings, Schwartz suggested that the individual black is more concerned than the individual white to use clothes to enhance his status.[26]

Similarly, in their analysis of the bra-burning incidents of the late 1960s, Morrison and Holden argued that an action that appeared silly or ridiculous to some observers could have reasonably had an important meaning to the participants:

> Substantively, de-emphasizing the breasts, and erotic de-emphasis in general, are not attempts to make women look like men (an accusation leveled at the earlier movement) or even an attempt

to prevent women from looking like women. They are attempts to prevent women from looking the way men want women to look and the way women have come to want to look *in order* to extract favors from men rather than relate to men as equals.[27]

As in the case of black males, the bra-burning incidents can be seen as an effort on the part of women to enhance their status, to stake a claim to equality.

Of course, one of the reasons mode of dress can be used in status-striving behavior is that we tend to evaluate each other by such things as clothing (a point that will be elaborated in the next chapter). Hoult showed in a early study that clothing was quite important to a group of students in judging the "attractiveness" of various male strangers.[28] Various other studies have shown that people relate to strangers in different ways depending upon the mode of dress.[29] Fashion has a social significance that enables the individual or a group to manipulate dress in order to maintain or change a status.

The Economics of Fashion

The last approach to the study of fashion that focuses on the functional significance is economic. Some theorists have looked at fashion as essentially an economic phenomenon. In fact, Veblen gave an essentially economic interpretation to fashion. As noted, he regarded fashion as one of the means by which the leisure class could demonstrate their affluence. The clothing worn by those in the upper classes were not only expensive but were dysfunctional for any productive purposes. In other words, the elite not only showed how much they could spend on clothing, but also demonstrated the fact that they did not have to engage in common labor. What people defined as "charming" in fashions—patent-leather shoes, linen, and lustrous cylindrical hat, and the gentleman's walking stick—were those things that indicated "that the wearer cannot when so attired bear a hand in any employment that is directly and immediately of any human use."[30]

Affluent men showed their wealth by displaying lavishly dressed wives. Such women were, of course, totally dependent in an economic sense upon their husbands. This, argued Veblen, meant they were the property of their husbands, who used them for display. "The homely reason for all this conspicuous leisure and attire on the part of women lies in the fact that they are servants to whom, in the differentiation of economic functions, has been delegated the office of putting in evidence their master's ability to pay."[31] The net economic effect of fashion for the entire society, therefore, was negative. Fashion, like many other pursuits of the leisure class, diminished efficiency and helped maintain social inequalities.

Veblen's argument that fashion has deleterious economic consequences was echoed half a century later by another radical analyst, Paul Gregory.[32] According to Gregory, sellers use brands, trademarks, and distinctive styles to try to sell at a higher price than their competitors. Through fashion, however, they attempt to sell more frequently than their competitors. Fashion limits consumer choices more than does brand differentiation because merchants will not carry goods that are considered unfashionable even if there is some demand for them. Fashion is also wasteful because new styles come out while the old styles are still quite usable. We discard goods not because they are worn or uncomfortable or unattractive, but simply because they are no longer considered fashionable. Finally, frequent changes in fashion show that we do not really have a true competitive system. Without the frequent changes, competition would take the form of price cutting, or improved quality, or both. Instead of reduced prices or improved quality, however, we have an effort to increase sales through changing styles. " 'New' fashions seldom change the product; they change the mind of the buyer."[33]

In spite of such radical critiques, and the obvious bearing of fashion on the economy, economists have dealt very little with the economic consequences of fashion.[34] One economist who has, Dwight Robinson, pointed out that fashion has some unique economic ramifications. Unlike any other kind of demand, fashion exploits the "versatility or partial fluidity of the factors of production in order to demonstrate command over currently disposable factors of production."[35] In other words, fashion means that the consumer pays—willingly—for impermanence, for the stamp of recency upon goods. This comes very near to what Veblen argued. In fact, Robinson asserts that people value scarce goods for their symbolic value, and that an important factor in purchases is the extent to which goods can be conveniently displayed. But where Veblen viewed the phenomenon of fashion with contempt and with dire statements about its undesirable consequences, Robinson simply says that economists may find themselves undergoing a kind of quasi-Copernican revolution if they begin to take fashion demand seriously.

One could argue that there are positive as well as negative economic consequences to fashion. After all, a considerable number of jobs are involved in the fashion business, many of which would be eliminated if styles were to become stable. The overall consequences of fashion for the economy, therefore, are complex and debatable. They are also quite significant.

DYNAMIC EXPLANATIONS OF FASHION

Dynamic explanations focus on fashion as a pattern of change. Thus, dynamic explanations address a different set of questions than functional explanations. Theorists who fall into the latter category explore the questions of the individual and social consequences of fashion, and of the motivations to be fashionable. Theorists who fall into the category of dynamic explanation explore the problem of how fashion changes or why it changes in a particular way.

Fashion as Diffusion

Anthropologists and sociologists have long been interested in the phenomenon of diffusion. A pioneering work was provided by the French sociologist, Gabriel Tarde, who wrote a work on "imitation" in 1890. By imitation, Tarde referred to the adoption of innovations. He tried to establish the laws by which innovations diffuse and are adopted. But the classic work in the study of the diffusion and adoption of innovations was not produced until 1962 when Everett Rogers published his review and synthesis of over 500 publications.[36] Rogers defined an innovation as any idea or any thing that is perceived as new. He identified four crucial elements in the process of diffusion and innovation: the innovation itself; the communication of the innovation; the social system in which the process occurs; and certain temporal aspects (in particular, the fact that different kinds of people adopt an innovation at different stages of the process).

Fashion may be analyzed as an innovation, and the spread of a fashion throughout a population may be explored using the various concepts employed in the study of the diffusion and adoption of innovations. Actually, the trickle-down theory could be seen as a form of diffusion theory, for it posits the spread of fashion as occurring from the upper to the lower classes. But the primary focus of trickle-down theory is the functional aspect of fashion rather than the pattern of change. The trickle-down theorist emphasizes the functions of fashion in the struggle for status.

To analyze fashion in terms of diffusion and adoption means to treat it as any other innovation and explore those factors that account for the spread, or lack of spread, of a new fashion. To refer back to the four crucial elements identified by Rogers, we could first examine characteristics of the fashion itself, such as its perceived compatibility with existing values and needs. We would not expect fashions that are defined as contradictory to our values—like "masculine" clothing on women—to be widely accepted. Second, we could explore the way in which fashion is communicated through the population. Diffusion studies have found that those who initially adopt an innovation—Rogers called them the innovators and early adopters—are primarily influenced by the mass media. The innovation diffuses to the rest of the population primarily by the interpersonal influence of the innovators and early adopters.

A third set of factors to examine are those in the social system, particularly the activities of change agents (such as advertisers and others who seek to get people to accept a new fashion) and opinion leaders (those individuals who are influential in the evaluation of new fashions). Finally, we could look at the reactions of those people who must first adopt, or refuse to adopt, the new fashion—the innovators and early adopters in a community who are key personnel in persuading others to accept or reject an innovation.

Using the diffusion and adoption approach, Grindereng looked at sales data from a department store and also obtained information from customers who had purchased items from the store.[37] She focused on the nature of the adopters in order to assess the trickle-down theory versus diffusion and adoption. She found that the pattern of use did not fit trickle-down theory. The new fashions were not first purchased by high-status individuals only, with subsequent sales being made to those from lower and lower status groups. Rather, she found fashion leaders (early adopters) in various social classes, so the pattern of diffusion was one of a simultaneous adoption across the strata and spread within strata, rather than adoption from the upper to the lower strata.

Diffusion and adoption theory has also been used to explain the lack of adoption of a new fashion. Reynolds and Darden investigated the failure of the "midi" skirt in the early 1970s as an instance of a rejected innovation.[38] They had identified a set of innovators and early adopters before the midi arrived in the stores (the initial adopters may be identified through such characteristics as education, attitude to change, and exposure to the mass media). The innovators and early adopters were then asked about their intention to purchase the midi, and the answers were largely negative. The researchers concluded that the midi would fail, since acceptance by innovators and early adopters is crucial to the success of an innovation. The new style did, in fact, fail, and a follow-up survey showed that the majority of innovators and early adopters had not purchased the midi. The new fashion did not diffuse because, in accord with diffusion and adoption theory, those people who must initially adopt it did not do so. Reynolds and Darden concluded, like Grindereng, that diffusion theory is more applicable to clothing fashions than is the trickle-down theory. Fashions are not adopted or rejected solely on the basis of how people in the upper socioeconomic strata respond to them.

Cycles of Fashion

The second dynamic approach to the study of fashion is the cyclic. One of the more well-known exponents of the cyclic nature of fashion was the anthropologist, A. L. Kroeber. On the basis of his study of changing fashions in women's dress, Kroeber argued that not only clothing styles, but civilization itself, must be seen as a rhythmic phenomenon, one that has "an existence, an order, and a causality as objective and as determinable as those of the subpsychic or inorganic."[39] With respect to women's fashions in particular, Kroeber found cycles of change over a long period of time, in such things as the width and length of skirts, diameter and length of waists, and decolletage. He pointed out that the rhythms of change could not be explained by particular individuals, for when "a swing of fashion requires a century for its satisfaction, a minimum of at least several personalities is involved."[40] Like others who have identified cycles

FIG. 2. Recurring cycles of the (a) back-fullness, (b) tubular, and (c) bell-shaped contours. (*Source: Agnes Brooks Young,* Recurring Cycles of Fashion, 1760–1937 *(New York: Cooper Square Publishers, 1966), pp. 14–16.*) Used by permission.

in social life, Kroeber viewed the social process as possessing a dynamic of its own that is independent of the will or the actions of particular individuals.[41]

Form as well as quantity has been used to identify cycles in female dress fashions. Young examined the form of skirts from 1760 to 1937.[42] She categorized all skirts into three fundamental types: the bell-shaped, back-fullness, and tubular contours. The bell-shaped skirt is illustrated by the hoop skirt that was fashionable around the time of the Civil War. The back-fullness contour was most strikingly represented by the bustle. The tubular contour was prominent in the "flapper" dress of the 1920s. By examining silhouettes of the changing styles over the 178-year period, Young concluded that women's fashions move through a series of recurring cycles. Each cycle lasts for about a third of a century. During a particular cycle, there will be annual changes, but the changes will be variations of the fundamental type. And for the period of her study, there were only the three basic types "which have succeeded one another in unchanging sequence over the past two centuries."[43]

Fashions other than those in female dress have been analyzed in cyclic terms. Robinson found a cyclical pattern in the changing fashions in shaving and trimming beards among English men from 1842 to 1972.[44] In fact, he found a close correlation between the cycles of skirt width measured by Kroeber and the cycles of beard frequencies (percentage of men having beards). Robinson points out that the invention and introduction of the safety razor had little effect on the cyclic pattern. Like Kroeber, he sees fashion as a process that operates in accord with its own dynamic:

> . . . fashion cycles display a regularity that puts them effectively outside the influence of external events. World War I had no discernible effect on the skirt width cycle; neither did that war disrupt the mode of shaving popular among men. Once a new fashion trend is set in motion, there is little—whether it be technological innovation, political edict, functional change, even basic economics—that can be done to stop it or change its course.[45]

Fashion as Erotic

James Laver, the noted historian of clothing and fashion, has argued that there are three principles that govern dress. First, there is the hierarchical principle, which states that people dress for status. Second is the utility principle, which says that people use dress for such things as warmth and protection from the elements. And the third principle is seduction, which states that we dress in order to attract those of the opposite sex. On the whole, says Laver, women's fashions follow the seduction principle. People have often assumed that clothes are worn for protection and as an expression of morality or modesty. Not so, says Laver, for "modesty is not the cause of clothing but its effect."[46] For instance, a woman does not cover her breasts because she is modest. Rather, she is modest because she has covered her breasts. After all, there are societies in which the breasts are never covered, and the people in those societies are not less moral or less modest than we are.

So far, our discussion of the erotic nature of fashion would seem to be a functional rather than a dynamic explanation. That is, the consequence of a particular fashion is that some portion of the female anatomy is defined as seductive. The explanation becomes dynamic, however, because it stresses the point that the part of the anatomy defined as erotic changes from one time to another. Psychologists have called this the "shifting erogenous zone" theory of fashion. As the psychoanalyst, Edmund Bergler, put it, fashion is basically "a series of permutations of seven basic themes, each theme being a part of the female body. . . . Parts of the body "appear" and "disappear" as the theme of fashion changes."[47] At one time the fashions may emphasize and partially expose the breasts. At another time the breasts will be covered and the fashion will focus attention on the legs. And so forth.

But why is it necessary to keep shifting the focus of attention? In the first place, according to the theorists, a woman is a desirable sexual object for a man, but he cannot focus his attention on the entire person. In order to maximize sexual attraction, the woman dresses in a way to secure the man's attention upon one part of her body. But in time the effect of a particular part diminishes so that she must shift the erogenous zone. As with anything else, novelty maximizes the appeal.

We can find empirical support for this theory as we have found for each of the others. We can, for example, trace out the extent to which various parts of the female body have been exposed or emphasized. A psychiatrist has noted the changes during recent decades:

> The mammaries were the wow of the fifties, the emphasis being on size. The buttocks were emphasized by tight skirts. Miniskirts shifted interest to the legs, and today was see renewed interest in the breasts, particularly the nipples, in the braless look.[48]

If we go back even further through history, we find considerable variations in ideas about what should and should not be exposed. At one time it was appropriate for a woman to expose her breasts but not her ankles. At other times she might expose her ankles but not her breasts. Some fashions have emphasized breasts (the "sweater girl" look), or the buttocks (the bustle), while others have de-emphasized them (the flapper). Bare legs, bare shoulders, and bare breasts have all been considered indecent at some times and fashionable at other times.

Laver gives an interesting personal illustration of the accuracy of the shifting erogenous zone theory. He says that in 1925 he noted in his diary that he found the newly exposed legs of women to be exciting. By 1930, "legs were a bore, and attention had to be directed elsewhere."[49] By the same token, the dress which was a bore by 1930 would have been declared indecent in 1915. Thus, fashion may be likened to "a game of hide-and-seek between seduction and prudery, and nothing is more astonishing than the things prudery finds itself able to accept, once it has grown used to them."[50]

Fashion and the Zeitgeist

The final dynamic explanation of fashion that we will discuss simply says that fashion, like every facet of culture, is a reflection of the Zeitgeist, the spirit of the times. In order to understand the changing fashions we must understand the changing society. For the clothes of a period are "significant expressions of the interrelation" of the various elements of the culture, including "the social and religious philosophies (as dress serves to symbolize them), the taste of an age, the economic and industrial progress, the development of dressmaking as a craft."[51]

If clothes express the spirit of the age, it follows that we can use changing fashions as an indication of a changing society. That is, one way to identify the point at which significant change is occurring is to note the important changes in fashion. As Clerget has argued, "a new style of dress is the visible sign that a transformation is taking place in the intellect, customs, and business of a people."[52] He gives the example of the adoption of European costume and the rejection of plaited hair during the rise of the Chinese Republic. Clerget also quotes Taine's observation that the advent of trousers marked the greatest change in history, the passing of Greek and Roman civilization into the modern. For nothing is more resistant to change than daily custom. In order to radically change customary dress, there must be a fundamental change in people. Therefore, the transition from the robes of the classical world to the trousers of the modern world represents a basic change both in civilization and in the people who comprise that civilization.

The notion that fashion is related to the spirit of the times is a very broad one. An analyst could hold both to it and to another theory simultaneously. For instance, although Flugel stressed social and sexual competition as the basis for any particular fashion, he also agreed that clothing fashions show a certain parallelism with such other fashions as architecture and interior decoration. This is because new fashions, whether in clothing or anything else, "if they are to be successful, must be in accordance with certain ideals current at the time that they are launched."[53] Social and sexual competition must be seen as operating within the broader framework of ideals, and any particular fashion is the outcome of both the ideals and the competition.

Similarly, Laver affirmed the importance of the Zeitgeist as a kind of broader framework within which the hierarchical, utility, and seduction principles work:

> In every period costume has some essential line, and when we look back over the fashions of the past we can see quite clearly what it is, and can see what is surely very strange, that the forms of dresses, apparently so haphazard, so dependent on the whim of the designer, have an extraordinary relevance to the spirit of the age. The aristocratic stiffness of the old regime in France is completely mirrored in the brocaded gowns of the eighteenth century. . . . Victorian modesty expressed itself in a multitude of petticoats, the emancipation of the post-War flapper in short hair and short skirts. We touch here something very mysterious, as if the Time Spirit were a reality, clothing itself ever in the most suitable garments and rejecting all others.[54]

It is not difficult to gather some evidence to support the notion that changing fashions reflect changes in societies. Indeed, it would be hard to dispute the argument that clothing, like everything else, reflects its age. One could use the changing fashions in clothing to help characterize the broad sweep of Western history. But even at a more micro level, there are instances of fashion changes that accompany basic social changes. Thus, Bush and London use the case of the disappearance of knickers to argue that fundamental changes in mode of dress indicate changing social roles and self-concepts within a particular society.[55] That which is in accord with the spirit of one age is completely discordant with the spirit of a new age. The mode of dress that is outrageous at one point in time may be considered typical at a later time. Or as Laver put it in his oft-quoted formula:

> . . . the same dress is indecent ten years before its time, daring one year before its time, chic (chic being defined as contemporary seductiveness) in its time, dowdy three years after its time, hideous twenty years after its time, amusing thirty years after its time, romantic a hundred years after its time and beautiful a hundred and fifty years after its time.[56]

CRITIQUE OF EXISTING THEORIES

We have given an overview of the major types of explanation of fashion. Theories may be divided into two major types—the functional and the dynamic. Functional explanations focus on the consequences or purposes of fashion—the functions served by fashion for individuals and societies. We found three different types of functional explanation, namely, the search for meaning and/or identity, the struggle for status, and fashion as an economic phenomenon. Dynamic explanations attend to the question of why and how fashion changes in a particular way. We identified four types of dynamic explanation: fashion as diffusion, fashion as cyclic, shifting erogenous zones, and fashion as a reflection of the Zeitgeist. There are other explanations, but we have covered those that are the most common.[57]

We have pointed out that there is empirical evidence to support each of the explanations (that is, each one seems to say something valid about the phenomenon of fashion), but we can also offer some criticisms of the existing theories. In particular, there are four problems that occur among the existing theories.

First, some of the theories confuse the part with the whole. This criticism has been leveled against the cyclic theory espoused by Kroeber. Turner and Killian have pointed out that "style consists of the total effect rather than single elements."[58] They note that Kroeber's own evidence shows differing rhythms for different parts or dimensions of the dress. Moreover, "specific embellishments are added or eliminated in irregular sequence" and "there is seldom a total repetition of style."[59]

In other words, while we may identify cycles of change in such things as skirt lengths or the general form of the skirt, we cannot say that fashion is a cyclical affair in the sense of precise repetitions.

Such things as skirt length may be inherently cyclical—what else can they do except go up or down? Wherever there is a finite number of alternatives, it is not surprising to find some rhythm of change among those alternatives. But it strains the imagination to argue that the knee-length skirt of the 1970s is a repetition of the knee-length skirt of the Bloomer costume.

Similarly, the erogenous-zone theory treats a part of the female anatomy as though that were the whole of fashion. But fashion can hardly be described in terms of only that part of the female anatomy which is being exposed or emphasized. Moreover, such an approach neglects male fashions and fashion in things other than clothing.

A second problem with existing theories is that they fail to account for all of the evidence. To argue that people follow fashion in an effort to find meaning or to experience a more fulfilling life, is not to explain why they will accept uncomfortable or unhealthy fashions. On the other hand, to argue that all fashion involves only status-striving behavior, is to overlook the fact that the search for meaning is a part of fashion, that fashion means more to people than just a struggle for status.

We have also seen problems with a particular status-related theory—trickle-down. Evidence has shown that there is a "trickle-across" pattern.[60] There may also be a "trickle-up" pattern. It has been argued that starting in the 1960s fashions diffused both from the young to the old and from lower to higher socioeconomic strata.[61] As one noted designer, Rudi Gernreich, put it, fashion now "starts in the streets." It seems evident that the course of fashion is more complex than that suggested by the trickle-down theory.

Similarly, to say that fashion is a reflection of the Zeitgeist is to ignore all the changes that occur within the same general spirit of the times. The Zeitgeist is a controversial notion to begin with. But even if we accept the validity of such a phenomenon, it is clear that fashion changes much more rapidly than the Zeitgeist. The spirit of the times undoubtedly sets a general framework that is reflected in fashions. But numerous different fashions can accord with the general framework. In order to understand the particular fashion at any time, and the rapid changes in fashion over time, we must employ some theory in addition to the Zeitgeist.

In sum, there is empirical support for each of the theories, but there is also empirical evidence that cannot be accounted for. Unquestionably, there is an element of seduction involved in dress. But if fashion were nothing more than a shifting emphasis on different parts of the female body in order to maximize sex appeal, it would be hard to explain why people react negatively to clothes that are defined as sexually revealing.[62] At some point, the various theories fail to explain the evidence that is available.

Third, the theories tend to focus on only a portion of the total process of fashion. The functional explanations tend to ignore the fact that fashion *is* a process, or at least they tend to ignore important aspects of the process. To see fashion in terms of individual identity and meaning, for instance, is to recognize an important element in fashion, but it may also result in overlooking the social structure within which the search for identity and meaning occurs. The individual's search must take place in the context of limited alternatives, and those alternatives exist prior to the individual. Diffusion theory also overlooks an important part of the process. The theory identifies those people who are likely to be the gatekeepers in the process (the opinion leaders, innovators, and early adopters), and it tells us the probable pattern of spread once the gatekeepers have accepted a particular fashion. But we are left in the dark as to why the gatekeepers themselves accept or reject any particular fashion.

We should note that some theorists would counter by saying that they did not intend to present an inclusive theory in the first place, but only wanted to understand a particular aspect of the process. To that extent, they no doubt have provided us with valid insights, but we are interested in a more comprehensive understanding. While recognizing the valid insights provided by the existing theories, we want to go beyond them and develop a more inclusive theory of fashion.

A final problem with the existing theories is the ambiguous or unrealistic linkage they make between structural and social psychological levels of social life. We have already noted the problem in the individual identity and meaning theory, where the significance of the social structure is ambiguous at best. In the cyclic theories, the significance of the social psychological level is ignored. For fashion is a supraindividual process that is external to, and coercive upon, the individual. This point was made by Kroeber explicitly, and earlier by Sumner:

> Fashion is by no means trivial. It is a form of the dominance of the group over the individual, and it is quite as often harmful as beneficial. There is no arguing with the fashion. . . . The authority of fashion is imperative as to everything which it touches. The sanctions are ridicule and powerlessness. The dissenter hurts himself; he never affects the fashion.[63]

Sumner did not argue for the cyclical nature of fashion, but, like those who do, he insisted that fashion is imposed on individuals so that social psychological processes are not useful in understanding the nature of fashion.

SCOPE AND METHOD OF THIS BOOK

Our purpose is to shed some new light on the fascinating but perplexing topic of fashion, and what is meant by fashion. Definitions range from the somewhat cryptic view of Emilio Pucci that fashion is "the vision of tomorrow realized today"[64] to the rather straightforward notion that fashion is simply "the thing that the most people do, express, or wear at any given time."[65] Many people distinguish between fashion and style. Some say that style is more enduring than fashion: "Fashion is fleeting. But good style, a thing of beauty, remains a joy forever."[66] There is a disparagement of fashion in this view, for fashion is defined as that which is more transitory (almost faddish) and less individualistic, while style is seen as that which adds creative individuality to fashion.[67]

We prefer the definition of Erwin and Kinchen:

> Style, in dress or any other art, refers to the characteristic or distinctive form, outline, or shape an article possesses. In dress, we speak of the hoop-skirt style, the princess style, and the shirtwaist style of garments. Silhouettes, shapes, and space divisions determine the style. If a style is popular at the present time, it is a fashion.[68]

Fashion, in other words, is simply the modal style of a particular group at a particular time. It is the style which is considered appropriate or desirable.[69]

The fashions we will discuss are basically clothing. But as others have pointed out, fashion is a pervasive phenomenon. There is fashion in art, literature, manners, architecture, and in virtually every facet of culture, including the physical sciences.[70] While we will not deal explicitly with these other areas, we believe that many of our conclusions will be applicable to fashion in general and not merely to fashion in clothing.

To investigate fashion we have searched both the popular and the professional literature. A considerable amount of the professional literature has been summarized above. Most of the discussion in the following pages is based upon the popular literature, buttressed wherever possible by professional studies. We have focused upon popular understandings because we agree that a significant part of the fashion process is the individual's search for meaning and identity. Moreover, we agree that humans behave on the basis of meaning. We do not accept the position of Sumner and Kroeber that fashion is externally imposed behavior. Human behavior, in fact, cannot be understood as long as we regard it as nothing more than the response to external stimuli or as the reflection of an overarching and overwhelming system of culture. Human behavior "is a function of the meaning attributed to objects, situations, and the anticipated consequences of the behavior."[71] The impact of the external environment upon behavior is important, of course, but it is not omnipotent and its impact is always mediated by the way in which the individual perceives and interprets it.

We shall attempt to gain a new understanding of the meaning of fashion to people by looking at what Americans have said about fashion in the popular media as well as by examining fashion behavior. Included in the popular media we have examined are books, magazine articles, and newspapers. We have looked at all fashion articles indexed in *Poole's Index* and the *Reader's Guide to Periodical Literature*. We have also looked at articles indexed in the *New York Times*. From the early part of the nineteenth century to the present, we have secured about 1000 relevant articles, that is, articles that discuss or bear upon the meaning of fashion rather than merely describing a current fashion.

The topics of discussion in the following chapters grew out of our reading of this literature. We had set up some initial topics on the basis of professional analyses, and these topics were modified and extended as we read through the popular literature. The result is, as we shall discuss in the following pages, seven general topics which we have grouped into three broad areas: the nature of clothes and fashion, fashion and various aspects of social life, and a theory of fashion.

Notes

1. Robert S. Lynd and Helen Merrell Lynd, *Middletown in Transition* (New York: Harcourt Brace Jovanovich, Inc., 1965), p. 200.
2. Lee Simonson, "Stay, Gentle Stays!" *The New Republic* 70 (April 27, 1932), p. 295.
3. Hendrik Willem van Loon, "You Can't Tame Fashion," *The New York Times Magazine,* April 25, 1943, p. 14.
4. Orrin E. Klapp, *Collective Search for Identity* (New York: Holt, Rinehart and Winston, 1969), p. 73 and *Currents of Unrest* (New York: Holt, Rinehart and Winston, 1972), p. 325.
5. Klapp, *Collective Search for Identity,* p. 114.
6. Georg Simmel, "Fashion," *International Quarterly* 10 (October, 1904): 130–55.
7. Edward Sapir, "Fashion." Pp. 139–44 in *Encyclopedia of the Social Sciences,* Vol. VI (New York: Macmillan, 1931).
8. René König, *À La Mode: On the Social Psychology of Fashion,* trans. F. Fradley (New York: The Seabury Press, 1973).
9. Gregory P. Stone, "Appearance and the Self," in Gregory P. Stone and

Harvey A. Farberman, eds., *Social Psychology Through Symbolic Interaction* (Waltham, Mass.: Ginn-Blaisdell, 1970), pp. 397–402.
10. *Ibid.,* p. 400.
11. Erving Goffman, *Encounters* (Indianapolis: Bobbs-Merrill, 1961), p. 108.
12. *Ibid.,* pp. 145–46.
13. Julia Ann Pinaire Reed, *Clothing as a Symbolic Indicator of the Self.* Unpublished Ph.D. dissertation, Purdue University, 1973.
14. *Ibid.,* pp. 116–17.
15. Quoted in Lawrence B. Rosenfeld and Jean M. Civikly, eds., *With Words Unspoken: The Nonverbal Experience* (New York: Holt, Rinehart and Winston, 1976), p. 85.
16. J. C. Flugel, *The Psychology of Clothes* (New York: International Universities Press, 1930), p. 138.
17. Murray Wax, "Themes in Cosmetics and Grooming," *American Journal of Sociology* 62 (May, 1957): 393.
18. Flugel, *loc. cit.*
19. *Ibid.,* p. 139.
20. Herbert Spencer, *The Principles of Sociology, Vol. II* (Wesport, Conn.: Greenwood Press, 1975), pp. 205–206. Originally published 1897–1906.
21. *Ibid.,* p. 210.
22. Thorstein Veblen, "The Economic Theory of Woman's Dress," *The Popular Science Monthly* 46 (December, 1894): 200.
23. Bernard Barber, *Social Stratification* (New York: Harcourt Brace Jovanovich, Inc., 1957), p. 150.
24. *Ibid.*
25. W. Godfrey Cobliner, "Feminine Fashion as an Aspect of Group Psychology: Analysis of Written Replies Received by Means of a Questionnaire," *Journal of Social Psychology* 31 (May, 1950): 283–89.
26. Jack Schwartz, "Men's Clothing and the Negro," *Phylon* 24 (Fall, 1963): 224–31.
27. Denton E. Morrison and Carlin Paige Holden, "The Burning Bra: The American Breast Fetish and Women's Liberation," in Robert R. Evans, ed., *Social Movements: A Reader and Sourcebook* (Chicago: Rand McNally, 1973), p. 579.
28. Thomas Ford Hoult, "Experimental Measurement of Clothing as a Factor in Some Social Ratings of Selected American Men," *American Sociological Review* 19 (June, 1954): 324–28.
29. R. Steven Schiavo *et. al.,* "Effect of Attire on Obtaining Directions," *Psychological Reports* 34 (February, 1974): 345–46. Apparently this tendency does not hold up under all circumstances, however. In an experiment involving public libraries, deviant-appearing individuals were as likely as those normally attired to receive help from librarians. See Howard W. Kroll and

Deborah K. Moren, "Effect of Appearance on Requests for Help in Libraries," *American Libraries* 8 (October, 1977): 489.
30. Thorstein Veblen, *The Theory of the Leisure Class* (New York: Mentor Books, 1953), pp. 120–21. Originally published 1899.
31. *Ibid.*, p. 127.
32. See Paul M. Gregory, "An Economic Interpretation of Women's Fashions," *Southern Economic Journal* 14 (October, 1947): 148–62 and "Fashion and Monopolistic Competition," *Journal of Political Economy* 56 (February, 1948): 69–75.
33. Gregory, "An Economic Interpretation . . . ," p. 156.
34. Dwight E. Robinson, "The Economics of Fashion Demand," *Quarterly Journal of Economics* 75 (August, 1969): 376.
35. *Ibid.*, p. 392.
36. Everett M. Rogers, *Diffusion of Innovations* (New York: Free Press, 1962).
37. Margaret P. Grindereng, "Fashion Diffusion," *Journal of Home Economics* 59 (March, 1967): 171–74.
38. Fred D. Reynolds and William R. Darden, "Why the Midi Failed," *Journal of Advertising Research* 12 (August, 1972): 39–44 and "Fashion Theory and Pragmatics: The Case of the Midi," *Journal of Retailing* 49 (Spring, 1973): 51–62.
39. A. L. Kroeber, "On the Principle of Order in Civilization as Exemplified by Changes of Fashion," *American Anthropologist* 21 (July, 1919): 263.
40. *Ibid.*, p. 260.
41. See Robert H. Lauer, *Perspectives on Social Change,* 2nd edition (Boston: Allyn & Bacon, 1977), chapter 2.
42. Agnes Brooks Young, *Recurring Cycles of Fashion, 1760–1937* (New York: Cooper Square Publishers, 1966).
43. *Ibid.*, p. 3.
44. Dwight E. Robinson, "Style Changes: Cyclical, Inexorable, and Foreseeable," *Harvard Business Review* 53 (November, 1975): 121–31 and "Fashions in Shaving and Trimming of the Beard," *American Journal of Sociology* 81 (March, 1976): 1133–39.
45. Robinson, "Style Changes . . . ," p. 126.
46. James Laver, *Clothes* (London: Burke, 1952), p. 3.
47. Edmund Bergler, "A Psychoanalyst Looks at Women's Clothes," *Cosmopolitan,* February, 1960, p. 52.
48. "Roundtable: Sex and Clothing," *Medical Aspects of Human Sexuality,* September, 1970, p. 152.
49. James Laver, "Fashion: A Detective Story," *Vogue,* January, 1959, p. 79.
50. James Laver, Modesty in Dress (London: William Heinemann Ltd., 1969), p. 38.

51. Elsie M. Frost, "Fashion—A Reflection of a Way of Life," *Journal of Home Economics* 40 (May, 1948): 245.
52. Pierre Clerget, "The Economic and Social Role of Fashion," *Annual Report of the Smithsonian Institution, 1913,* p. 763.
53. Flugel, *op. cit.,* p. 152.
54. James Laver, *Taste and Fashion* (London: Burke, 1937), p. 250.
55. George Bush and Perry London, "On the Disappearance of Knickers: Hypotheses for the Functional Analysis of the Psychology of Clothing," in Mary Ellen Roach and Joanne Bubolz Eicher, eds., *Dress, Adornment, and the Social Order* (New York: John Wiley & Sons, 1965).
56. Laver, *Modesty in Dress,* p. 40.
57. One theory that we have not yet discussed, that of Herbert Blumer, will be treated in the last chapter when we offer our own theory.
58. Ralph H. Turner and Lewis M. Killian, *Collective Behavior,* 2nd edition (Englewood Cliffs: Prentice-Hall, 1972), p. 153.
59. *Ibid.*
60. See also Charles W. King, "A Rebuttal to the 'Trickle Down' Theory," in Gordon Wills and David Midgley, eds., *Fashion Marketing* (London: George Allen & Unwin Ltd., 1973), pp. 215–27.
61. Sheldon Zalaznick, "Fashion from the Streets," in Lois M. Gurel and Marianne S. Beeson, *Dimensions of Dress and Adornment* (Dubuque, Iowa: Kendall/Hunt, 1975), p. 83. See Michael and Ariane Batterberry, *Mirror, Mirror: A Social History of Fashion* (New York: Holt, Rinehart and Winston, 1977), pp. 94–5 for an example (admittedly unusual) from the fifteenth century. The slashing and putting of outer garments began among low-status soldiers who were repairing their tattered clothes.
62. See *Psychology Today,* June, 1977, p. 90.
63. William Graham Sumner, *Folkways* (Boston: Ginn, 1940), pp. 194–95. Originally published 1906.
64. Quoted in the *New York Times,* July 19, 1964.
65. Frank L. Walton, "There Will Always Be Fashion," *The New York Times Magazine,* March 21, 1943.
66. Floyd DeForest Boyer, "Style or Fashion?" *American Home,* May, 1946, p. 30.
67. Amy Gross, "What Style Is—and Isn't—All About," *Mademoiselle,* September, 1974, pp. 123+, and Elizabeth Hawes, "Fashion Is Spinach," *Reader's Digest,* June, 1938, pp. 49–50. See also William M. Fine, "Fad, Fashion, or Style?" *Saturday Review,* February 5, 1977, pp. 52–53.
68. Mabel D. Erwin and Lila A. Kinchen, *Clothing for Moderns,* 3rd edition (New York: Macmillan, 1964), p. 39. This definition stems from Nystrom's 1928 work, in which fashion was defined as "nothing more or less than

the prevailing style at a given time" (Paul Nystrom, *Economics of Fashion*, New York: Ronald Press, 1928, p. 4).
69. Anne Hollander, *Seeing Through Clothes* (New York: The Viking Press, 1978), p. 350.
70. Diana Crane, "Fashion in Science, Does It Exist?" *Social Problems* 16 (Spring, 1969): 433–41.
71. Robert H. Lauer and Warren H. Handel, *Social Psychology: The Theory and Application of Symbolic Interactionism* (Boston: Houghton Mifflin, 1977), p. 303.

PART I

THE NATURE OF CLOTHES AND FASHION

chapter 1

What Mean These Clothes?[1]

In a lecture on discoveries and inventions, Abraham Lincoln asserted that the first important discovery of man was the fact of his nakedness, and the first invention was the fig-leaf apron. This, according to Lincoln, was the origin of clothing, "the one thing for which nearly half of the toil and care of the human race has ever since been expended."[2] Although Lincoln correctly pointed out the fundamental importance of clothing to the human enterprise, he did not raise the question of *why* clothing was invented. After all, not all people feel compelled to clothe their nakedness.

Those who do ask the question of why people use clothes, typically answer in terms of three basic functions. Clothing, it is said, is used for protection, for adornment, and because of a sense of modesty. As Mrs. Haweis wrote in 1879, the "three great requirements" of the art of dress are "(1) to protect, (2) to conceal, (3) to display."[3] Undoubtedly all three functions are a part of the meaning of clothing (although all three do not apply to all peoples), but they barely begin to explain the full meaning.

Clothes are used for multiple reasons, and any particular style communicates information to observers. In this chapter, we will explore the full meaning of clothing in general, and of fashionable clothing in particular. We will show that there are numerous and important meanings attached to the clothes that people wear. Much of our subsequent discussion will be more understandable in the light of the materials in this chapter. It will be clear that, given the meaning of clothing, an individual cannot ignore fashion with impunity.

CLOTHING AS NONVERBAL COMMUNICATION

Our approach in this chapter will be to view clothing as a form of nonverbal communication. Several disciplines have been involved in a growing number of studies on a variety of modes of nonverbal communication, including the meaning of gestures, intonation, eye contact, facial expressions, and interpersonal distance. Clothing is a form of "structural nonverbal communication" as opposed to the "kinetic nonverbal information" of gestures, movements, and so forth.[4] Goffman pointed out that all kinds of nonverbal communication (which he called "body idiom") tend to be institutionalized in any society, with some of them likely "to be regularized and accorded a common meaning."[5] Furthermore, an individual may stop talking, but he or she cannot stop communicating. Through nonverbal communication, or body idiom, we are constantly saying something to others.

What are the regularized and common meanings attached to clothing in American society? According to Stone, clothing enables individuals to establish an identity and to give indications of the kind of people they are and of their mood.[6] In addition, clothing can indicate social status or can be used to manipulate status, as illustrated by the person who said, "My new clothes had put me instantly into a new world."[7]

A different assessment of the meaning of clothing is offered by Knapp, who argues that clothing is clearly a means of communication, but that it would be impossible to list all of those things that are invariably communicated.[8] He argues that such a list would vary both by situation and by time.

A host of writers in the popular media have also insisted that clothing communicates information. In the early part of the nineteenth century, for instance, *Godey's Lady's Book and Magazine* warned its readers to "be careful that our fashions are not inconsistent with good sense and pure morals."[9] In other words, the clothes we wear can tell something about our character, and those who wish to maintain a good reputation will attend to their dress. As the magazine pointed out, "the woman who is careless and indifferent of her personal appearance loses half her influence."[10]

Americans have been so convinced that dress tells something important about the character of the wearer they have made it the subject of legislative action. For example, in the 1920s, laws regulating dress were proposed in a number of states.[11] In Utah a proposed bill would have allowed a woman to be fined and imprisoned for wearing a skirt in public that was more than three inches above the ankle. An Ohio bill would have limited to two inches the amount a woman's throat could be displayed by a blouse or evening dress, and the Ohio legislature was also asked to pass a law prohibiting any female over the age of fourteen from wearing a skirt which went above the instep.

The communicative nature of clothing is learned at an early age, as children and young people are taught about the meanings of their clothes. We will note some examples in later chapters, but here we might point out a 1970 publication of the government for 4-H Club members entitled *Clothing Speaks*. The manual begins by reminding the young people of the communicative nature of dress:

> Clothing and appearance speak a silent and subtle language. Clothes are an expression of social behavior; they develop within a social situation. Clothes are an important way of helping you figure out other people.[12]

Thus, both professional and popular writers have argued that clothing is an important form of nonverbal communication. We are led back to the question of what exactly are the regularized and common meanings of clothing in our society. In our view, the professional analyses are partially right. It is true that clothes communicate something of an individual's identity, value, mood, and status. But they communicate more than that, as numerous popular writers have insisted, and what they communicate varies by time and place. But the variations are not numberless. Furthermore, the variations occur within stable categories, as we shall detail in the following text. Based upon the meanings which have been stated in the popular media, we would argue that clothes are a form of nonverbal communication which have a limited number of social meanings, and those meanings—at least at an abstract level—are stable over time.

We want to emphasize the term "social meanings," for the communication is not idiosyncratic. It may be true that the primary purpose of manipulating our appearance is "self-presentation, that is, sending messages about the self."[13] But as Goffman pointed out, some meanings become regularized and shared within a society. The meaning of the message to the receiver is therefore dependent upon the social context and not merely on the sender's individual desires. Stone's work focused upon what the wearer tries to say. Our concern is with social meanings which are assigned to clothing, with the way in which people define the wearer and his or her clothing in everyday life. Meanings are attributed both to the kind of clothing and to the manner in which it is worn. And for American society, we have found a relatively stable set of social meanings. Throughout the nineteenth and twentieth centuries, Americans have consistently defined clothing as: reflecting certain personality traits of the wearer; reflecting the character or morality of the wearer; an indication of the wearer's conformity or nonconformity with social expectations; a useful indicator of social desirability; a measure of status; a means of identifying and evaluating groups and their members; and an indicator of the state of the union. We shall look at each of these in turn, and a number of the ideas we touch upon will be elaborated in subsequent chapters. Here we shall get an overview of what clothes have meant to Americans.

CLOTHING AND PERSONALITY

As noted in the last chapter, some recent investigations have shown that clothing does indeed reveal information about the wearer's personality. That point has been made by writers in the popular media since at least the beginning of the nineteenth century. In 1827, an anonymous author drew a number of parallels between the manner of an individual's dress and the personality of that individual. In most cases, said the author, a gentlemen's or lady's dress gives us a general idea of the mind and tastes of the wearer.[14] A slovenly dressed man will "most probably chew tobacco . . . talk loudly, swear like a trooper, and wind up the week with a carouse." A woman who dresses in a slovenly fashion will have a disordered home, including "an assortment of undarned stockings in a corner closet, and the bed will always have an impression of her form."

The idea that something negative is indicated when an individual wears clothes in an inappropriate manner (that is, when the individual's clothes are dirty, worn, or sloppily arrayed on the body), is a recurring one. Books of etiquette assure us that there is a direct relationship between manner of dress and the nature of the individual. He who is negligent of his dress is a negligent type of person generally.[15] As a 1936 writer put it, "Sloppy clothes or a disorganized wardrobe indicate sloppy and disorganized thinking."[16] Worse, inappropriate manner of dress may reflect emotional problems. A psychiatrist reported that his depressed patients often showed the intensity of their problem by their outward appearance. Patients who could no longer cope with their existence tended to look disheveled or wear clothes that clashed.[17]

On the other hand, to wear one's clothes neatly is to show positive qualities of character, including self-respect. As the editor of the *New York Times* wrote in 1879, a man owes it to himself to be properly clothed, for

> dress is the most obvious mark of personal dignity, and the factory girl's neat, and sometimes too showy attire proves, as well as the city belle's laces, satins, and jewels, that the outside appearance is supposed to affirm the worth of what goes with it. In spite of too frequent extravagance, we must in honesty allow that carefulness in dress is, on the whole, the sign of a due self-respect.[18]

Not only the manner of dress, but the kinds of clothing worn, indicate the kind of people we are. In the nineteenth century, a woman was supposed to wear different dresses for different purposes and different times of the day. If she did not wear what was appropriate, her reputation could suffer. For example, a woman's guide to "perfect gentility" noted that a woman should wear a small muslin cap and a loose robe upon first rising. It was not considered good taste for a woman to appear at breakfast without being laced at all, for that would "give an air of untidiness to the whole appearance."[19] However, she could only receive intimate friends or people who have urgent busines in that attire. To neglect to take it off as soon as possible would be to "expose one's self to embarrassments often very painful, and to the appearance of a want of education."[20]

Men as well as women show their nature by their dress. Why, asked a writer in 1905, would a man wear a starched, white shirt? What does such a shirt mean? It has nothing to do with modesty and very little to do with protection. Rather, the starched shirt is symbolic, "giving an effect of metallic crispness far removed from the soft finish of textile fabrics, and helping to cry aloud the real song of the shirt, 'I am clean!' "[21]

For both men and women, then, dress is more than protection, adornment, or modesty. Both professional and popular writers have insisted that it is an extension of the individual's personality. We have already noted the work of Julia Reed concerning this relationship. Various other professionals, using experimental methods or clinical observations, agree that dress reflects personality. Such attributes as sociability and a sense of insecurity have been linked with varying types of clothing.[22] A psychiatrist has asserted that people who dress for comfort are secure and can relate well to others, while tight, uncomfortable clothing reflects insecurity and perhaps a sense of inferiority.[23] And a study of clothing as a form of communication concluded that, while there are some differences between males and females, there is a relationship between dress and personality for both sexes.[24] For example, males in the study who were concerned about practicality in dress (rather than style or attractiveness), were more likely to be inhibited, cautious, rebellious, dissatisfied, and uninterested in making and retaining friends. Practical-minded females, on the other hand, were likely to be more clever, enthusiastic, confident, outgoing, and unwilling to be led by others.

If the style and manner of one's dress is an extension of one's personality, it follows that one inevitably communicates information about one's self through dress. The individual cannot avoid the revelation. Rightly or wrongly, others will draw conclusions on the basis of dress. In 1852, the editor of a woman's magazine said that "every woman walks about with a placard, on which her leading qualities are advertised."[25] A 1913 writer agreed that no one can avoid revealing his or her personality through dress. We must learn, she said, the "one great lesson" that an individual's dress

> will either reveal or betray. There is a vast difference between the costume in the closet and when it is worn. That difference is the spirit of the wearer. Besides, all the good or bad qualities which clothes so inevitably show are also shown in the face and the manner. Acquire the habit, then, of dressing well. It will be all the easier for you to appear and act well. Self-respect is always well dressed, while self-contempt is down at the heel.[26]

Moreover, according to both professional and popular writers, clothing is not only an extension of personality; to some extent, the way one's personality is perceived by others is determined by your clothing. That is, the wearer's personality is defined in accord with social meanings *whatever the intent of the wearer may have been.* An individual may not have intended to convey the information and may be unaware that it has been conveyed. The editor of *Godey's* advised his readers that dress "reveals, more clearly than speech expresses, the inner life of heart and soul in a people, and the tendencies of individual character."[27] Furthermore, some good qualities of an individual can be obscured or forgotten because of the negative information communicated by inappropriate or slovenly dress. A woman, said *Godey's* editor, may be "an angel of goodness, a Minerva in wisdom, a Diana in morals, a Sappho in talent," but all will be forgotten if her dress is soiled or her bonnet is improperly arranged on her head.[28] Nor have such statements been confined to the past. In the 1970s, writers still warned the readers of popular magazines that they would be judged on the basis of their dress. As one put it, the impressions given by our clothing can be the strongest of all the signals we send to others, making it impossible to dress neutrally; "whatever you wear makes a statement of some kind."[29]

The information given by clothes may not only be unintended but contrary to the wearer's desire or intent. An individual may be telling others something that he or she does not want to say. The editor of a woman's magazine warned his readers in 1869 to give careful thought to clothes, because young women do not always recognize that particular styles encourage familiarity on the part of men.[30]

The editor assumed that young women did not want to encourage such familiarity, and were being subjected to it because of their blind obedience to the reigning fashions. His assumption is questionable, but he was certainly correct in pointing out that clothes do convey meanings to others which can be contrary to the wearer's desire.

For example, young women in the 1920s liked to think of themselves as a liberated generation, but a male observer in 1926 argued that their clothing showed otherwise.[31] Women of his day, he said, were "poor creatures" who had to get about in skirts too narrow for a natural stride and in high heels that made long walks a torture. The entire costume of the day loudly proclaimed a message of bondage: "I am designed not to be useful, but to be ornamental; I suffer the agonies of cold and pinched feet, and I spend hours in elaborate cosmetic ministrations; I am—or I long to be—an expensive and pampered parasite."[32]

Finally, there is the example of the New York nun who exchanged her traditional habit for street clothes and who certainly did not intend for people to react to her as did one older Catholic woman: "You used to symbolize everything good and holy and chaste to me. Now you're just human like everybody else."[33] Perhaps the nun thought she was communicating her sense of identity with other people through her new clothing style. The outcome, for at least one woman, was the opposite of the nun's intent, however, For what we communicate does not depend merely upon our desire or intent, but upon the meaning ascribed to our clothing by others.

In sum, throughout the last two centuries popular writers have insisted that the well-dressed individual is also an individual with positive personality traits, while the poorly dressed individual is expressing his or her negative traits. And the revelation of personality occurs independently of the intent of the wearer. As a psychologist advised the readers of a woman's magazine in 1971, choice of clothing "goes beyond whimsy; it tells others a great deal about you. What you wear is an expression of conscious taste and preference. . . . It's also a portrait, largely unconscious, of the way you see yourself ('I am delicate, helpless,' or 'I am a swinger')."[34]

CLOTHING AND MORAL CHARACTER

The moral meaning of clothing in American society primarily is rooted in Christianity. Both in the Bible and in Christian writings there is a tradition that associates dress with morality. We have already noted that one commonly identified function of clothing is to express one's modesty, an idea that has its roots deep in Christian history. St. Augustine developed a lust-shame theory of the origin of clothing that influenced subsequent Christian thought.[35] For example, a Massachusetts minister wrote a tract in 1728 in which he advised his children and, in doing so, clearly outlined the lust-shame theory of clothes.[36] It was, he argued, the sin of our first parents (that is, Adam and Eve), that made it necessary for us to wear clothes. Since their sin, we are clothed because of our sense of shame and in order to prevent sin.

Undoubtedly, there is interaction between clothing and modesty. Some groups, such as the Shakers, have clearly adopted particular styles of clothing out of a sense of modesty and a desire to minimize any erotic feelings. On the other hand, total nudity also seems to do away with the sense of shame and to minimize erotic feelings. In the 1920s, George Bernard Shaw said the sex appeal of women was diminished by the trend towards nudity, and a clothing trade magazine agreed that the charm of women had not been enhanced by the new styles; "better for women if their limbs were wrapped in mystery."[37] Dr. Ernest Seton, a well-known naturalist, went even further and said clothing is a threat to morality. The health and morality of the nation's women will increase in direct proportion to the brevity of their dresses, and will be at a maximum when they wear nothing at all.[38]

Some empirical support for the advocates of nudity was provided by an observer of a nudist colony who said nakedness ceased to arouse any curiosity. "Since there is nothing to focus the attention on any specific part, one has merely the impression of the body as a whole, and sex differentiae no longer possess special significance."[39] Furthermore, a sense of immodesty develops if an individual seems to be trying to conceal any part of his or her body.

It would appear that our sense of modesty and shame is as much a result of our being clothed as it is a cause of our clothing. Nevertheless, the Christian tradition has insisted upon the linkage between dress and modesty, and between dress and morality. Nearly all of the early Christian writers warned against the evil practice of decorating the person, that is, of wearing ornate or expensive clothes. Tertullian, for instance, writing around the first part of the third century, spoke of women who tried to be both Christian and fashionable as acting out of either "simple ignorance" or "from hypocritical motives."[40] It is wrong, he argued, to attempt to alter that which God has given to us. Rather than fancy dress and cosmetics, women ought to clothe themselves in "the silk of honesty, the fine linen of righteousness, and the purple of chastity." At some point or other, virtually every kind of bodily covering has been condemned as immoral, with "immoral" having a number of different meanings.

Clothes and Immorality

Clothing may be immoral and corrupting either when the individual is consumed by the passion to be fashionable, or when a particular fashion is defined as inherently immoral. That is, a particular fashion may be defined as improperly erotic or as a subversion of a proper role. We shall illustrate this with respect to women's fashions. On the other hand, even if the fashion itself is not objectionable, people can act immorally by their passion for fine clothes. And both males and females can be taught to have that passion, though *Godey's* editor considered a male ardor for splendor in dress to be far worse than that of a female. It is, he said, bad enough to raise vain females, but downright shocking to turn boys into vain men. For of all the weaknesses that we might find in a man, "what is more despicable than an inordinate love of dress, added to an exorbitant desire for admiration of himself?"[41]

Depending upon the writer's perspective, "immoral" may mean anything from irresponsibility to sin. In any case, the consequences are serious. The woman who devotes herself to the pursuit of fashion may commit a whole series of immoral acts, including: wasting her time; losing opportunities to improve herself morally and mentally; neglecting the education of her children and charitable activities; and disturbing her husband's peace or seriously embarrassing him by her extravagance.[42]

As in the case of personality traits, it is not simply the kind of clothes but the manner of wearing them that is important. One writer admitted that she looked down on any man or woman who was content to wear cheap clothes, for to be content in a shoddy outfit is like being content in a dirty house or languishing in a lazy mental attitude. She agreed with the argument "that a cheap coat makes a cheap man; the man who is content to wear a cheap and shabby coat has a serious lack in his character; and so with the woman who is willing to wear a shoddy dress and a dowdy hat."[43]

Typically, immorality and clothing is discussed in the context of the Christian faith, so that the immoral behavior being discussed is called sin, or is at least more serious than mere irresponsibility or moral deficiency. American writers followed the early Christians in attributing great moral importance to dress. The Quakers, for example, insisted upon the strict regulation of clothing as a requisite for Christian living. William Penn called "excess in apparel" a "costly folly" and told his followers: "If thou art clean and warm, it is sufficient; for more doth but rob the Poor, and please the Wanton."[44] Ministers warned that Christians can break one or more of the Ten Commandments by their adoption of improper dress.[45] Fashion torments the conscience, ruins morality, and is an enemy of religion, so that a man or woman cannot be both fashionable and moral and religious.[46]

An example of the way in which dress can ruin morality is provided by the relationship between prostitution and clothing. According to Lucy Hooper, who wrote in 1874, research showed that the greater number of women who entered the profession did so because of their love of dress. "Sin led to the invention of dress, and now dress lures the souls of the weak and vain among women into sin."[47] The same connection between dress and prostitution was mentioned by others as late as 1914.[48] There is probably some truth to their observations since later studies have shown that prostitutes usually have inadequate income from previous jobs. Money, or quick financial gain, has been given as the strongest motive for becoming a prostitute.[49] In other words, it is not that fine clothes possess some intrinsic temptation that can lure the innocent into degradation (as the above writers assumed). Rather, fine clothes are one aspect of a way of life that is desired by those who struggle at the subsistence level, and who, in some cases, may accept prostitution in an effort to move from the latter to the former. But for writers in the popular media, the passion for fine clothes was inherently corrupting to the

FIG. 3. Clothes are tied up with morality, as shown by this disapproval of an 1898 mini-skirted bathing suit. (Source: Library of Congress.)

rich and poor alike. It is little wonder, then, that Christian writers expressed with fervor the need for every Christian to avoid the sartorial sins. As one nineteenth-century woman vividly described the problem:

> When Satan can once inspire a Christian with a strong desire to be fashionable, he just waits till he sees the poor victim boldly wearing his livery, and then leaves him contentedly to seek other prey. He knows that he has secured a heavy mortgage on that soul. If there is an object of pity on earth it is the fashionable Christian.[50]

That which is sinful in dress has varied somewhat by denomination and also over time. For example, in a small Missouri town in the 1930s, appropriate female attire varied from "dressing up" for services in the Christian Church to extreme plainness (including no makeup or jewelry) in the Holiness Church. The preachers called sunsuits for small children immodest. Slacks for women were also called immodest—bordering on the immoral—in 1937, but were considered respectable and even desirable by 1939.[51] The moralists do not agree with each other, but in every age they have insisted that particular styles are sinful and that the end result of their adoption would be the corruption of the wearer.

Immoral Women's Fashions

It is female fashions which are usually the subject of discussions about immorality. In dress, as in other matters, the double standard has prevailed in America. We shall discuss this matter further in subsequent chapters; here we will simply note that the woman has been considered the virtuous member of society, the one responsible for the maintenance of morality. In every generation, therefore, her clothing has been closely analyzed to determine whether she is fulfilling her role.

Has woman fulfilled her role as the moral leader? If we judge her performance on the basis of her clothing, we would have to conclude that she has often offended moral sensibilities. A good deal of moral outrage has been expressed periodically about women's fashions, especially when a new fashion was defined as either obliterating sexual differences or as being overtly erotic. In the middle of the 18th century, the *Boston Gazette* or *Country Journal* published an article about the "new sect of Evites," a group of fashionable ladies who decided to appear publicly dressed with nothing other than "the original Fig-Leaf."[52] The article was a satire and a warning to the women of Boston, whose fashionable clothing had reached the point where "there remains no further step to be taken except absolute Nakedness."[53]

Attacks on the immoral nature of women's clothing picked up in the middle of the nineteenth century. The Bloomer costume appeared, was attacked viciously as a destroyer of the God-ordained female role, and quickly abandoned as a result of the assault. The primary objection to the Bloomer was the trousers, which seemed to most contemporaries to erase the distinction between the sexes. As *Godey's* editor noted a few years later, the most morally refined and Christian nations were precisely the ones in which there were fundamental differences between the dress of men and women.[54]

Another nineteenth-century fashion that was denounced was the false calves of the 1860s. Women were wearing hoop skirts, which sometimes allowed their calves to be seen. Corset makers began selling padded calves for those who didn't feel they were sufficiently endowed by nature (similar to the padded bras of other generations). The false calves were vehemently denounced as demonstrating indecency and immodesty. The women who wore them (you cannot call them ladies, said a New York editor) may not be capable of educating children to fear God and fulfill their duty to others.[55]

Neither honorable intentions nor reasonable arguments could stay the wrath of the moralists once they decided that a particular style was immoral. In 1890, the girls of Muncie, Indiana were wearing loose woolen shirts in the summer for coolness and comfort. An editor in the town called the style disgusting. A girl might as well wear a night gown on the street, he said, as one of the "female blouse rags. No girl possessing any self-respect or any regard for the opinion of respectable people will wear one."[56]

In the first quarter of the twentieth century, women's fashions underwent radical changes, and the denunciation of them as erotically immoral was frequent. A number of writers argued that women were adopting styles only suitable for (and used by) prostitutes. In some instances, the denunciation was more than verbal. In 1913, a young woman was arrested in Richmond, Virginia for wearing a slit skirt. She was jailed, fined, and then ordered to leave the city.[57] In the same year, a Chicago alderman, shocked by the slit skirt, tried to have a bill drafted by the Health Committee to make the skirt illegal.[58] And a Connecticut firm took steps to make the skirt a thing of the past among its female employees. The management ordered all of its female employees to wear respectable dress. The order obviously meant that slit skirts would not be tolerated, and to make certain the women would know about the new order, a note was placed in each pay envelope.[59]

The moralists were frantic in the first two decades of this century. They saw morality, chastity, modesty, and the femininity of women all being destroyed.[60] And they took numerous and varied steps to quell the new styles. In a 1918 speech, a woman tried to appeal to the sense of patriotism, arguing that it was "true patriotism" to control the emotions and impulses and that young women must learn to dress properly so as not to sexually attract or arouse young men.[61] In New York, a group of members of the Federation of Women's Clubs tried to get the organization to adopt a resolution stating that the women of New York would do everything possible to dress modestly and to persuade dress designers to accept their own responsibility for decency in fashion. The resolution was tabled, largely because many of the women did not feel they could do anything about the problem.[62]

During the 1920s, there was a veritable crusade against the short skirts. Prominent women spoke out against the new styles. The YWCA made a concerted effort to get working women to adopt what it defined as a "moral" dress.[63] Ministers railed against the sinful fashions of the day, and a large number of them advocated a moral dress that had elbow-length sleeves and a hem that was exactly seven and one-half inches above the floor.[64] But neither the appeal of patriotism, the warnings of moral corruption, nor the threat of sumptuary legislation stemmed the process of change. The majority of people rejected the definitions of the moralists, though they did not deny that clothing reflects the moral worth of an individual or that certain styles of dress can be properly called immoral.

The moral implications of clothing styles continued to be debated into the 1950s, 1960s, and 1970s. In 1954, women's fashions gained the attention of the Pope, who asked Catholic bishops throughout the world to act against indecency in dress. Summer modes of dress in particular, said the Pope, were having "spiritually ruinous effects" on people.[65] The next year, an Illinois priest began the practice of tagging wedding gowns and formal dresses to show that they met modesty requirements. According to the priest, tags with the inscription "Marilyke Modest Dress" could be found in various stores in most states.[66] Actually, the Catholic clergy were most concerned about bathing suits, but felt that little could be done except to speak out in editorials, articles, and sermons. A 1963 editorial in *America* is representative of the Catholic viewpoint. It said that the manufacturers of women's bathing attire were attempting to outdo each other in the "daring" styles they were offering to "gullible girls." The styles were setting low moral standards by emphasizing *female* instead of *feminine*. Obviously, said the editor, traditional standards of Christian modesty were in the process of being undermined.[67]

Debates and discussions about the moral nature of various styles continued in the 1970s. There seemed to be little more that could be done to reveal the female body after the miniskirt, the braless look, and the topless and see-through fashions. By 1978, the new styles were said to be "one veil short of nudity."[68] The judgment was quite similar to the eighteenth-century Boston editor's comment about fashions being one step removed from nakedness. But whereas the Boston editor saw moral danger, a 1978 psychiatrist viewed the styles as simply part of the cycle of fashion and pointed out that dress reflects rather than influences morality.[69] Preachers and other moralists continued to despair over women's dress, but the general public was far more tolerant than our forebears. That the generation of the 1970s accepted styles that would have been considered immoral by previous generations does not mean the moral significance of dress disappeared, of course, it only means there was a new definition of what is moral and what is immoral.

Clothing and Morality

If clothing is associated with immorality, it follows that it should also be associated with morality. Indeed, the proper use of clothing has been said to be conducive both to individual morality and to social order. Fashion, argued Arnold Bennett, is good, not evil, for it is an expression of a social convention, and conventions are the essence of social order. In other words, without such conventions as fashions in clothing we would face the awful possibility of anarchy.[70] In his study of child-rearing practices in early America, Greven said that the clothing of infants and small children was profoundly important as a means of social control. The same clothes were put on boys and girls—long dresses with aprons and petticoats. Clothing styles therefore indicated

> the feminization of children; and since being female meant being perceived as weaker, inferior, submissive, and obedient, the clothing of children became a part of the overall process of discipline. . . . All had wills that needed breaking and desires that needed to be subdued and suppressed.[71]

Individual morality has also been associated with proper clothing. George Fox, who was called the "President of Fashion" in the latter half of the nineteenth century, believed that "no civilized man is apt to commit a crime in a good suit of clothes. An easy and graceful garment is incompatible with a deed of violence."[72] Similarly, the editor of the *New York Times* pointed out that the well-to-do women of his city who dressed fashionably were among the noblest of people, spending a good part of their lives in benevolent and charitable work. The fashionable women of his city, he asserted, assist by word and deed anyone that they can. "The actually fashionable woman of New York follows the fashion of goodness which she sets."[73] This, incidentally, was a rare editorial, the only one we found in the *New York Times* that praised the women who tried to be fashionable. There are those, of course, who are consumed by the passion to have fine clothes and to be fashionable. But, insisted the editor, in New York City nineteen out of every twenty fashionably dressed women are setting the standards for moral behavior by vigorously engaging in charitable and benevolent activities.

Almost a century after the writers just mentioned, another observer made the relationship even stronger. Not only are good clothes associated with good morals, but immoral behavior may be transformed into moral behavior by adopting the proper clothing. Thus, if you have a delinquent child, provide that child with the proper attire and you will get a different kind of behavior. For the delinquent who is washed and clothed well behaves just as the rest of us who are clean and well clothed.[74] The periodic debate over dress codes for adolescents, carried on by parents, writers, and educators, suggests that a good many people agree that moral behavior can be created, at least in part, by the appropriate clothes.

CLOTHING AND CONFORMITY

A third kind of information communicated by clothing involves conformity—an individual's dress tells us whether that individual is likely to conform to social expectations. Conformity includes moral behavior, but it includes much more—in general, expectations about roles and norms. In other words, can we expect a particular individual to fulfill our expectations about normative behavior generally? The individual's clothing helps us to answer the question, for the individual's behavior with respect to dress is generalized to that individual's overall behavioral pattern. A person may be defined either as respectable (and, therefore, predictable) or as a rebel, purely on the basis of dress.

To some extent, those clothes considered fashionable at any particular time reflect various roles. Books of etiquette exploit the desire of most people to conform by detailing role-appropriate clothing. The books tell us such things as the appropriate dress for funerals, for parties, and for various other social functions. Occupational roles also tend to have normative styles. The funeral director may be expected to dress conservatively. The professional may have to wear "dress" clothing, or at least be attired neatly and expensively. The assembly-line worker wears those clothes that allow freedom of movement and which can be dirtied freely, while the nurse dresses in a uniform that reflects the cleanliness of her work.

Role-related clothing is not necessarily as rational as some of the above examples would suggest. Traditionally, male members of Congress dress in suits and ties. When a presidential order aimed at conserving energy set summer themostats at 78° in all public buildings in 1979, a Representative from Texas appeared in the House in a sport shirt. He was ordered out of the chambers by the Speaker, who asserted that legislators would not be allowed to come to the House improperly attired. To many people, a sport shirt makes more sense under the circumstances. But the function of role-related clothes is not necessarily to make sense; it is to indicate to others that the individual can be trusted to conform to social expectations about his or her behavior. This function will be underscored when we examine the role-related dress that has historically generated the most controversy—that defined as appropriate to sex roles (chapter 3).

It is understandable that we would want to know whether other people will conform to our expectations, at least in a general way. A capricious or totally unpredictable world is unsettling at best and terrifying at worst. Conformity in dress reassures us as we interact with others. We feel comfortable as the nurse attends us in her neat, white uniform, but it would be disconcerting to be confronted by a nurse in a disheveled outfit, part of which was white and part a sporty print.

Nevertheless, there is also a tradition of individualism in our country. We pointed out earlier that an individual may alter his or her dress in order to express role distance and affirm individuality.

Such an individual, because of the importance of conformity, runs the risk of being considered something of a maverick who is likely to be a nonconformist in other ways. If the break is a radical one, a rejection of normative dress, the individual will be defined as a rebel. Thus, those who want to maintain their respectability will be careful to wear those styles defined as appropriate for their roles, even if what is considered appropriate at one time is defined as unsuitable or unhealthy or absurd at another time. As a 1907 writer pointed out, people will wear the dress that is considered appropriate to their station in life even if it means "to paint one's body, or tattoo one's face, to deform one's feet, to displace one's internal organs, or to wear stiffly starched linen."[75]

An individual who has lost some respectability may regain it by the appropriate use of clothing, showing thereby that he or she can now be trusted to conform generally to social expectations. For example, in 1978 Hamilton Jordan, an aide to President Carter, made headlines by some untoward behavior, including heavy drinking and questionable relationships with women. Jordan had been tieless for years, contrary to the conventional dress of Washington. But following the stories in the newspapers he began to dress "almost contritely" in a suit and tie.[76] In essence, he was requesting that he be restored to respectability and was implicitly telling others that his behavior would subsequently be more in accord with social expectations.

CLOTHING AND SOCIAL DESIRABILITY

If clothing tells us something about an individual's personality, moral character, and tendency to conform to social expectations, it follows that it also tells us about the social desirability of that individual. That is, we can determine from an individual's clothing whether or not we would like to interact with that person. As a popular writer succinctly put it in 1974, a person's dress is the evidence we use to make immediate judgments and to categorize the person "as one of Us or one of Them, and which particular Them."[77] Professional studies support the point that clothing is used to evaluate social desirability. In one study, male and female college students were shown photographs of a female student wearing four different outfits, two fashionable and two out-of-fashion. Both males and females rated the young woman in the photographs as more sociable when she was in fashionable clothing than when she wore the out-of-fashion clothes. The findings were particularly noteworthy in view of the presumed de-emphasis of style on college campuses at the time. The researchers concluded that whether or not there is a de-emphasis on clothing, style distinctions continue to be noticed. Furthermore, "there are style distinctions inherent in costumes and items of apparel which affect the formation of the impression of the sociability of the wearer."[78]

First, then, clothing tells us whether we want to interact with, support, or help another person. In the 1920s, according to the *Literary Digest,* people used dress to a considerable extent to evaluate political candidates, so candidates should carefully consider the dress they adopt for any particular appearance. "Clothes not only make the man," said the editor, "but they make votes also."[79] The article went on to note the problems of a certain J. Sloan Fassett who had run for governor of New York. Fassett was unaware that New Yorkers, both rich and poor, frowned upon careless dress. He made the mistake of speaking to a poor section of the city dressed in less expensive clothes than he had used elsewhere. He also concluded his speech in his shirt-sleeves. The result was that the people rejected him. They said the man wore "his fancy shell for his swell friends," but that they were apparently not good enough for the man's best. At the polls, they let the candidate know their feelings.[80]

The wives of political candidates have also been subjected to scrutiny in terms of the clothes they have worn. In the 1972 campaign, a *New York Times* article noted that the wives of presidential candidates all claimed that clothing styles were no longer an issue. In contrast to the 1960 campaign, when the report that Mrs. Kennedy spent $30,000 a year on Paris fashions caused a stir, the 1972 campaign was said to be marked by a lack of interest in the wives' mode of dress. Nevertheless, the article went into considerable detail on the styles of the various women, and also noted that Mrs. Muskie kept a notebook of what she wore in order to avoid the mistake of wearing the same dress a second time in the same city.[81]

If we dress differently for different groups of people, as did J. Sloan Fassett in his campaign, the change will have meaning both for us and for them, though the meaning may not be the same. Whatever Fassett's intent, his informal attire was defined by the people as evidence of his disparagement of them. They saw his behavior as a public act of status degradation, and that made him undesirable for interaction or support. On the other hand, in her study of working-class families, Lillian Rubin was sensitive to the possibility of status degradation through her dress. She reports that she dressed very carefully when she interviewed her respondents for she would be expected to look like a professional woman (even though she came from a working-class background herself). "Anything else could be taken as a sign of disrespect, both for myself and my hostess. For those who have lived on the edge of poverty all their lives, the semblance of poverty affected by the affluent is both incomprehensible and insulting."[82]

Thus, social desirability works in both directions across socioeconomic lines. We noted earlier that people react to others differently depending upon mode of dress. The individual who dresses as a rebel (for example, a hippie), or as one in a lower socioeconomic stratum is less likely to receive help from others in most situations. On the other hand, those who dress down for people in the lower strata are likely to be defined as engaging in status degradation and as therefore undesirable to support or to help.

In addition to general interaction, writers have identified a number of specific kinds of social desirability involved in evaluating clothing. We can, for one, define people as potentially desirable for friends on the basis of their dress. In 1911, mothers were advised to be careful in selecting clothes for their daughters who were going to boarding school, for the friends the daughters would make could rest upon the first impressions created by dress.[83] A number of studies of high school student bodies have shown the importance of dress in popularity. There is a significant relationship between personal appearance and social acceptance, especially for girls.[84] Again, the particular kind of clothing defined as an indication of desirability changes from one generation to another; but each generation evaluates the individual in accord with dress norms. In essence, the individual can say, "Based on the way you are dressed, I can tell whether or not I would like to know you better."

In the nineteenth century, it was said that a man might even evaluate a prospective wife on the basis of her dress. If a man is prudent and sensible, if he prefers to look before he leaps, he "may safely predicate of the inner lining from the outer garment, and be

FIG. 4. How a Business Woman Should Not Dress. (*Source:* Ladies' Home Journal, *November, 1907.*) © 1907 LHJ Publishing, Inc. Drawings by Anna Speakman. Reprinted with permission of Ladies' Home Journal.

thankful that he has this, at least, to go by."[85] In both the nineteenth and twentieth centuries, employers have used the dress of people to evaluate them as potential employees. A 1907 article, for example, showed two sets of drawings of women; one set dressed well and the other dressed sloppily. The commentary stressed the difference in social desirability between the two. The ones who were dressed neatly and appropriately, the article pointed out, were clearly more desirable people with whom to interact. The well-dressed business woman "impresses you first and last with her calm, dignified efficiency." You know that she will attend to business and do it well. And you know this by her dress. On the other hand, one of the poorly dressed young women was trying to impress people by her elaborate, out-of-place outfit, including "jingly, 'near-gold' bracelets, blue beads, clicking French slippers, and last night's violets." The woman, as her employer well knew, was more interested in men and ice cream than in business.[86]

A more contemporary effort in the evaluation of business dress is that of John Molloy, a dress consultant for businesses and corporations. According to Molloy, clothes can either make or break the aspiring young executive. He has conducted numerous experiments to assess the significance of clothing and to buttress his argument about their impact on business careers. In one piece of research, he surveyed 100 corporate executives to determine their attitudes about dress. Among his findings were the following:

1. 95 said their company had an unwritten dress code and two reported having a written dress code;
2. 96 said a number of their employees would be more likely to get ahead if they knew how to dress;
3. all 100 said they would send their own sons to a course on how to dress for business;
4. 72 said they would delay a promotion for a man who did not dress properly;
5. 84 said their company had turned down people solely for appearing at an interview improperly dressed.[87]

On the basis of such findings, Molloy advises people who want to succeed to attend carefully to their dress. As he said in an interview, you must realize "that what you wear immediately establishes your authority, credibility and likability."[88]

Is it legitimate to evaluate people on the basis of their clothing? Is it fair to an employee, or potential employee, to use his or her dress as a measure of suitability? Molloy identified some attitudes of executives that legitimated their stance on proper dress for employees. Over half of the executives believed that dress affects the efficiency of the worker and all of them said that dress affects the general tone of an office. Molloy himself conducted an experiment that lends substance to their attitudes about efficiency. He studied two branch offices of a corporation, one in which there was a dress code for all men in positions of authority, and in the other, the men dressed more casually. A time study showed the dress-code office to be more efficient. An unwritten dress code was instituted in the second office, and Molloy gave the executives there a series of lectures on dressing for authority and effectiveness. At the end of a year, the first office was performing as well as it had before, and the efficiency of the office with the new dress code had improved markedly.[89]

Long before Molloy's work, however, books of etiquette and manners implicitly or explicitly legitimated evaluation on the basis of clothing. A 1940 book of manners for young people noted the fact that we are judged by our clothes and then affirmed the rightness of making such judgments. After all, said the author, if a young person does not think enough of himself or herself to be neatly dressed, others will properly decide that that young person does not have the kind of manners that would make him or her a desirable friend or acquaintance.[90]

In sum, clothing is a common way to evaluate the social desirability of others. It is defined as a legitimate basis for evaluation even though a number of people have pointed out that the individual's dress may communicate unintended and even false information. Different modes and manners of dress function like stereotypes. They are shorthand methods of evaluating others, allowing us, without having to take the time to know others in depth, to decide how to relate to them and whether we want to interact further with them.

CLOTHES AS AN INDICATOR OF STATUS

As often observed, a fifth kind of information communicated by clothing is the status of the wearer. In all societies, clothes have been related to status. Even where the typical outfit was minimal and where clothing was unnecessary for protection, as in ancient Egypt, the clothes that were worn indicated the status of the wearer.[91] In ancient Rome, all classes of people wore the toga. But the type and condition of the material of the toga could vary by status, and the tunica, worn beneath the toga, showed the status of the wearer by the width of a purple stripe.[92]

In some societies, status distinctions have been regulated by law. But even where there are no sumptuary laws, people of differing status wear different kinds of clothes. Thus, those who assert that we can identify the status of another by that person's dress have a good deal of evidence to support them. Over time and across societies, there is a tendency for particular kinds of clothing to reflect a particular status. (In chapter 4 we will discuss how fashion relates to *status-striving behavior* as opposed to the *status-related information* discussed here.)

In the United States prior to the twentieth century, the prevailing view was that clothing did and should reflect socioeconomic differences. In 1853, a popular fashion magazine advised its female readers on the proper course of action if a "poor woman" should receive the "gift of a lady's dress fully trimmed all over." Should the poor woman simply use the dress as she received it? By no means! Rather, "all conspicuous and needless trimmings" should be removed, and various other modifications should be made. Otherwise, the poor woman might "begin to think that she looked so like a lady with this full-trimmed dress, that sundry unbecoming airs would be likely to creep over her."[93]

One of the ways those in the upper strata could demonstrate their status was through the adoption of useless accessories, ranging from jewelry to lap dogs. In the antebellum South, a young lady might take her Sunday walk accompanied by living accessories—her black house servants. The servants would follow her in the order of their own status, each dressed in differing amounts of finery according to status.[94]

In the latter part of the nineteenth century, and increasingly in the twentieth century, voices are heard that claim that clothing styles have become democratic. Particular social classes do not, and should not, according to many observers, have distinctive styles of dress. In 1879 a St. Louis editor criticized "feminine flunkeyism."[95] A "flunkey," said the editor, is one who considers herself superior but is afraid to "risk the natural test of the equality of man." The flunkey is anxious to be distinguished from the lower strata by some outward sign or badge, such as fine clothing. Male flunkeyism appeared first, but it is no longer to be found in America, where even the President "walks along the streets entirely undistinguishable from the citizens of the Republic, so far as costume is concerned." Unfortunately, warned the editor, the nation might be faced with a period of feminine flunkeyism, for a foremost female fashion writer pointed out that genteel American women were seriously discussing how to dress in order to distinguish themselves from those women who work for a living.

In contrast to the earlier view that clothing does and should reflect status differences, the St. Louis editor argued that clothing might but should not. Other writers also complained about the tendency of women to desire status-related kinds of clothing.[96] But a number of twentieth-century observers asserted that American clothing styles now express a *lack* of status distinctions. As the St. Louis editor pointed out, men's dress ceased to express status distinctions long before the twentieth century.[97] During the first quarter of the twentieth century, many people believed that women's fashions had also been democratized. Among other things, the rapid development of ready-made clothing was identified as the prime reason for the lack of status distinctions in clothing. Shop after shop, said a 1921 writer, shows the same gown. Thus, women's clothes are democratic. The same outfit is appropriate for all classes of women.[98] Moreover, the democratization of clothing applied to all aspects of dress. However else democracy might have failed, "in the feet of American women it is triumphant. Class distinctions are utterly impossible with modern shoes and stockings."[99]

In addition to mass production techniques, a number of other technological developments were said to facilitate the democratization of clothing. Basically, the other developments were a variety of improved and quicker methods of transportation and communication, including the exposure of the bulk of women to new fashions through the mass media.[100] Technology combined with ideology to implement American ideals in the realm of clothing.

But have the ideals really been implemented? Has clothing ceased to have any status implications? It seems to us that the note of democratic triumph has sounded prematurely. Clothing styles have not yet lost their status implications, either for men or women. Molloy says that one of the first things he researched was the status implications of various clothing styles. On the basis of observations and experiments, he found that a beige raincoat is defined as higher status than a black raincoat. When a man wears a beige raincoat, therefore, he can expect to be treated with more respect than if he wears a black raincoat.[101]

Those who question some of Molloy's methods might take note

of Reed's research, which showed socioeconomic background as the best of discriminators between high fashion and nonfashion clothing style groups.[102] Or consider John Corry's observation in 1974, that New York clothing styles are no longer used to make political statements but rather to express the two things they did in the past—gender and social class.[103] Or listen to people connected with major department stores describe, in 1977, the current status symbols in clothing.[104]

In spite of what has been said, American clothing retains its status significance. Then why have many people argued that our clothes have been democratized? The contradiction is only apparent. Democratization means there are no class-specific styles. However, through one's choice of designer, brand, or cost, or through the display of "good taste," one is still categorized by one's dress. In the past, an individual's status defined that individual's appropriate clothing style. Ascription gave way to achievement, and now one's clothing style helps define one's status. As Bernard Barber pointed out, fashion now fulfills the two functions of maintaining class distinctions and simultaneously supporting our ideological equalitarianism.

CLOTHING AND GROUP MEMBERSHIP

The norms of groups generally include some that are related to appropriate dress. Clothing may enable us to identify an individual as a member of a particular group. Moreover, the clothes worn by group members may communicate information about the entire group (and, of course, about each person who is a member of that group). For instance, a religious group may try to communicate something of their morality or their ideology through dress. The Amish have strict rules about dress.[105] There is a sameness that reflects equality among the members. Clothing must also show modesty and reflect sex differences. The Amish are pacifists, and therefore reject buttons on their outer garments or Sunday clothes because buttons are regarded as military appurtenances. Hat styles reveal age differences. The varied styles may not be noticeable to an outsider, but the Amish regard them as quite significant for they "indicate whether people are fulfilling the expectations of the group. A young man who wears a brim that is too narrow is liable for sanction."[106]

Groups develop dress norms for various reasons. Occupational groups have often developed norms as a badge of identity, or because the style is believed to be functional for the work. At the turn of the century, one would invariably find an undertaker in black, a bank clerk with collars at least three inches high, an actor with a silk hat and tan boots, a musician in a velvet coat, and a golf player in a red necktie.[107] Such distinguishing styles were simply badges of identity.

Some groups use dress style both as a badge of identity and as a way of expressing something about their characteristics. Earlier in the century, members of the American diplomatic service wore spats in order to symbolize their cosmopolitanism.[108] Juvenile gang members in more recent times assert both their identity and their toughness through a uniform mode of dress. Such groups as Hell's Angels, the Black Panthers, and the Yippies have used distinctive clothing styles to express hostility and aggression against American society. A feminist has raised the question of whether a woman in America in the 1970s can "live a 'liberated' life in a lace blouse," and notes that radical feminists in Boston adopted battle fatigues and heavy boots so they could avoid altogether the appearance of sexual beings.[109]

On the other hand, groups may insist upon certain styles in order to express their respectability or their elite status. Particular kinds of clothing may be required for an adolescent to be accepted into the "in" crowd in high school. In his national survey of high school students, Coleman asked, "What does it take to get into the leading crowd in this school?" For girls, being well dressed came just behind a good personality and good looks. As one girl put it: "Wear just the right things, nice hair, good grooming and have a wholesome personality."[110]

Full participation in any group demands conformity to group norms, whether the group is composed of the workers in an office or the members of an adolescent gang. Where a particular kind of dress has become normative, the individual will have to accept the style. In their study of groups of adolescent boys, the Sherifs noted that "among the narrowest ranges of individual variation permitted in the groups was the latitude of acceptable clothing."[111] There was considerable difference in the styles of various socioeconomic groups, but within the group the boy had little room for individuality in dress.

The power of group norms is also illustrated by the young woman who said of her blue jeans: "I do not feel part of my friends unless they are on."[112]

Once the individual adopts the requisite dress, we presumably know something about that individual's character. The boy or girl who is part of the "leading crowd" in school is personable and has the qualities necessary for leadership and success. The man or woman who is a member of a religious sect shows by plainness of dress that he or she is pious and has an other-worldly orientation. The feminist in fatigues is expressing her hostility against a male-dominated society. The point is that these are not simply individual qualities, but shared qualities of all members of the group.

CLOTHES AND THE STATE OF THE NATION

The final category of social meanings of clothing which is found in the popular media relates to the state of the nation. "Clothes," said a writer shortly after the turn of the century, "always have been and always will be an outward and visible sign of national growth, or decadence."[113] The editor of the *New York Times* agreed, but said this is particularly true of female dress. "Our national character is more reflected in the clothes of our women than in anything else."[114] When our women do not know how to dress with taste and without spending needlessly large sums of money, we may be sure that there are problems with the nation. The reason we may draw conclusions about nations, about a whole people, on the basis of styles worn by individuals is that certain styles tend to prevail throughout a society. Consequently, we can discover important facts about the people by analyzing their dress. In particular, clothing has been said to communicate information about the tastes, the principles, the character, and the mood of a nation.

Just as an individual might "overdress" and reveal a lack of taste, an entire nation can be faulted similarly. In 1860, the editor of *Godey's* said that overdressing and over-furnishing were national sins against good taste.[115] Of course, the styles of a previous generation often appear to be uncomely (recall Laver's formula in the last chapter). Writing in 1909, Hoeber characterized the styles between 1820 and 1880 as the "outcome of utter fatuity, of vile taste and really ingenious incongruity."[116] But even the contemporary styles have been labeled as anything from obnoxious to outrageous. The editor of the *New York Times* agreed that it would be "barbarous" to ask for a national calamity in order to change the "hideous glaring fashions" of 1910, but those fashions, he insisted, were an offense to the sight, a perversion of the tastes of the coming generation, and a destroyer of the charms of even the loveliest of women.[117]

More importantly, according to a number of observers, we have subverted our principles by the kind of clothing we define as fashionable. In particular, we have thwarted our democratic principles by insisting on fashions that are inappropriate to the American situation (see chapter 5). It has been argued that Americans cannot create a truly democratic society without a style of dress that is appropriate to such a society. And the dress reformers continually reminded people that we could hardly claim to be democratic when the clothes of half the people of the nation (that is, the women) expressed a subservient and passive role.

Clothing has also been thought to say something about the character of a people. The subservience of women to an unending series of ugly fashions, argued one writer, would make the sheep a better national emblem than the eagle. The eagle, after all, is a proud, independent creature "who looks as if he did his own thinking." Consequently, the eagle is an inappropriate symbol for a nation that is in bondage to fashion.[118] The question of individualism and the way in which fashion relates to individualism is a recurring one. Whereas most people have seen ready-made clothing as a democratizing process, one saw it as a threat to individualism. How can a woman be an individual under a system of "forced standardization" of styles? "Can she be anything but commonplace?"[119]

Others have seen a loss of our valued individualism in our easy acquiescence to every new style. In 1955, an award-winning designer claimed that American women could be the best dressed in the world if they would only express their individuality in their clothing instead of being slaves to every new fashion.[120] There is a dilemma in this for the individual, however. For individualism in dress, as we have already seen, can quickly be defined as rebellion, as deviance, or as a lack of taste. In clothing, as in other things, the "rugged individualist" in America is admired more in the essay than in life.

Various other aspects of character have also been linked with

FIG. 5. A cartoonist expressed the idea that the flapper costume was ruining the morals and manners of American women. (*Source:* Life, *June 14, 1928.*)

clothing styles. The flapper costume of the 1920s was said to show a decline of morals and manners among young people. The continuing changes in fashions were said to be "just one more manifestation" of the restlessness of Americans.[121] The eagerness of people to follow every new style shows "that they are empty at the core."[122] Styles adopted by particular groups have been said to reveal the character of group members, such as the teenage fashions of the 1950s which were thought by many people to be the "signs of epidemic lunacy in the younger generation."[123] Different observers have quite differing interpretations, but all agree that we can tell something about the character of a people by the prevailing style of clothing.

Finally, the dominant dress of a nation may indicate the national mood. In 1940, the editor of the *New York Times* noted, with a sense of despair, the contradiction between advertised styles of women's clothes and the front page news. Although there was war in Europe, the American mood was a carefree one. Women's hats reflected that mood, which one would not have guessed from the news.[124] By the 1960s and 1970s, the mood was stressed more than the morality or character. In 1972, the *New York Times* commented on the new fashion of "children's" clothes for adult women, suggesting that the style captured the mood of the country. For adults were turning away from the complexities of modern life to "the reassuring simplicity of childhood." The country was weary of drugs, weary of strife, weary of the continual assault on old values and norms. We were in the mood to return to "the good old days when rules were laid down and life was simpler."[125] Similarly, in 1974 the turn toward more conservative fashions was explained as a desire for a more quiet and relaxed way of life after the hectic 1960s.[126] National trends in fashions reflect the mood of a whole people, who live in a changing and therefore mood-altering world.

CONCLUSIONS

When we first plunged into our research on the meaning of clothing and fashion, we anticipated finding patterns of change over time. Instead, we found a number of stable categories with a small number of variations within the categories. Throughout the nineteenth and twentieth centuries, and in some cases throughout earlier centuries as well, Americans have insisted that clothes communicate the seven kinds of information detailed earlier. There have been variations within the seven categories, in the sense that some meanings only appear at particular times. For example, no one in more recent times suggests that a woman in the lower socioeconomic strata is guilty of wrong behavior if she wears the clothes typical of women in the upper strata. But people do still insist that there are status-related meanings to clothing. There are some historical variations within the seven categories, but the categories of meanings themselves are to be found in every age.

Obviously, the meanings assigned to clothing are not trivial. To the extent that people act upon meanings, an individual's life could be significantly affected by his or her manner and mode of dress. Precisely, then, how important is the information communicated by clothing as a basis for interaction? The available evidence indicates that we do tend to relate to others on the basis of what their dress communicates to us. This is not true, of course, with long-standing relationships. But we do tend to use dress as one important basis for secondary relationships—interacting in interviews, in customer and client relationships, and with strangers in various situations. Such relationships can be a crucial part of an individual's career or an individual's sense of acceptance and self-worth.

In sum, Americans have consistently defined clothing as a very important form of nonverbal communication. That communication is used to pattern interaction and to make various judgments about the individual. A nineteenth-century writer captured the essence of the matter in saying: "We are all unconscious disciples of that wonderful gospel of Sartor Resartus, convinced of the 'unspeakable significance and symbolism' of clothes . . . and of the tangible and mystic influence of clothes upon the world at large."[127] The question of fashion—the clothing defined as appropriate and desirable—becomes, therefore, one of considerable significance.

Notes

1. Some of the ideas and materials in this chapter appeared in our paper, "The Language of Dress," published in the *Canadian Review of American Studies*.
2. *The Collected Works of Abraham Lincoln, Vol. II,* ed. Roy P. Basler (New Brunswick, NJ: Rutgers University Press, 1953).
3. Quoted in James Laver, *Clothes* (London: Burke, 1952), p. 8.
4. Paul F. Secord and Carl W. Backman, *Social Psychology,* 2nd edition (New York: McGraw-Hill, 1974), pp. 43–47.
5. Erving Goffman, *Behavior in Public Places* (New York: The Free Press, 1963), p. 33.
6. Gregory P. Stone, "Appearance and the Self," in Gregory P. Stone and Harvey A. Farberman, eds., *Social Psychology Through Symbolic Interaction* (Waltham, Mass.: Ginn-Glaisdell, 1970), pp. 397–402.
7. Gregory P. Stone, "The Circumstance and Situation of Social Status," in Stone and Farberman, *op. cit.,* p. 227.
8. Mark L. Knapp, *Nonverbal Communication in Human Interaction* (New York: Holt, Rinehart and Winston, 1972), p. 82.

9. Quoted in Robert Kunciov, ed., *Mr. Godey's Ladies: Being a Mosaic of Fashions & Fancies* (New York: Bonanza Books, 1971), p. 7.
10. *Ibid.*, p. 18.
11. James Laver, *Modesty in Dress* (London: William Heinemann, 1969), p. 25.
12. U.S. Department of Agriculture, *Clothing Speaks . . . 4-H Members' Guide* (Washington, D.C.: U.S. Government Printing Office, 1970), p. 5.
13. Michael Argyle, "Non-verbal Communication in Human Social Interaction," In Edwin P. Hollander and Raymond G. Hunt, eds., *Current Perspectives in Social Psychology*, 4th edition (New York: Oxford University Press, 1976), p. 190.
14. "Fashion in Dress," *Southern Literary Journal and Magazine of Arts* 2 (1827): 526.
15. Lily Haxworth Wallace, *The New American Etiquette* (New York: Books, Inc., 1941), p. 655.
16. Elinor G. Hayes and Marjorie Shuler, "Do Clothes Make the Woman?" *Independent Woman* 15 (December, 1936): 395.
17. *New York Times*, December 27, 1957.
18. *New York Times*, November 2, 1879.
19. Emily Thornwell, *The Lady's Guide to Perfect Gentility* (Philadelphia: Lippincott, 1876), p. 118.
20. *Ibid.*, p. 119.
21. Charlotte Perkins Gilman, "Symbolism in Dress," *The Independent* 58 (June 8, 1905): 1295.
22. Seymour Fisher, *Body Experience in Fantasy and Behavior* (New York: Appleton-Century-Crofts, 1970), p. 57.
23. Liz Smith, "Why You Wear What You Do," *Today's Health* 51 (October, 1973): 36–37.
24. Lawrence B. Rosenfeld and Timothy G. Plax, "Clothing as Communication," *Journal of Communication* 27 (Spring, 1977): 24–31.
25. "Chitchat for September," *Godey's Lady's Book and Magazine* 45 (September, 1852): 302.
26. Grace M. Gould, "Motive in Dress," *Woman's Home Companion* 40 (March, 1913): 62. See also Bertha Holley, "Psychology in Woman's Dress," *The Forum* 61 (June, 1919): 749.
27. "Fashions of Dress and Their Influence," *Godey's Lady's Book and Magazine* 70 (April, 1865): 370.
28. "Chitchat upon New York and Philadelphia Fashions for February," *Godey's Lady's Book and Magazine* 68 (February, 1864): 210.
29. Emily Cho, with Linda Grover, "Looking Terrific," *Family Circle*, September 27, 1978, p. 103.

30. "Decency in Female Dress," *The Ladies' Repository* 29 (November, 1869): 393.
31. H. Ruggles, "Fashion and the Female," *The Independent* 96 (February 20, 1926): 219–20.
32. *Ibid.*
33. Trucia Kushner, "Finding a Personal Style," *Ms.*, February, 1974, p. 84.
34. Joyce Brothers, "Why Some Women Prefer Daring Fashions," *Good Housekeeping* 173 (July, 1971): 58.
35. For a discussion of Augustine's views, see Stanford M. Lyman, *The Seven Deadly Sins: Society and Evil* (New York: St. Martin's Press, 1978), pp. 56f.
36. George Weekes, *A Discourse Delivered One Hundred and Fifty Years Ago* (Cambridge: Press of John Wilson and Son, 1876), pp. 1–3.
37. C. Willett and Phillis Cunnington, *The History of Underclothes* (London: Michael Joseph, 1951), p. 257.
38. *New York Times,* January 6, 1921.
39. Howard C. Warren, "Social Nudism and the Body Taboo," *Psychological Review* 40 (March, 1933): 182.
40. "On Female Dress," in Anne Fremantle, ed., *A Treasury of Early Christianity* (New York: Mentor Books, 1953), p. 67.
41. "Chitchat for October," *Godey's Lady's Book and Magazine* 47 (October, 1853): 380.
42. "The Influence of Fashions," *The Ladies' Magazine and Literary Gazette* 5 (January, 1832): 2–3.
43. Juliet Virginia Strauss, "When a Man Thinks of Woman as a Pretty Fool," *Ladies' Home Journal* 29 (January, 1912): 16.
44. William Penn, "Some Fruits of Solitude," in Charles W. Eliot, ed., *The Harvard Classics* (New York: P. F. Collier, 1909), p. 346. See also Nathaniel Ward, "Woman's Fashions," in George Mayberry, ed., *A Little Treasury of American Prose* (New York: Charles Scribner's Sons, 1949), p. 21. Ward lived c. 1578–1652.
45. George Weekes, *op. cit.,* pp. 5–7.
46. "Fashion," *Pennsylvania Freeman* 2 (July 8, 1837): 68.
47. Lucy H. Hooper, "Fig Leaves and French Dresses," *Galaxy* 18 (October, 1874): 510. See also Mrs. Burton Harrison, "Some Sins of Society," *Outlook* 50 (December 22, 1894): 1090.
48. See Otto E. Probst, *Secret Sins of Society and Philosophy of the Sexes* (Chicago: American Publishing House, 1901), p. 41, and "The Ideas of a Plain Country Woman," *Ladies' Home Journal* 31 (August, 1914): 26.
49. Robert H. Lauer, *Social Problems and the Quality of Life* (Dubuque: Wm. C. Brown Company Publishers, 1978), p. 112.

50. Mrs. H. C. Gardner, "Fashions," *The Ladies' Repository* 27 (May, 1867): 261.
51. James West, *Plainville, U.S.A.* (New York: Columbia University Press, 1945), pp. 39–177.
52. See Robert F. Seybolt, "Dress Reform in Massachusetts," *New England Quarterly* 3 (No. 2, 1930): 333–38.
53. *Ibid.*, p. 335.
54. "Fashions of Dress and Their Influence," *Godey's Lady's Book and Magazine* 70 (April, 1865): 370.
55. Quoted by R. W. Richmond, "When Hoops Did Tilt and Falsehood Was in Flower," *American History Illustrated* 6 (no. 1): 26.
56. Robert S. Lynd and Helen Merrell Lynd, *Middletown: A Study in American Culture* (New York: Harcourt Brace Jovanovich, Inc., 1929), p. 160.
57. David L. Cohn, *The Good Old Days* (New York: Simon & Schuster, 1940), p. 299.
58. *New York Times*, May 15, 1913.
59. David L. Cohn, *op. cit.*, p. 300.
60. See Kenneth A. Yellis, "Prosperity's Child: Some Thoughts on the Flapper," *American Quarterly* 21 (Spring, 1969): 45 and Linda Hall, "Fashion and Style in the Twenties: The Change," *The Historian* 34 (May, 1972): 487.
61. Jeannette Throckmorton, "Fashions as Affecting Public Health," *American Journal of Public Health* 8 (November, 1918): 819.
62. *New York Times*, November 1, 1919.
63. Linda Hall, *op. cit.*, p. 467. See also "A New Crusade for Longer Skirts," *The Literary Digest* 88 (January 16, 1926): 31–32.
64. Roderick Nash, *The Nervous Generation: American Thought, 1917–1930* (Chicago: Rand McNally & Co., 1970), p. 146.
65. *New York Times*, August 21, 1954.
66. *New York Times*, June 12, 1955.
67. "Female or Feminine," *America* 109 (August 3, 1963): 107.
68. Patricia Shelton, "Nudity in Fashions: Will Society Bare It?" *St. Louis Post-Dispatch*, May 1, 1978.
69. *Ibid.*
70. Arnold Bennett, *Things That Have Interested Me*. Second Series (New York: George H. Doran, 1923), p. 66.
71. Philip Greven, *The Protestant Temperament: Patterns of Child-Rearing, Religious Experience and Self in Early America* (New York: Alfred A. Knopf, 1977), p. 46.
72. George P. Fox, *Fashion: The Power That Influences the World* (New York: Sheldon & Co., 1871), p. 21.
73. *New York Times*, October 18, 1878. See also, Helen Gilbert Ecob, *The*

Well-Dressed Woman, 2nd edition (New York: Foster & Wells Co., 1893), pp. 252-53.
74. Lawrence Langner, *The Importance of Wearing Clothes* (New York: Hastings House, 1959), pp. 141-42.
75. A. G. Noyes, "Practical Protest Against Fashion," *The Independent* 63 (August 29, 1907): 509.
76. *Time,* July 24, 1978, p. 80.
77. Amy Gross, "What Style Is—And Isn't—All About," *Mademoiselle,* September, 1974, p. 123.
78. Barbara Hunt Johnson, Richard H. Nagasawa, and Kathleen Peters, "Clothing Style Differences: Their Effect on the Impression of Sociability," *Home Economics Research Journal* 6 (September, 1977): 62.
79. "Clothes in the Making of a Candidate," *The Literary Digest* 82 (September 6, 1924): 82.
80. *Ibid.*
81. Judy Klemesrud, "As a Campaign Issue, Fashion Is Out of Style," *New York Times,* April 4, 1972.
82. Lilian Breslow Rubin, *Worlds of Pain* (New York: Basic Books, 1976), p. 16.
83. *New York Times,* September 10, 1911.
84. Kenneth L. Cannon, Ruth Staples and Irene Carlson, "Personal Appearance as a Factor in Social Acceptance," *Journal of Home Economics* 44 (November, 1952): 710-13. See also James S. Coleman, *The Adolescent Society* (New York: The Free Press, 1961), pp. 53-55.
85. "Chitchat for September," *Godey's Lady's Book and Magazine* 45 (September, 1852): 302.
86. "As Business Women Should and Should Not Dress," *Ladies' Home Journal* 24 (November, 1907): 25. For a more recent statement, see Amy Gross and Nancy Axelrad Comer, "Power Dressing: A Report on Combat Gear for the Trip to the Top," *Mademoiselle* 83 (September, 1977): p. 188f.
87. John T. Molloy, *Dress for Success* (New York: Peter H. Wyden, 1975), p. 28.
88. "Does What You Wear Tell Where You're Headed," *U.S. News & World Report* 85 (September 25, 1978): 59.
89. John T. Moloy, *op. cit.,* pp. 23-24.
90. Eleanor Boykin, *This Way, Please* (New York: Macmillan, 1940), p. 32.
91. Robert Selbie, *The Anatomy of Costume* (New York: Crescent Books, 1977), p. 6.
92. Michael and Ariane Batterberry, *Mirror, Mirror: A Social History of Fashion* (New York: Holt, Rinehart and Winston, 1977), pp. 50-52.

93. "The Economics of Clothing and Dress," *Godey's Lady's Book and Magazine* 48 (May, 1853): 421.
94. Jane Dorner, *Fashion* (New York: Crescent Books, 1974), p. 57.
95. *St. Louis Post-Dispatch,* January 14, 1879.
96. See, e.g., 'Als Ik Kan," Craftsman 10 (May, 1906): 263–65.
97. See also Charles M. Connolly, "Reform in Men's Dress," *Munsey's Magazine* 25 (September, 1901): 864–70 and Harvey Maitland Watts, "The American Miracle," *The Forum* 73 (March, 1925): 373–78.
98. Agnes Repplier, "The Drolleries of Clothes," *The Independent* 107 (December 3, 1921): 225.
99. Florence Guy Woolston, "If a Worm Could Know," *Harper's Monthly Magazine* 144 (February, 1922): 394.
100. Pola Stout, "The Spirit of Style," *Saturday Review* 47 (October 24, 1964): 45.
101. John T. Molloy, *op. cit.,* pp. 15–18.
102. Julia Ann Pinaire Reed, *Clothing as a Symbolic Indicator of the Self,* unpublished Ph.D. dissertation, Purdue University, 1973, p. 119.
103. John Corry, "About New York: Clothes Are in Fashion Again," *New York Times,* October 23, 1974.
104. R. W. Dellinger, "Keeping Tabs on the Joneses," *Human Behavior,* November, 1977, p. 48.
105. Lois M. Gurel and Marianne S. Beeson, *Dimensions of Dress and Adornment* (Dubuque: Kendall/Hunt, 1975), pp. 59–60.
106. *Ibid.,* p. 60.
107. F. A. Bruce, "Philosophy of Clothes," *Current Literature* 34 (February, 1903): 263.
108. *New York Times,* July 31, 1930.
109. Trucia Kushner, *op. cit.,* p. 51.
110. James S. Coleman, *op. cit.,* p. 37.
111. Muzafer Sherif and Carolyn W. Sherif, *Reference Groups: Exploration into Conformity and Deviation of Adolescents* (New York: Harper and Row, 1964), p. 170.
112. *New York Times,* June 16, 1972. See also, Flanders Dunbar, M.D., "Why Teens Dress That Way," *Parent's Magazine* 37 (August, 1962): 42–43.
113. "Dress and Its Relation to Life," *Craftsman* 11 (November, 1906): 269.
114. *New York Times,* May 16, 1909.
115. "Over-Dress," *Godey's Lady's Book and Magazine* 60 (January, 1860): 89.
116. A. Hoeber, "American Social Life in Illustration," *The Bookman* 28 (February, 1909): 555.
117. *New York Times,* May 16, 1910. See also Katherine Fullerton Gerould,

Modes and Morals (New York: Charles Scribner's Sons, 1920), pp. 46–49.
118. "The Apotheosis of the Commonplace," *Scribner's Magazine* 51 (March, 1912): 378.
119. Ruth Brown Reed, "Parade of Wooden Women," *The Forum* 85 (February, 1931): 92.
120. *New York Times,* April 27, 1955.
121. "Our Bondage to Style," *The Literary Digest* 98 (September 1, 1928): 53.
122. Winifred Raushenbush, "The Idiot God Fashion," in Samuel D. Schmalhausen and V. F. Calverton, eds., *Women's Coming of Age* (New York: Horace Liveright, Inc., 1931): 445.
123. Lester Rand, "Kaleidoscope of Teen-Age Fads," *New York Times,* October 17, 1954.
124. *New York Times,* December 14, 1940.
125. *New York Times,* June 29, 1972.
126. "The New Fashions: 'Man as Man and Woman as Woman'," *U.S. News & World Report,* September 16, 1974, p. 58.
127. "Fetish of Clothes," *Current Literature,* 26 (October, 1899): 336.

chapter 2
What is Fashion?

"Fashion," wrote Mrs. H. C. Gardner in 1867, is an "earthly goddess" that has made religion a secondary concern to most people: "Some of us would be satisfied to reconcile the two, if such union were possible; we would like to see them harmoniously sharing the throne of sovereignty, but the first article in the creed of the universal woman is this, 'There is but one god, and that is Fashion.' "[1] The earthly goddess has intrigued not only popular writers like Mrs. Gardner, but philosophers, moralists, playwrights, and social scientists. Fashion is one of those elusive phenomena of social life that is a part of everyone's experience, the object of numerous analyses, and a continuing source of perplexity and uncertainty. As Charlotte Gilman wrote in 1905, fashion is a simple enough subject if we simply follow it unthinkingly, but it is quite complex when we try to subject it to any serious treatment.[2]

We have already seen the diversity of explanations of fashion in professional analyses. In this chapter we shall see a similar variety in popular writers, who, like their professional counterparts, have attempted to capture and express the essential meaning of fashion, and to explain the inexorable changes in fashions.

MEANING AND METAPHOR

We are symbolic creatures. Some thinkers argue that it is our ability to use symbols that distinguishes us from the lower animals. As an anthropologist put it, the symbol "transformed our anthropoid ancestors into men and made them human."[3] The most important set of symbols we use is our language, and one of the most interesting and useful linguistic symbols is the metaphor.

A metaphor is a shorthand device for expressing a complex meaning. It is

> a way of knowing—one of the oldest, most deeply embedded, even indispensable ways of knowing in the history of human consciousness. It is, at its simplest, a way of proceeding from the known to the unknown. It is a way of cognition in which the identifying qualities of one thing are transferred in an instantaneous, almost unconscious, flash of insight, to some other thing that is, by remoteness or complexity, unknown to us.[4]

Metaphors arise out of the matrix of experience. We attempt to capture the essence of something complex in our experience by encapsulating that essence in a metaphor. In turn, the metaphor becomes a channel for the experiences of others. If my experience with the perplexing phenomenon of fashion leads me to label it an earthly goddess, the label will, in turn, help to construct the meaning of fashion for others. To the extent that different people employ a particular metaphor to think about, or write about, some phenomenon, that phenomenon has a common meaning for them.

We have chosen, therefore, to explore the question of the meaning of fashion to Americans by examining the metaphors applied to fashion in popular writings. In books, essays, and articles in popular magazines, Americans have used a variety of metaphors to discuss fashion. But the metaphors they have used are not idiosyncratic. We find different people in the same and in different eras applying the same metaphors. The earthly goddess reveals herself in differing ways, but she appears to a number of people in each of those ways. Consequently, we are able to construct categories of imagery into which the metaphors fall. In all, seven types of imagery express the meaning of the various metaphors: force, tyranny, divinity, royalty, irrationality, mystery, and deviousness. These seven types may be grouped into two broader categories of power and nonrational images. Metaphors reflecting both of the broader types can be found throughout the nineteenth and twentieth centuries.

METAPHORS OF POWER

There are four different kinds of imagery that have the theme of power—force, tyranny, divinity, and royalty. Each of these suggests something different about the exercise of power. But each also emphasizes the fact that power is being exercised, that fashion is not merely something out there that is available to us, but something that has an inescapable impact upon our lives.

Force

First, there is the image of force. The metaphors that express this image vary in the extent of forcefulness, from the idea of exerting influence to the notion of being virtually omnipotent. George Fox, the "President of Fashion" in the 1870s, subtitled his book on fashion, "the power that influences the world." He gave numerous examples of the ways in which fashion influences people and their behavior. "The serenity produced by a perfect fitting suit puts one in good humor with all mankind," he wrote with assurance.[5] He attributed to fashion the same kind of power that others reserve for religion or drugs.

Generally, however, those who have written about fashion's power have been more negative in their assessment. Fashion is a force in the individual's life, but it is an overwhelming force. According to most writers, the individual is not merely influenced by fashion, rather, the individual is overpowered by an irresistible and external force. We become subservient to fashion, falling short of the ideal of an autonomous person. In the face of fashion, we are no longer self-directed but other-directed.

If we are directed by an external force rather than by our own reason or inclinations, we may be unable to act in accord with our own best interests. At one level, this may mean nothing more than that we wear those styles that are unflattering or that fail to effectively complement our natural appearance. A 1917 writer lamented the fact that women insist on being fashionable "however unbecoming it may be to themselves individually."[6] A 1931 writer told of a woman who wanted to buy a velvet hat without a brim because such a hat would be most becoming to her at her age and with her type of skin. But after considerable searching she had to abandon her desire because "the all-powerful Dame Fashion dictated felt hats or those of similar materials made without brims."[7]

As we shall discuss later, one of the functions of fashion is to allow the individual to enhance his or her natural attractiveness and to hide unattractive features. But those who yield unthinkingly or servilely to Dame Fashion may find themselves uglified. Fashion is more than merely unflattering to them, it is an unseemly force that twists their potential beauty into ugliness.

A few writers argued that all fashions uglify. In the unforgettable words of one nineteenth-century advisor on love and beauty, "Taste has a disease which is called Fashion. It is a sort of microbe which has the effect of distorting and *exaggerating* everything it takes hold of."[8] Commenting on the practice of making the waist smaller by the use of a corset, the same advisor pointed out that fashion, which is "the handmaid of ugliness," was "too vulgar to appreciate the exquisite beauty of slight and subtle curvature."[9]

Most people do not agree that fashion is always an uglifying force. Most would not even go as far as the woman who claimed that fashions "make inevitably, nine years out of ten, for the greatest ugliness of the greatest number."[10] Most of those who comment on the uglifying impact of fashion refer to a particular fashion at a particular time. Incidentally, the intensity of reactions to a fashion defined as uglifying illustrates the importance of the prevailing style to people. People react vehemently to things that a later age regards as trivial. For instance, bangs became a fashionable hair style in St. Louis in 1881. One woman, incensed over what she regarded as a "barbarous custom," wrote the editor of the local paper and said that if God had intended for His children to wear bangs He would have made our hair grow forward, like it does on puppies, instead of backward like it does naturally.[11]

At times, fashion has been more than uglifying; it has been a destructive force, as physicians, educators, and feminists insisted throughout the nineteenth century (see chapter 6). In spite of these negative consequences, fashion is extremely difficult to resist. Its power is awesome. "Few, save the reformer and the recluse, ever willingly become conspicuous by defiance of the passing mode."[12] It is generally useless to argue, to ridicule, or to malign. Those who try to show the undesirability of a particular fashion are "trying to outshout the whirlwind."[13] Most people will simply follow the changing fashions meekly like sheep. And some people, called by the editor of the *New York Times* in 1922 the "feather-brained,"[14] will accept any new fashion at all, no matter how ludicrous. Some of us may believe that we are making a choice when we select our clothes, but the notion that we have free will is only a "gay illusion," since we can only select within the extremely narrow limits of fashion. "The choice has really been made for us by something which sees to it that we all like the same things at the same time."[15]

Obviously, those who have contemplated the power of fashion have seen it as potent. Fashion is neither meek nor weak. It is a force so potent that people have followed its dictates even when common sense or the advice of physicians or the laments of feminists stressed the deleterious consequences. There are, of course, more than negative results from following fashion. The fashionable individual is able to share the power exerted by the earthly goddess:

> One may describe it and its suzerains unlimitedly; but the thing itself, Fashion, which to the worldly minded always conveys the last supreme grace—what is it? It is a bauble, a toy, a trifle light as air; but to him who possesses it, a scepter of infinite power.[16]

Tyranny

Each of the other three images that we have grouped under the general category of power also stress the forceful nature of fashion, but combine forcefulness with another image that suggests the kind of power that is being exerted. The most frequently used of all the power images is that of tyranny. As in the case of the image of force, the tyrant is potent; in fact, the tyrant possesses overwhelming power. In addition, the tyrant knows no authority other than his own as he establishes law. And the subjects of the tyrant are slaves.

The extent of the tyrant's power was expressed vividly by Paul Poiret, the noted twentieth-century designer. Even sovereigns of states and kings of finance and industry, he argued, are "under the despotism of Style, which is an intolerant dictator." We have no choice in the matter of fashion, for it "controls and rules" our decisions. Fashion is "like an astral influence" that "weighs upon our freedom of will. This tyrant is twice a despot, since he rules women and sways the action of men."[17] As with any tyrant, the rule of fashion is absolute; it has virtually complete control over people's minds so that no appeal to a higher law is even possible.[18] Furthermore, this "tyrannical rule of Dame Fashion" is not only powerful but ancient, because from the beginning "the womanly instinct to be attractive led woman to regard dress as a means to an end."[19] In other words, the tyrant has gained power by convincing us that he will amply satisfy our hunger to be attractive. As Frank Parsons, president of the New York School of Fine and Applied Art, put it, fashion is "one of the greatest of earth's autocrats" because it appeals to our "elemental desires, appetites, vanities, and self-interest."[20]

The preceding statements show that metaphors are not used flippantly or unthinkingly. Fashion is not called a tyrant, or an autocrat, or a despot, because it is cute to do so—the metaphors are used because they capture something of the meaning of the phenomenon. And the writers who use them often draw out the implications of the metaphor in consistent terms. This point is underscored by the frequent use of the term "slaves" to refer to those who diligently obey fashion.

If fashion is a tyrant, then those who are quick to obey are the tyrant's slaves. Americans have always prized freedom, so those who see fashion as a tyrant have been quick to condemn both the tyrant and its subjects. The feminists who were involved in the movement for rational dress were particularly scathing in their attack both on fashion and on fashion's slavish followers. In an 1891 article on "fashion's slaves," Mrs. B. O. Flower recalled two cartoons and a poem that had appeared in print some years earlier. One cartoon showed a poor man's wife, who was the "slave of toil," while the other showed a well-dressed, affluent woman, who was the slave of fashion. The poem was titled, "Sister Slaves:"

> *You think there is little of kinship between them?*
> *Perhaps not in blood, yet there's likeness of soul;*
> *And in bondage 'tis patent to all who have seen them*
> *That both are fast held under iron control.*
> *The simpering girl, with her airs and her graces,*
> *Is sister at heart to the hard-working drudge;*
> *Two types of today, as they stand in their places;*
> *Whose lot is the sadder I leave you to judge.*
>
> *One chained to the block is the victim of Fashion;*
> *Her object in life is to be perfectly dressed;*
> *Too silly for reason, too shallow for passion,*
> *She passes her days 'neath a tyrant's behest.*
> *Thus pinioned and fettered, and warily moving,*
> *Lest looping should fail her, or band come apart:*
> *What room is there left for thinking or loving?*
> *What noble ambition can enter her heart?*[21]

Feminists and other dress reformers were not the only ones to give the followers of fashion the name of slave. A great many writers agreed with the 1914 observer, who said that if we accept the dictionary definition of slavery as involving moral or physical bondage, then we cannot deny that "the world today is filled with women slaves."[22] For women never get weary of discussing dress or the changes in fashion, and they behave just "as fashion dictates" while at the same time they judge other women by the extent to which those other women also obey the decrees of fashion.

Most writers identify women rather than men as the slaves of fashion. Some have even contrasted women's slavish behavior with the more rational, utilitarian approach of men. But an occasional writer cast men into the role of slaves also. Arnold Bennett differed from most male observers when he argued that women are no more foolish than men in the matter of clothing. Men are enslaved to fashion, and if they do occasionally escape from some oppressive fashion, they will strive to return to prison.[23] As an example of the man who rushes back to prison, Bennett gave the case of the return of the top hat in the 1920s to its old position of tyranny over the male head. Another author argued that men are even more bound than women by fashion, that in the matter of fashion the average man is "pigeon-livered and lacks gall."[24] But most refer to women when they discuss the slaves of fashion.

As a tyrant with slaves, fashion oppresses and subjugates with ruthlessness. Frances Russell, one of the leaders of the nineteenth-century rational dress movement, wrote that fashion is a "fiend" who is "bent upon the hopeless subjugation of one-half the human race, and, through their degradation, upon the extinction of the sentiment of freedom in all humanity."[25] We cannot be a nation of free people as long as we acquiesce to the tyranny of fashion. A twentieth-century writer, elaborating upon the same image of tyranny, called for revolt by women who were "groaning under the whimsical whip of Fashion" and eager to escape the dictates of the tyrant.[26]

Alexander Pope said that whatever makes a man a slave takes away half his worth. The critics of fashion have a good deal to say about the demeaning consequences for the tyrant's slaves. In addition to robbing us of our freedom, fashion robs us of money, blocks us from following more fulfilling pursuits, jeopardizes our health, and, as we have already seen, plunges us into the stagnant waters of immorality.[27] As Pope Pius said in 1940, women who were bowing to the tyranny of fashion were like "insane persons who unwittingly throw themselves into fires and rivers."[28] At worst, the slavery is said to be a direct and quick path to destruction. At best, we are made into servile and ridiculous creatures, as a St. Louis editor noted in 1890, in commenting on women who are "ridiculously submissive slaves" to the whims of fashion:

> Twice within the last week have I been unable to recognize old friends because of their hats. Think of women who have reached years of discretion and crows-feet, wearing those monstrosities in the poke shape that shoot up in front like a sort of milliner's airbrake. They were undoubtedly meant only for girls, but the birthday forgettors have claimed them for their own, and they'll keep them until they are out of fashion.[29]

Will Americans always be enslaved to fashion? Will the tyranny never end in this land of liberty? Those who employ the metaphor of tyrant stress the difficulty of resistance that is implied. The power of the tyrant is awesome. As a 1921 writer put it, a woman would not deform her body to produce an "hourglass" waist out of personal vanity, rather, women have been the victims of that which is "more powerful than vanity, the inexorable decrees of fashion."[30] In the face of those decrees, all other authority—whether ecclesiastical, marital, or medical—is ignored.[31]

Nevertheless, tyrants can be overthrown. At some point, the trampled human spirit rises up and begins the grim struggle for freedom. The dress reformers of the nineteenth and early twentieth centuries took this approach. They labeled fashion a tyrant, but they rejected the "inexorable" nature of fashion's laws. They advocated revolt. Many despaired of the unwillingness of women to engage in the revolution, but at least it was an option. "It is proven," Mrs. Flower wrote, "that there is in this day manhood grand and noble enough to encourage this righteous rebellion against the tyrannical dictator, fashion." And if those men would only endorse the efforts of women, the latter would be able to rebel.[32]

Some writers even went so far as to argue that fashion only continues to tyrannize us because we allow it. We may be slaves, but we are willing slaves. If we had sufficient strength of character, we could revolt against the tyrant. This argument was supported by pointing out that "the most abject slaves of fashion are to be found among the barbarous races and classes," those who lack a high and independent character.[33] The slavery of well-to-do and less barbarous Americans is no less real, but the potential for revolt is with us, awaiting only our willingness.

Royalty

The image of royalty does not occur very often, but when it does, fashion is portrayed as a monarch who exercises complete control of the subjects. In 1879, the editor of the *New York Times* pointed out that only on rare visits do Americans see anything of the Old World nobility. On the other hand, "there is one sovereign who holds his court everywhere in our America, and who insists upon everywhere establishing his caste, nobility, and throne." That sovereign, of course, is fashion. And nowhere on earth is its reign as powerful as it is in America, "since here it has no rivals in its exclusiveness and no tribes or classes outside of its sway."[34]

The royal image, like that of tyranny, stresses the fact that fashion follows its own laws which are established by its own authority. It is not the majesty, or the elegance, or the beauty of royalty that is in the minds of the writers, but royalty's power. Fashion is a "Queen" whose "sway is absolute" and whose "word is law," so that "her decrees go forth and nations hasten to do her bidding with an eager compliance that shames the followers of Christ."[35] Some Americans may scoff at the notion that we have a reigning monarch. But "if you doubt that she is queen," asserted a 1929 writer, "try to ignore her suggestions."[36] When the Queen has spoken, one does not go one's own independent way with impunity.

But a Queen is not necessarily a tyrant. The tyrant subjugates us and exploits us in behalf of his own interests and well-being. The monarch at times may act in ways that are detrimental to our well-being by decreeing that we shall wear those things that are physically harmful or aesthetically undesirable. As a nineteenth-century writer lamented, at the word of the "many-minded empress" good things may be banned and "the preposterous becomes popular, absurdities are defensible, monstrosities grow endurable, and all the laws of symmetry and taste are set at naught." But at other times, the monarch acts in a benevolent fashion and decrees a style that enhances our well-being. A 1901 writer observed that the "royal dame" had allowed women to adopt the golf skirt, which was "the only rational thing she has invented since the shirtwaist, which she now decrees must be relegated to the past."[38] The benevolence of the royal dame is limited. She gives with one hand and takes with the other. But, unlike the tyrant, she does sometimes act in behalf of our well-being. Her power brings us some happiness as well as some burdens.

Divinity

The last of the power images, divinity, stresses the power of fashion by focusing on the commitment of the devotees. We are not slaves of a tyrant; we are, rather, committed with great devotion to a divine being. We are not the subjects of a monarch whom we have not chosen; we are the dedicated followers of our god. Fashion is a god or goddess, and like all divinities, it elicits religious fervor in the form of total commitment. It may be, in the words of Amelia Bloomer, a "fickle goddess" whom we serve, but the commitment is not diminished by the ungodly traits.[38]

As a form of religion, then, fashion has its creed, and that creed is accepted by the devotees.[39] Furthermore, there are rituals to be conducted in the religion of fashion. Women pray to the little god and offer him incense in the form of "smooth silks, the ivoried innocence of lace, the icy invitation of crystal, the forest mystery of jade, the embittered blue of turquoises, the glow of pink pearls, voluptuous satins, and the sensuous electricity of fur."[40]

Critics of religion have often made a distinction between faith and reason. The one, they argue, is contrary to the other, so that we must either be a people of faith *or* a people of reason. To support the argument, they may cite the famous declaration of the ancient theologian, "I believe *because* it is absurd." Critics of the devotees of fashion likewise distinguish between faith and reason. The devotees live by faith, not by reason; the god they serve is an "idiot."[40] The decrees of the god or goddess are to be obeyed rather than understood. The devotees give up their reasoning to the god, allowing fashion to do their thinking for them.[42] In fact, the abdication of reason is necessary because there is no pattern to the changing styles, at least none which is comprehensible to males according to an 1860 writer:

> . . . for ladies' tastes and fashions are without rule, rhyme, or reason, and more inconstant than the moon. . . . Fashion is the goddess of woman, because she is like woman, *"Varium et mutabile semper"* . . . she is a household goddess, who presides over all the domestic concerns, and regulates family affairs and expenditures, by means of her votaries, the ladies, who alone can comprehend her requirements, and interpret aright her oracles and her revelations.[43]

As with any divine being, fashion is jealous of her followers; she will brook no rival for her authority. Thus, if a Christian can be filled with a strong desire to be fashionable, Satan leaves that person "contentedly to seek other prey" for he "knows that he has secured a heavy mortgage on that soul."[44] No one can serve more than one

FIG. 6. For some people, woman's slavery to fashion inevitably meant an abandonment of religion. (*Source:* Life, *1915.*)

god. Those who choose to follow fashion are at the same time choosing to reject the authority of any other divine being. One gets the impression from a number of the writers that it is as incongruous to be both fashionable and Christian as it is to be both a Christian and a Buddhist.

Those who argue for the incompatibility of devotion both to fashion and to something else, have a valid point. In the nineteenth century, it took an incredible amount of time for a woman to be fashionable. A number of changes were required throughout the day for various times and activities, and each outfit could be composed of as much as thirty or more pounds of clothing for some styles. In the twentieth century, a woman may be fashionable without devoting nearly as much time and energy to the task. But it is still possible to religiously pursue the goddess. In discussing the "evil effects of the dress-cult," a 1912 writer said that one can almost assert that the more the amount of time women spend in pursuing fashionable dress, the less they have of such qualities as competence, humor, and intelligence.[45] A 1972 newspaper story described women who spend enormous amounts of money and time on clothing ($100,000 or more a year). In some cases, they buy more than they can possibly wear. When asked why she bought so many, one responded, "I don't play bridge or golf. What would I do afternoons if I didn't shop?"[46] The true contemporary devotee of the goddess shops in order to buy fashionable clothes in order to look attractive when she shops. For the contemporary devotee, as well as for her counterparts through the last two centuries, the conclusion of Mrs. Gardner is apt: "There is but one god, and that is Fashion."

METAPHORS OF NONRATIONALITY

As those who label fashion a god or goddess illustrate, the two categories of power and nonrationality are often mixed. We shall discuss this further, but first we will look at the three kinds of nonrational images. Each of them reflects some kind of nonrational behavior, but each gives a different flavor to the nonrationality.

Irrationality

In the image of irrationality, fashion is said to be not merely without reason, but even contrary to reason. Fashion is often spoken of in terms of its "follies," that is, it lacks sense, it is unreasonable. "Twin sisters ever are Fashion and Idiocy."[47] Often, the follies of fashion are illustrated by recalling freakish styles of the past. A 1919 writer suggested a set of tableaux illustrating American fashions through the ages that could be used for entertainment. Each tableau would be introduced by someone who was dressed up as "Folly." As an introduction to the entire set, Folly was to give the following:

> *For three hundred years,*
>   *In the domain of fashion,*
> *The dressmaker's shears*
>   *Have been cuttin' and slashin';*
> *But don't be alarmed*
>   *At any new style.*
> *We've had something worse,*
>   *If you'll look back a while;*

> *The old "Godey's Book,"*
> *If it could but speak*
> *Would tell us the story*
> *Of many a freak.*[48]

A 1948 textbook for high school students said that we can find many follies by looking at books on historic costume. Among the outstanding "freaks of fashion" were the high headdress popularized by Marie Antoinette, the "Merry Widow" hat which was fashionable around 1907, and shoes with long toes, including those worn by men in England in the fifteenth century which had points half a foot long.[49]

There are a number of reasons why various writers maintain that fashion is irrational. In the first place, they argue that its irrationality is illustrated by its nonutilitarian nature. When a particular style is more comfortable than its predecessors, or when it provides better protection, or when people agree that it is more attractive, the new style makes sense. But it is pointed out time and again that the history of fashion is replete with styles which had no utilitarian value whatever. The editor of the *New York Times* in 1875, echoed the sentiments of every generation of Americans when he declared that the fashion of his day contravened the laws of health and the principles of comfort. Indeed, they violated the "intrinsic rules of beauty."[50] A 1970 writer added to the list—fashion also totally disregards cost as well as comfort and beauty.[51]

Critics of fashion insist that we should not get the impression there is no utility to clothing or to new styles at all. In fact, it is pointed out that a number of styles were quite useful when introduced but became nonutilitarian with time. For example, buttons on the sleeves of men's jackets have no useful purpose. The practice is said to have originated when Napoleon was angered by watching his soldiers wipe their noses on their sleeves. Napoleon first added braid to the sleeves, but the wiping continued. Finally, he had buttons sewn on all the sleeves of his men and that effectively stopped the habit. Similarly, the grenadier cap originally was designed for a select group of soldiers who were assigned to throw grenades. The tall, brimless cap allowed the soldiers to fulfill their task without knocking the cap off their heads, but over time the cap became increasingly tall and decreasingly useful. "It finally evolved as the absurd and towering bearskin cap of the nineteenth century."[52]

FIG. 7. The nonutilitarian nature of fashion was illustrated by, among others, the bustle of 1889. *(Source: Library of Congress.)*

Sleeve buttons and bearskin caps are harmless. What has incensed the critics are not the harmless styles, but those that are painful, frustrating, or aggravating. When a style is positively harmful in some way, then it is truly irrational. And there are endless examples of such styles in history, styles which were quite fashionable and quite contrary to comfort or convenience, or even health.

An 1832 writer complained that fashion in his day was frustrating desired kinds of behavior.[53] "Who," he asked, "has not felt vexed, nay absolutely angry" at being unable to come "within reasonable earshot of a lady by the vast masses of envelopes in which she is rolled, when being in a tender mood he has wanted to say something pretty to her, without being particularly desirous it should be heard by every one near." The same fashions, he pointed out, have ended some "good old customs." Two women, for instance, who have been separated for a long time, would formerly have rushed into each other's arms and embraced "according to the rules of the sentimental." But that behavior was precluded by fashion. In fact, were the two to attempt such an embrace, "what a tremendous concussion, what a terrible crash of whalebone, cordage, hoops, etc., would be produced." Similarly, it used to be customary for a man to give a kiss of friendship to a pretty cousin "or any other clever female friend," but the fashions of the day have surrounded women "by a row of defenses, like an enemy shut up in a strong garrison, which it is impossible to carry either by storm or siege." When fashion so frustrates desired behavior and quells good old customs, it is nothing less than irrational.

Another complaint involving the nonutilitarian nature of fashion is the way in which fashions have tormented or disfigured the human body. An 1881 writer said that people's comfort is never considered. Clothing is not fitted to the human body; rather, a woman must make her body conform to the shape of the style and endure the "pinches, distortions, and exposures." In fact, lamented the writer, from her head to her feet, a woman is subjected to the "tortures of dress:"

> Pins stick her in places that she cannot reach at the time; garters are too tight and stop the circulation of blood in her limbs; corset steels break and the sharp ends prod her sides; changes from the flannels of every day to the bareness of evening costumes give her shivers and neuralgia . . . and above all, she is sure to itch in numerous places. I have known moments when I would have given my purse and contents for a good claw at the calf of my leg.[54]

Bernard Rudofsky dramatically illustrated the disfiguring aspect of fashion when he had an artist create models of the female body as it would have appeared had the clothes of various eras been formfitting.[55] For example, the bustle suggests a four-legged woman, a kind of short-bodied, female centaur. The dowager of 1904 appeared to have a huge, single breast. The hobble skirt gave the appearance of a single leg which was bifurcated near the bottom. And the flapper is hardly recognizable as female; it is simply a pole with legs, arms, and a head.

A final complaint about the nonutilitarian nature of fashion points to the contradiction of certain fashions with efficient behavior. In 1890, a St. Louis editor said the heavy amounts of rain were making dress reformers of the city's women. The streets had become "pure adhesive liquid mud," a fact appreciated by every woman who had to make her way through it "tilting forward to prevent the back of her dress from dipping into every puddle and accumulating a generous quantity of alluvial deposit on the front of her gown, to be wiped off on the tops of her six dollar French kid boots, to their utter demoralization."[56] The contrast with men walking under the same conditions was obvious. It makes no sense for one half of the population to be dressed in a style that inhibits the kind of activity that is relatively easy for the other half. But women—at least in America—have typically been the victims of styles that contradict efficient behavior. Sometimes they have acquiesced to, or even supported, inefficient styles. In 1910, the woman's amateur tennis champion of the United States addressed the debated question of whether women should wear corsets while playing golf or tennis. She asserted that she wore them herself and felt they were "desirable for many reasons," including the fact that most players looked better with them.[57] At other times, as we shall see, women have revolted against irrational styles, including those that made them inefficient in various activities.

Are the complaints about the nonutility of styles a thing of the past? Looking backward, Americans may be inclined to think that we have passed out of the dark ages of fashion and into the modern era, that we have sloughed off the irrationalities of our forebears. Certainly, health damaging styles like the corset (see chapter 6) have been discarded. And some American designers like Claire McCardell have stressed the point that clothes must be comfortable or they make no sense. Nevertheless, fashions in the 1960s and 1970s were not always as sensible as Americans liked to believe. Critics were quick to point out that the follies of Dame Fashion continue. What makes sense, they asked, about the miniskirt when a women has to bend down or sit down comfortably? Or what makes sense about jeans for women that fit so tightly they can be put on only with great effort? What makes sense about a young man tottering on high-heeled shoes? The fashion of each generation seems irrational (especially from the perspective of other generations), although each may be irrational in its own way.

The use of "folly" to label fashion illustrates one kind of irrationality—the nonutilitarian and positively harmful aspects of fashion. Fashion has also been called irrational because it is fickle. That is, it keeps changing in an apparently capricious manner. You can't predict it. You know it will change, for change is its nature, but you can never be sure in which direction, for fickleness is also its nature.[58] Fashion, it has been said, is like "a beautiful, smooth-cheeked boy, who paints his finger-nails to-day and his toe-nails to-morrow, and smiles complacently."[59] Such changes can only be called irrational. They are arbitrary and they are senseless. Obviously, fashion is temperamental and fickle as it runs from one "unreasoning extreme" to another.[60] If fickle fashion ever decrees a style that is generally satisfactory, one wary writer pointed out, we should be quick to seize upon it and approve it, for the changes are usually from one senseless style to another.[61]

Because fashion is a fickle or capricious process, it should not be blindly followed. Fashion and its devoted followers are simply a perfect picture of the blind leading the blind. The irate Mrs. Flower argued, in fact, that we shall be positively harmed if we blindly follow fashion, for "health, posterity, and all the instincts of the higher self are ruthlessly sacrificed to the fickle folly of fashion's criminal caprice."[62] She argued that only when common sense and reason triumphed over "an effete conventionality, the caprice of fashion, and the cupidity of man," would woman be able to attain "the plane to which absolute and impartial justice must, and will eventually, assign her."[63]

For a third set of writers who saw fashion as irrational, the words fickleness and folly were too mild. Like Mrs. Flower, they may have seen fashion as folly and as capricious, but they also saw it in much more intense terms; blind, absurd, mad, or even insane.[64] An 1858 writer illustrated the absurdity of fashion by pointing out that she "performs freaks" among both "savage" and civilized people; "if the Chinese beauty pinches her foot out of every natural proportion, the New York belle compresses her waist till she looks like an hourglass."[65] We should not scoff at the "savage" Chinese until we remedy the absurdities in our own midst. A 1946 writer gives us an image of fashion as an insane person who is imposing her own irrationality upon us. Fashion, he declared, can run berserk, issuing decrees about every aspect of our lives, all of which "have nothing to do with what we *are.*"⁶⁶ One reaches the apex of irrationality when one dresses, eats, acts, and thinks in ways that are fashionable but contrary to one's essential being.

How can we cope with this irrational process? Some writers argued that although fashion was an irrational process, the exercise of reason and judgment could offset any potential ill effects. An individual simply had to use his or her common sense or reason and refuse to accept every new style unthinkingly.⁶⁷ But generally, the image of irrationality has suggested less scope for resistance than the images of power. After all, one can always rebel against a tyrant, even if the rebellion is unsuccessful at first. But how does one cope with an irrational process? How does one deal with caprice? How does one even maintain one's well-being in the context of fickleness? The point is that humans do not function well in a capricious world. We all have a need to make sense out of our world, to have at least some sense of orderliness, regularity, and security. One of the boons of modernity is the increasing rationalization of certain aspects of life. We prefer and function better in a world that is lawful than we do in one that is battered around arbitrarily by capricious demons. It is understandable, therefore, that those who see fashion as irrational react so negatively to it.

Mystery

The image of mystery suggests that fashion is unconnected with reason. It is not irrational. It does not offend or contradict the reason. Rather, it is a process which is not amenable to rational analysis. It follows no known laws. We cannot even construct laws that apply to it. It is like the wind blowing at will, now one way and then another. But the way in which it will blow in the future is unknown, for the same Heaven that hides the book of Fate conceals the future of fashion.⁶⁸ The mystery of fashion eludes the human intellect. We can only say that fashion is a "strange and wonderful creature" that sways us through a kind of magic.⁶⁹

Even though fashion as a mystery is a nonlawful process, it does not offend us like an irrational process. For there is no threat in a mystery as there is in the irrational. On the contrary, we are attracted to the mysterious, there is a fascination in it. It is little wonder that when the mysterious edict of fashion arrives "all classes hasten to obey, from the shopgirl on four dollars a week to the woman with unlimited money at her disposal—all are actuated by the same impulse; all are united in chasing the phantom 'style.' "[70] It is a chase. It is not the slave obeying the tyrant. It is not the devotee performing his or her ritual. It is not the blind following the blind. It is the pursuit of fascination. Therefore, whenever a style receives "the magic touch of fashion," that style will prevail.[71]

The disappearance of a style from fashion may be as mysterious as the appearance of a new style. In either case, we will heed the mysterious call. A 1928 observer pointed out one of the "mysterious pronouncements" of fashion that occurred in 1921—veils were no longer fashionable. Veil manufacturers reacted indignantly and then fearfully. They tried various kinds of advertising. They even tried to convince women that Paris approved of veils. "But the women obeyed the mysterious voice. They always do. The veil business disappeared overnight."[72]

There is no rationality to such a phenomenon. It is simply a mystery. And the more one studies fashion, the more one may come to the conclusion of one lifelong student that fashion has "nothing to do with beauty, modesty, or utility, and that it is a great natural force. We use it, just as we do electricity, but we do not know what it is."[73]

The image of mystery, like that of irrationality, evokes a feeling of helplessness. The primary emphasis is not on helplessness, but the image is there. We stand somewhat perplexed and awed in the face of mystery. Reason and will are both inadequate to deal with that which casts its spell over us like a sorcerer. And yet for all that, we yield willingly, drawn by the fascination of that which transcends our minds yet stirs our hearts.

Deviousness

The final image is also nonrational. As a devious phenomenon, fashion is portrayed as that which acts immorally rather than reasonably. In its deviousness, fashion tricks us or fools us. Reason is not an effective defense because fashion makes use of cunning. In particular, the American woman is the "butt of Fashion's dirty joke," for she has been led to believe such fallacies as the superiority of French designers and the necessity for changing styles every six months.[74]

As a devious creature, fashion keeps us off guard. It alternately grieves and consoles us.[75] We are led to believe that fashion is our friend, only to be deceived and betrayed and then cajoled back into friendship. As a trickster, fashion makes us believe that we are attractive when we follow her decrees. The real result, however, is that we are uglified. In fact, "whole nations have been dressed absurdly, uncomfortably, unbeautifully," and because they buy rather than make their clothes, women have lost their discernment.[76] The ultimate in deviousness has occurred when we are so confused by the incessant tricks that we have lost all powers of judgment.

The interesting thing is that we are not a people easily duped. We have made impressive advances in every kind of endeavor, but no matter how sophisticated we have become in other matters, we continue to fall into the traps set by fashion. By 1947, a national news magazine could still talk of fashion being "up to its old tricks—peddling, as Oscar Wilde observed, 'that by which the fantastic becomes for a moment universal.' "[77]

PATTERNS OF USAGE

The metaphors discussed above span more than one hundred and fifty years of American history. Enormous changes occurred during those years. Among others, the nineteenth century was characterized by a greater belief in absolutes than that which prevailed in the twentieth century. In fact, a dominant strand of thought in the nineteenth century was deterministic. According to this line of reasoning, humans have little control over their destiny. The universe is governed by laws that are "almost as rhythmic and predictable as the new machinery spawned by the Industrial Revolution."[78] However, another strand of American thought in the second half of the nineteenth century argued otherwise. Some Americans saw an open society rather than one hemmed in by deterministic laws. They envisioned a world "in which almost everything could be challenged and changed by man's growing intelligence."[79]

Both strands of thought suggest that we can understand the process of change. Indeed, for most thinkers, the future held a better, more satisfying life. Whether largely determined or created primarily by human effort, the path that lay ahead was upward towards utopia. Periods of economic woe, political corruption, and war assailed the faith in progress, but could not crush it. And with the rapid industrializing of the nation after the Civil War, praise for the nation and its future abounded. For instance, an 1890 writer spoke of the "marvellous developments of physical science which have characterized the progress of civilization," the "wonderful acceleration" of the progress, and the fact that science is "a great comforter, civilizer, and enlightener."[80]

American optimism and faith in progress gave way to an encroaching pessimism after World War I. Phenomena were increasingly viewed as relative rather than as absolutes. Uncertainty and doubts about the meaning of life challenged the old confidence in America's God-given destiny. By the late 1920s, many young Americans had rebelled only to become disillusioned with their own rebellions, and our culture was pervaded by beliefs in "the meaninglessness of society, the absurdity of purposeless nature, and the richly textured mood of combined pleasure and isolation."[81] The society then faced the even more shattering experiences of the Great Depression and World War II, so the American's world after 1929 "in all its aspects seemed out of order; luck, chance, irrationality" confronted the American everywhere.[82] But the American's faith in the future refuses ultimately to be defeated. The belief in progress, and in the possibility of human action creating that progress, was reflected in the various movements for civil rights in the 1950s, 1960s, and 1970s. And various polls in the 1960s and 1970s showed the majority of Americans still believed in progress; even when they did not believe that the nation as a whole had a brighter future, they asserted the progress of their own personal lives and expectations for an even better future.

Thus, during the time we are studying, America moved from a pastoral to an industrial to a postindustrial society. Changes in life-styles have been enormous. After all, it was not until after World War I that we became an urban nation according to the census, that the majority of homes had electricity, and that the home appliances we now take for granted became readily available and commonly used. Through all the changes, our faith in progress has fluctuated but has never been eradicated. In broad terms, we have a greater sense of the relative nature of existence and of the nonrational elements of life than did our nineteenth-century forebears. But we still believe in our ability and in our right to control our own destiny.

With this social context in mind, we would expect certain patterns to appear in the use of the metaphors of fashion. The greater mechanistic and deterministic emphasis of the nineteenth century, and correspondingly greater emphasis on the nonrational in the twentieth century, would lead us to expect an increasingly larger proportion of nonrational metaphors over time. The fluctuations in our sense of control over our destiny and our faith in progress as we have been buffeted by wars and economic problems, would lead us to expect some short-term variations as well as the long-term trend. The continuing value on autonomy would lead us to expect the use of negative metaphors, or metaphors with negative connotations, whenever fashion is perceived to threaten our freedom of choice.

Only the last of the three expectations is fulfilled when we examine the patterns of usage. Fashion is labeled in negative terms whenever a writer sees the goddess as a threat to our autonomy. But there is no significant trend—neither long-term nor short-term. We examined the patterns over the entire period, 1825 to 1978, in terms of the overall usage, for each twenty-five-year period, for the nineteenth versus the twentieth centuries, and for the pre-1919 versus the post-1919 period. A little over half of the metaphors (52.6 percent) fall into the power images. This does not vary significantly regardless of the time periods into which the metaphors are divided. There is no significant trend either in the two broad categories (power and nonrational), or in any of the seven subcategories discussed.

In spite of the vast changes in our society, in spite of the enormous gains in knowledge, in spite of all our sophistication and progress, fashion remains as perplexing and elusive as ever. We know it is powerful and we know it does not operate in accord with the laws of human reason. But as a 1973 article in the *New York Times* put it, who knows what fashion is? The "elusive idea even baffles experts."[83] Indeed, the present work was undertaken in part because fashion eludes the grasp of understanding today quite as much as it did for Mathew Carey in 1838 when he called it "a most arbitrary, inexorable, and capricious tyrant."[84] The earthly goddess remains, now as then, cloaked in mystery and holding firm to her scepter of power.

CONCLUSION

Fashion stands upon the twin pillars of power and nonrationality. The importance of both themes is illustrated by the fact that the metaphors fall almost equally into the two broad categories. The point is underscored by the fact that nearly a third of the writers use both kinds of metaphors in their discussions of fashion. As a 1930 writer expressed it, Dame Fashion shows her power when she issues her decrees. At the same time, she plays boundless pranks on us, for she is a "fickle old girl."[85]

Thus, one aspect of the meaning of fashion in popular writings, is its power and nonrationality. Fashion has a powerful impact upon human life but that impact cannot be grasped in accord with any laws of human reason. A second aspect of the meaning of fashion is implicit in the metaphors—fashion is very important to us. The vividness of the metaphors, and the intensity of the discussions in which those metaphors are employed, testify to the importance. We do not bother to construct such imagery, or speak with such emotion, about those things which are trivial or peripheral to human life. The prevailing style—whether in clothing, architecture, scientific theory, or any other matter—is a central concern. The earthly goddess lives at the core of our social life. Sometimes we may praise her, and sometimes we may damn her. But we can never ignore her!

Notes

1. Mrs. H. C. Gardner, "Fashion," *The Ladies' Repository* 27 (May, 1867): 260.
2. Charlotte Perkins Gilman, "Why These Clothes?" *The Independent* 58 (March 2, 1905): 269.
3. Leslie A. White, *The Science of Culture* (New York: Farrar, Straus & Giroux, 1941), p. 22.
4. Robert A. Nisbet, *Social Change and History* (New York: Oxford University Press, 1969), p. 4.
5. George P. Fox, *Fashion: The Power That Influences the World* (New York: Sheldon & Co., 1871), p. 360.
6. M. H. Mason, "The Tyranny of Fashion in War Time," *The Nineteenth Century* 81 (March, 1917): 673.
7. Blanche W. Rollinson, "Dame Fashion," *Practical Home Economics* 9 (March, 1931): 92.
8. Henry T. Finck, *Romantic Love and Personal Beauty* (New York: Macmillan, 1887), p. 352.
9. *Ibid.*, p. 379.

10. Katharine Fullerton Gerould, "Dress and the Woman," *Atlantic Monthly* 108 (November, 1911): 619.
11. *St. Louis Post-Dispatch,* January 5, 1881.
12. Elizabeth Robins Pennell, "For Fashion's Sake," *The North American Review* 224 (September, 1927): 391.
13. "Crazy Mixed-Up Kids," *Collier's* 133 (February 19, 1954): 110.
14. *New York Times,* February 7, 1922.
15. Stella Mary Pearce, "The Spirit of the Times—and the Fashion," *The New York Times Magazine,* May 9, 1954, p. 21.
16. Nancy M. W. Woodrow, "How Fashions Are Set," *Cosmopolitan* 33 (July, 1902): 253.
17. Paul Poiret, "Who Sets Our Styles?" *The Forum* 80 (August, 1928): 187. See also Mrs. Merrifield, "Dress as a Fine Art," *Godey's Lady's Book* 46 (April, 1853): 324; "Follies of Fashion," *Harper's New Monthly Magazine* 18 (February, 1859): 310; E. L. Godkin, "The Rationale of Fashions," *The Nation* 5 (November 21, 1867): 419; Ida M. Tarbell, "The Great Problem of Clothes," *Ladies' Home Journal* 30 (April, 1913): 26; "Nina Wilcox Putnam," *The American Magazine* 75 (May, 1913): 34.
18. Carrie A. Hall, *From Hoopskirts to Nudity* (Caldwell, Idaho: The Caxton Printers, 1938), p. 21.
19. Margaret Woodward, "Sanity in American Fashions," *Country Side Magazine & Suburban Life* 19 (September, 1914); 153.
20. Frank Alvah Parsons, *The Psychology of Dress* (Garden City, N.Y.: Doubleday, Page & Company, 1923), pp. 324–25.
21. B. O. Flower, "Fashion's Slaves," *The Arena* 4 (September, 1891): 408.
22. "The Slaves of This Century," *The Craftsman* 26 (April, 1914): 120. See also B. O. Flower, "The Next Step Forward for Women: Or, Thoughts on the Movement for Rational Dress," *The Arena* 6 (October, 1892): 638; "Emancipating Slaves of Fashion," *The Literary Digest* 44 (December 14, 1912): 1154; "Is a Nation's Character Revealed in Its Dress?" *The Craftsman* 25 (March, 1914): 623.
23. Arnold Bennett, *Things That Have Interested Me,* Second Series (New York: George H. Doran, 1923), p. 65.
24. James C. Bayles, "Courage in Dress," *The Independent* 70 (May 4, 1911): 957.
25. Frances E. Russell, "Woman's Dress," *The Arena* 3 (February, 1891): 357.
26. "Nina Wilcox Putnam," *op. cit.,* p. 34.
27. These points will be discussed fully in chapter 7.
28. *New York Times,* October 7, 1940.
29. *St. Louis Life* 2 (November 15, 1890): 12.
30. Agnes Repplier, "The Drolleries of Clothes," *The Independent* 107 (December 3, 1921): 224. See also "Costume versus Criticism," *Godey's Lady's*

Book 58 (March, 1859): 271; Nancy M. W. Woodrow, *op. cit.,* p. 254.
31. Frances M. Steele, "Extravagance in the Dress of Women," *The Arena* 9 (April, 1894): 656. See also Alice Walker, "Out of Fashion," *The Ladies' Repository* 18 (March, 1858): 158.
32. Hattie C. Flower, "Eight Months' Experience in the Syrian Costume," *The Arena* 9 (February, 1894): 326.
33. James Parton, "The Clothes Mania," *Atlantic Monthly* 23 (May, 1869): 538. See also "Concerning Dress-Worship," *Southern Magazine* 4 (1869): 190–94.
34. "Fashion in America," *New York Times,* March 2, 1879. See also Frances Anne Allen, "Fig Leaves," *American Mercury* 13 (January, 1928): 65.
35. "Fashion," *The Ladies' Repository* 29 (August, 1869): 110.
36. "Beauty Conquers the Beast," *Collier's* 84 (September 14, 1929): 70.
37. "Fashion," *The Ladies' Repository* 29 (August, 1869): 110. See also B. O. Flower, "Fashion's Slaves," *The Arena* 4 (September, 1891): p. 411.
38. D. C. Bloomer, *Life and Writings of Amelia Bloomer* (New York: Schocken Books, 1975; first published 1895), p. 81.
39. Katharine Fullerton Gerould, *op. cit.,* p. 617.
40. Winifred Raushenbush, "The Idiot God Fashion," in S. D. Schmalhausen and V. F. Calverton, eds., *Woman's Coming of Age* (New York: Horace Liveright, 1931), p. 424.
41.. *Ibid.*
42. Carrie A. Hall, *loc. cit.*
43. G. Fitzhugh, "Domain of Fashion," *De Bow's Commercial Review* 29 (1860): 695. See also Lucy H. Hooper, "Fig Leaves and French Dresses," *Galaxy* 18 (October, 1874): 508; O. F. Yonge, "Some Causes of Change in Dress," *The Living Age* 223 (October 7, 1899): 38.
44. Mrs. H. C. Gardner, *op. cit.,* p. 261.
45. Mary Roberts Coolidge, *Why Women Are So* (New York: Arno Press, 1972; first published 1912), p. 168.
46. *St. Louis Post-Dispatch,* September 18, 1972.
47. Henry T. Finck, *op. cit.,* p. 485.
48. Maude Williams, "The Follies of Fashion," *Woman's Home Companion* 46 (March, 1919): 39.
49. Lucy Rathbone and Elizabeth Tarplety, *Fabrics and Dress,* new and revised edition (Boston: Houghton Mifflin, 1948), p. 3.
50. *New York Times,* October 8, 1875.
51. Normal Lobsenz, "Mini-Midi-Maxi Madness," *Good Housekeeping* 171 (August, 1970): 61.
52. Peter F. Copeland, "Our Ancestors as Fashion Plates," in L. M. Gurel and M. S. Beeson, eds., *Dimensions of Dress and Adornment* (Dubuque, Iowa: Kendall/Hunt, 1975), p. 31.

53. "Fashion," *Boston Literary Magazine* 1 (November, 1832): 338–39.
54. *St. Louis Post-Dispatch,* March 17, 1881.
55. Bernard Rudofsky, *Are Clothes Modern?* (Chicago: Paul Theobald, 1947), pp. 48–49.
56. *St. Louis Life* 1 (March 15, 1890).
57. May G. Sutton, "Women and Dress," *Harper's Bazaar* 44 (May, 1910): 327.
58. See Mary Brooks Picken, *The Secrets of Distinctive Dress* (Scranton, Pa.: International Textbook Press, 1918), pp. 6f.; "Up or Down—It's Fashion," *The New York Times Magazine,* September 7, 1947, p. 15; Mrs. Bettina Ballard, "Women and Fashion," in J. E. Fairchild, ed., *Women, Society & Sex* (New York: Sheridan House, 1952), p. 229.
59. Winifred Raushenbush, *op. cit.,* p. 445.
60. See "Follies of Fashion," *Harper's New Monthly Magazine* 18 (February, 1859): 310; "Follies and Fashion," *New York Times,* October 28, 1866; B. O. Flower, "Parisian Fashionable Folly versus American Common Sense," *The Arena* 8 (June, 1893): 131; Elizabeth Smith Miller, "Reflections on Woman's Dress, and the Record of a Personal Experience," *The Arena* 6 (September, 1892): 493; Helen G. Ecob, "A New Philosophy of Fashion," *Chataqua* 31 (December, 1900): 607; Franklin S. Clark, "Who Sets Fashion—and How?" *The Review of Reviews* 31 (January, 1930): 53.
61. "Fashion as a Dress Reformer," *The Independent* 86 (October 23, 1913): 152.
62. B. O. Flower, "Fashion's Slaves," *The Arena* 4 (September, 1891): p. 418.
63. B. O. Flower, "The Next Step Forward for Women . . . ," *The Arena* 6 (October, 1892): p. 636.
64. See Mrs. Merrifield, "Dress—as a Fine Art," *Godey's Lady's Book* 46 (April, 1853): p. 325; Frances E. Russell, "Freedom in Dress for Woman," *The Arena* 8 (June, 1893): 70; "Coercion of Fashion," *Current Literature* 28 (June, 1900): 377.
65. Alice Walker, *op. cit.,* p. 160.
66. Floyd DeForest Boyer, "Style or Fashion?" *American Home* 35 (May, 1946): 33.
67. See Grace Margaret Gould, "The Afflicted in Appearance," *Woman's Home Companion* 38 (October, 1911): 94; Agnes Repplier, *op. cit.,* p. 224; Mary Alden Hopkins, "Woman's Rebellion against Fashion," *The New Republic* 31 (August 16, 1922): 331; Elizabeth Hawes, "New Women Make New Styles," *Scribner's Magazine* 90 (September, 1931): 299.
68. Grace Margaret Gould, "Miss Gould's Fashion Talk," *Woman's Home Companion* 38 (October, 1911): 92; "What Women Will Wear in 1915," *Current Literature* 32 (March, 1902): 315.

69. Elizabeth Hawes, "Fashion Is Spinach," *Readers' Digest*, June, 1938, p. 49.
70. Julia Cruikshank, "Economic View of Fashion," *The Arena* 27 (April, 1901): 387.
71. "Style Sells the Goods," *The Literary Digest* 95 (October 8, 1927): 78. See also Frieda Inescort, "The Tyranny of They," *Harper's Monthly Magazine* 79 (May, 1927): 791–92; "Fashion's Effect on Business," *The Literary Digest* 96 (February 25, 1928): 18.
72. Henry Eckhardt, "Style and Business," *Magazine of Business* 54 (August, 1928): 145.
73. Quoted by Winifred Raushenbush, "Fashion Goes American," *Harper's Magazine* 184 (December, 1941): 75.
74. Elizabeth Hawes, "Fashion Is Spinach," *Readers' Digest*, June, 1938, p. 50.
75. Franklin S. Clark, *op. cit.*, p. 53; Agnes Repplier, *op. cit.*, p. 224.
76. "Is a Nation's Character Revealed in Its Dress?" *The Craftsman* 25 (March, 1914): 622–23. See also "Beauty, Not Novelty, the Purpose of Fashion," *The Craftsman* 11 (January, 1907): 520.
77. "Fashion: Counter-Revolution," *Time* 50 (September 15, 1947): 87.
78. George E. Mowry, *The Era of Theodore Roosevelt and the Birth of Modern America, 1900–1912* (New York: Harper and Row, 1958), p. 16.
79. *Ibid.*, p. 17.
80. R. H. Thurston, "The Border-Land of Science," *The North American Review* 150 (1890): 67.
81. Loren Baritz, "The Culture of the Twenties," in S. Cohen and L. Ratner, eds., *The Development of an American Culture* (Englewood Cliffs: Prentice-Hall, 1970), p. 168.
82. Warren Susman, *Culture and Commitment, 1929–1945* (New York: George Braziller, 1973), p. 13.
83. Isadore Barman, "What is Fashion? Who Knows?" *New York Times*, September 16, 1973.
84. Mathew Carey, *Philosophy of Common Sense* (Philadelphia: Blanchard, 1838), p. 54.
85. "Dame Fashion's Influence," *National Republic* 18 (May, 1930): 13.

PART II

FASHION AND SOCIAL LIFE

chapter 3 | Fashion and Human Nature

What is man? asked the Psalmist. The answers have been diverse, ranging from the pride to the refuse of the universe. If we rephrase the Psalmist's question, and ask what is man and what is woman, we will discover that most thinkers do not conceive of human nature in unitary terms. There is a male nature and there is a female nature. There are some similarities, of course, but most observers of the human scene have ascribed some fundamental differences to the sexes. Furthermore, there has been congruence between views of male nature and female nature on the one hand, and ideas about the appropriate dress for males and females on the other. We will look first at the dual nature of humans and then at the ways in which fashion interacts with those notions about the nature of males and females.

THE NATURE OF MALES AND FEMALES

Historically, males have asserted that whatever else female nature may be, it is inferior to that of males. Some of the most enlightened males in the history of the world have held women in low regard. Plato thanked God that he was born a Greek rather than a barbarian, a free man rather than a slave, and a man rather than a woman. Aristotle declared that woman is an unfinished man, left standing on a lower plane of development. There are still men who would agree that woman is in some sense inferior. A more enlightened view, we believe, is one that consigns the notion of the male's natural superiority to the realm of an ideology that has justified male exploitation. Nevertheless, there are many differences in the attitudes and behavior of the sexes. How much of the sexual variation can be attributed to biology and how much to society? Are the differences innate, or do they merely reflect diverse social roles? Experts from various disciplines have addressed these questions, and their answers have generated as much controversy as satisfaction.

Gender or Role?

While the question of the extent to which attitudes and behavior are a function of gender or of role has not been settled, there is sufficient evidence to make a number of conclusions. An important part of the evidence is the research conducted by Margaret Mead in the 1930s, among three primitive tribes in New Guinea. She concluded that the meaning of being a male or a female is primarily the result of cultural conditioning rather than of any biological imperatives. She said that many—perhaps even all—of the traits that we think of as masculine or feminine are really as "lightly linked" to gender as the clothing or manners that are assigned to men and women at any particular time.[1] Among the Tchambuli, she found males and females were virtually the opposite of our own ideals. Women were in command, took the lead in matters like mating, and dealt with such practical concerns as fishing and trading. The men behaved much as our traditional women. They worried about their appearance, their jewelry, and their competition with other males for female attention.

On the basis of such evidence, Chafetz has drawn a number

of conclusions about the relative importance of gender and social role with respect to attitudes and behavior.[2] First, most of the traits which are thought of as masculine or feminine are not innate. They are not the result of biological imperatives. In fact, those traits which are defined as masculine in one society may be considered feminine in another. Second, the data on hormones and chromosomes suggest a few tendencies that are innate to gender. But these are only *tendencies,* and they can be moderated or even reversed by social factors. For example, if it is true (some say it is and some say it isn't) that male hormones tend to make men more aggressive, social factors may moderate the tendency or even make men less aggressive than women (as among the Tchambuli). Third, any innate differences are a matter of degree rather than of kind. This means it would not be true in any case to say that men are aggressive and women are passive. Rather, it may be true that men are more *inclined* to aggressiveness than women. Similar statements could be made about other traits.

In essence, then, there are some differences in the sexes that are rooted in human biology. But these differences seem to be mainly tendencies, and the tendencies can be moderated or even reversed by social factors. The primary basis for different attitudes and behavior between the sexes is to be found in social factors. In particular, the role assigned to the male or to the female is a crucial factor in determining (and in understanding) behavior.

The Traditional Female Role

For the most part, role and gender are equated. That is, people tend to think that the role reflects the innate characteristics of individuals. For instance, if a wife is supposed to be submissive to her husband, it is because, among other things, women are innately passive and submissive. As we describe the traditional role of women in America, therefore, we are also describing the traditional American view of female nature.

For the bulk of Americans, women have been thought to be complex creatures who are in some ways inferior and in some ways superior to men. Physically, intellectually, and emotionally, women are inferior; morally, they are superior. These notions flowered in the nineteenth century, and have not yet wilted in the minds of many Americans.

The inferiority of women was given a scientific basis by nineteenth-century physicians. Studies of the head and brain were used to put females, along with blacks, in an inferior position of development. Virtually every type of analysis of the brain and its functions suggested female inferiority to nineteenth-century researchers.[3] Naturally, then, women could not compete with men in sports, business, education, government, and so forth.

> For medical science in the late nineteenth century, woman's place in nature rested ultimately on biological laws. The only method to achieve equality, wrote one physician, was to "unsex" the species, a process naturally repugnant and contrary to normal sexual instincts. The division of labor reflected centuries of evolutionary race development and corresponded accurately to the differentiation of physical and psychical structure.[4]

On the other hand, women have been defined as superior in the moral and spiritual realm. Women, it has been said, possess a higher nature than men and have been called to a nobler task in life. Women, it was commonly asserted, are more virtuous than men. They are gentler, kinder, more modest, long-suffering, and spiritually attuned.[5] God bestowed upon men "mechanical ingenuity and physical strength;" to women, He gave "moral insight or instinct and the patience that endures physical suffering."[6] The elevation of women did not consist in "becoming like a man, in doing a man's work, or striving for dominion of the world."[7] Rather, God had given to women the moral power of the world.

In spite of her many-faceted inferiority, then, woman was a superior creature because she had the greatest of all callings. The stability of society and the grandeur of the nation depended upon the conduct of its women. They were "the silent, throbbing heart, sending, by its strong pulsations, every drop of the flowing life-blood to the life-sustaining oxygen of moral purity."[8] If the sacred fires of patriotism were to be kept alive in the hearts of the people, it would be done by the wives, mothers, and daughters of the land. Women, said the editor of *The Ladies' Wreath* in 1849

> are the guardian spirits, who are to watch over and nourish the flame on the altar of our liberties. Their teachings and example, if true to their mission, will furnish the Republic with a conservative

power, more reliable than paper constitutions, or bill of rights, and will throw around it a wall of defence, more effective than frowning batteries or naval armaments.[9]

Of course, women were supposed to perform their vital role within their homes. In the home, the dedicated mother would raise, nurture, and educate her children. "In the right education of her children," the editor of *Harper's* assured American mothers, "she exerts a far purer and more effective political power, than she could ever wield through the freest admission to the ballot-box or the caucus."[10] In the home, the devoted wife could provide her husband with a haven from the rigors of the business world, encouraging him in his pursuits, supporting him in every noble endeavor, and curbing his less noble tendencies. In her home, a woman wielded a "reforming power," inculcating religious precepts in her children and guarding over the morals of her sons as well as her husband. A man's susceptibility to female influence, it was said, is one of the most powerful controls over his behavior. Without it, one gentleman observed, "we would degenerate into brutes."[11]

Women were not flawless, of course. Even in the moral and spiritual realm they had their weaknesses and had to guard against temptation. They were warned that the greatest threat to their virtue was vanity. It could cause a woman to seek after luxury rather than spiritual riches and become a captive of fashion rather than a slave of righteousness. All women had to be vigilant in the face of such temptation, for the well-being of the nation depended upon their continued purity.

In sum, women have traditionally been defined as creatures who are inferior to men in most respects, but who are morally and spiritually superior. Women, therefore, need not feel their contribution to society is any less important than that of men. In fact, women, through their devotion as wives and mothers, provide the bedrock upon which the more intelligent and stronger men can erect a prosperous civilization. As long as American women remain true to their calling, the nation will flourish. As one editor said in the middle of the nineteenth century:

> Beautiful by the hearth—beautiful at the domestic board—beautiful in her ministering of charity—beautiful in her guiding counsels to

infancy, in her tender, pious solicitudes for manhood—as the sister, the wife, or mother—the women of America have been performing their high and holy mission . . . a soft, steady, exhausting lamp—guiding the virtuous to safety and to God.[12]

The extent to which such sentiments have been expressed in popular literature has varied from time to time. But the response to the new wave of the Women's Movement which began in the 1960s, showed that a great many Americans still agreed that woman's place is in the home, that women are basically meant to be wives and mothers, and that the well-being of the nation depends upon women's willingness to accept their proper role.

Fashion and Sex Roles

All societies differentiate between males and females. The meaning of maleness and femaleness may vary considerably, but each society has its own notions of appropriate roles for the sexes. These roles are also believed to express basic gender differences. That is, the roles assigned to men and women are believed to be a logical outcome of the nature of men and women. Most people, therefore, do not think of gender and role as two quite different phenomena. The roles are merely mirrors of gender differences.

Furthermore, in every society there is appropriate dress for males and females. In his extensive study of dress in preindustrial cultures, Ernest Crawley found that "the great bifurcation of dress is sexual."[13] All cultures make a fundamental distinction between the clothing appropriate to males and that which is proper for females. Sex-appropriate clothing is believed, like the roles generally, to express gender differences. Clothing reflects the duality of human nature. In societies where there is fashion in clothing, the changing styles are supposed to stay within the bounds of gender propriety. That is, fashion is supposed to always allow men to be truly masculine and women to be truly feminine (as, of course, masculinity and femininity are currently defined in the society).

As suggested, we would argue that clothing styles reflect role differences rather than gender differences. And, as we shall discuss further, clothing styles help to maintain those role differences. It is important to keep in mind, however, that the distinction between gender and role is not generally made. The failure to make the distinction accounts for some of the intensity of conflict over certain styles. For example, when American women wanted to wear trousers, they were not merely trying to change a role; rather, they were believed to be making an assault on human nature itself, a nature that had been created and ordained by God.

FASHION AS REVELATION: QUALITIES OF THE SEXES

In discussing clothing as nonverbal communication, we pointed out that styles may tell us something about the nature of entire groups of people. For Americans, fashion has always revealed some basic facts about the two largest groups—men and women. The duality of human nature, it has been argued, is clearly evident in fashion behavior.

The Life of Reason

The people of Erewhon, as described in Samuel Butler's utopian novel, deliberately developed their "unreasoning" abilities. Professors of Inconsistency and Evasion helped young people in their study of Unreason. Like any heir of the Enlightenment, the young Englishman who visited the Erewhonians considered the emphasis on unreason an absurdity. The heights of human well-being can only be reached through the life of reason.

Americans share Butler's distaste for unreason. We have always valued and admired the person who demonstrates rationality and practicality in his or her life. There are, consequently, overtones of anger or despair, or even disparagement, in the observations of those who compare male and female fashions. For they assert or assume that male fashions demonstrate reason and practicality, while female fashions show that the fair sex is also the sex without much sense.

A mid-nineteenth-century writer noted that "many of the distinctive features of modern male dress may be explained on the obvious principle of convenience and common sense."[14] A host of others have agreed with that basic conclusion. Men dress for utilitarian reasons. They want clothes that do not interfere with their activities. They want to be comfortable. They want to be protected from the elements. In essence, as the editor of the *New York Times* put it in 1911, men's clothes in America "suit our climate, our occupations, and our pastimes and do no violence to our democratic spirit. That is about all that can be said about them, but it is probably enough."[15]

And what of women? A woman will accept anything if it is defined as fashionable, even the "most arrant nonsense."[16] Since our clothing reveals something about our character, it follows that the person or the group of people that accept senseless styles must be senseless individuals. It is not that women are totally lacking in sense. It is, rather, that they fail to use it consistently in their lives. Unlike men, they do not live a life of reason. And nowhere is the female propensity for senselessness more evident than in the realm of fashion.

The failure of women to employ their reason in responding to fashion has been noted by a series of writers throughout our history. In the seventeenth century, Nathaniel Ward wrote that he honored any woman who honored herself by her dress. But he could not understand those women who had so little sense "as to disfigure themselves with such exotick garbes, as not only dismantles their native lovely lustre, but transclouts them into gant bar-geese, ill-shaped shotten shell-fish, Egyptian Hieroglyphicks, or at the best into French flurts of the pastery."[17] A nineteenth-century physician, writing about the need for reform in female dress, said that all of the deleterious physical consequences of the contemporary fashion could be avoided "if ladies would only allow themselves to be guided by reason and common sense. Let dress be made at once a subject of rational consideration."[18]

Many male observers have expressed frustration because women seem so unable to recognize the irrationality in their dress that is apparent to men. In 1868, the editor of the *New York Times* reacted angrily to the new fashions in women's hats "which women are stupid enough to accept." He argued that women would have considerable illness and "premature wrinkling and roughness" of their skins as a result of their hats. The whole incident, he claimed, showed the way in which fashion "needs wander away into extravagant vagaries to satisfy her capricious followers" and reflected "an irreconcilable stupidity which is being very fast developed in the otherwise sharp and wide-awake characters of our women."[19]

In the face of fashion, women fail to use whatever powers of reason they may otherwise possess. In the struggle between common sense and fashion, fashion always wins where women are concerned.[20] Unlike men, women do not have the capacity for dealing in a rational and practical way with all matters of life. Even the dress reformers, who often exalted women and claimed that female dress did not reflect the true nature and potential of women, sometimes lapsed into expressions of despair or contempt. They had to acknowledge that women's subservience to the contemporary fashion was at best puzzling and at worst evidence of a creature who was not equal to men. Thus, Frances Russell concluded that "the average dress of the average woman pronounces against her the verdict: fickle, frivolous, incompetent!"[21]

For some writers, women's lack of reason and practicality in the matter of fashion was worse than unreason. It was a distortion, or even perversion, of reason. For most women, argued the editor of the *New York Times* in 1878, life is a constant struggle for and with clothes. For the male observer, it was clear that women were the losers in the struggle. But to women, it appeared they were the winners. For clothes are the "natural master" of women, and "to be conquered by them appears to her like glorious victory."[22] That can only be seen as a setting of reason on its head, a complete distortion of the rational process.

The perversion of reason appeared in war time, when any reasonable, practical individual would have recognized the importance of saving and sacrifice. But in the middle of "the greatest war of the world," said a 1916 writer, women managed to take time to change clothing styles, "an act so shameless that the most brazen of men must have blushed for it."[23] It apparently never occurred to the writer that far more men than women were involved in the design and promotion of new styles. Men, after all, act reasonably. A year later, in 1917, the *New York Times* carried an article about women gardeners and their contribution to the war effort. Unfortunately, the article noted, the women were using the money they had saved (or made, by selling the produce) to buy new clothes. What a perversity when a man has his wife and daughters tell him that before they can save money on vegetables they must have large sums of money to buy nice, feminine clothing in which to garden![24]

For most observers, then, the greatest part of American history has been characterized by the utter senselessness of women with respect to fashion. Many writers like to contrast female behavior with male. They note that some men have indeed exhibited a lack of reason with regard to dress. We need only remind ourselves of the sartorial splendor of Louis XIV or the foppery in England at various times. Vanity has afflicted males as much as females at certain points in history. But men fought with vanity, overcame it, and emerged as rational victors. Women, it seems, will never follow suit, for they lose whatever reasonable faculties they have when confronted by the demands of the earthly goddess.

We should point out that there are dissenting voices. Not every observer agrees with the preceding paragraph. A 1955 writer pointed out that men's clothes are not the practical, comfortable things they are claimed to be. Rather, "men's clothes are about as comfortable as a fur coat in the tropics and as sensible as high heels on a hike."[25] Another has argued that many aspects of male dress are nothing less than unnecessary (and therefore nonrational) remnants of nineteenth-century English riding clothes, including the waistcoat, the tie, and vents in suit jackets.[26] Such attire had important functions for the horse-riding Englishman in the late nineteenth century, but are without any practical purpose now.

Confronted with these arguments, the other writers we have discussed might respond by pointing out that the last two authors are both women. And if women lack sense in the wearing of clothes, can they be any more reasonable in writing about them? But the sword of critical analysis cuts in both directions. If it can be argued on the one hand, that women have typically lacked reason with regard to fashion, it can be argued on the other hand, that men have lacked reason not only with respect to their own clothes but with respect to their expectations for women. As a turn-of-the-century writer pointed out, men have not been the consistently rational creatures they perceive themselves to be, for they "condemn and criticize the very things in their own wives and sisters that they run after and admire in the sisters and wives of other men."[27] Thus, men always harp about women wearing "common-sense" shoes, but they would never say that a woman who wore the shoes had pretty feet. They see a woman in French heels and note that she has pretty feet but needs to take off the French shoe and wear a pair of common-sense shoes. "Poor things, they don't know that only the French shoe can show the outlines of a pretty foot. Men are so peculiar."[28]

While the dissenters appear to be as logical in their arguments and as firm in their evidence as those who argue that fashion exhibits the lack of female reason and practicality, the latter group has been heard far more often than the former. If we were to accept the arguments of the majority, we would have to conclude that fashion behavior clearly demonstrates the rational, practical nature of the male and the capacity of the female to be utterly senseless and impractical.

The Life of Submissiveness

Traditionally, the male is assumed to be the assertive or aggressive sex, while the female is assumed to be passive and submissive. Most of the writers who saw such qualities manifested in fashion behavior agreed with the traditional view. Those who used the metaphor of the slave pointed out that it was women, not men, who were enslaved to the tyrant. But even those who have not seen fashion in such dramatic terms have pointed out the submissive nature of females and the assertive behavior of males in response to fashion.

The submissiveness of the female can be seen in her lack of independence and courage in the face of fashion's demands. A nineteenth-century writer in St. Louis pointed out the problems that women were having in walking through the streets in rainy weather, "tilting forward" to keep the backs of their dresses from dragging through every puddle but thereby "accumulating a generous quantity of alluvial deposit" on the fronts of the dresses. "And all this for a stupid prejudice in favor of a certain kind of dress—all this because she has not independence enough to wear what is suitable, without regard to the fact of its being fashionable."[29]

Why do women lack the independence of character in the realm of fashion? For wome writers, women are innately submissive, incapable of acting in the aggressive manner of males. For others, women have a tendency to be submissive, but they are not biologically determined to be so. An editor in 1921 argued that woman's enslavement to fashion was "not the ordinary story of woman's victimization" in a world dominated by men. For woman "accepts of herself" the decrees of fashion and "rushes to embrace it." It is a "woman-made" enslavement that we witness when we look at fashion behavior.[30]

If the servitude is indeed voluntary rather than innate, if women are submissive because of habit or custom or societal pressures, then there is some hope for change. The dress reformers clung to this hope through many a frustrating battle. They exhorted women to exercise their will and throw off the shackles of an oppressive fashion. They sought the help of men, asking them to encourage and support women. Elizabeth Miller, who helped popularize the Bloomer costume during its brief appearance in the 1850s, speculated that higher education for women was the "one grand outlook" that might release them from the "thraldom to fashion, which presents such a hopeless aspect."[31] It would seem that Mrs. Miller's "grand outlook" became another impotent factor, for a hundred years after she appeared in her Bloomers, a generation of well-educated women was still being described as submissive to fashion.

The frustration of those who hoped for change was inevitable in the face of the total commitment of women to their servitude. According to most observers, women's submissiveness is not tempered by a measure of indpendence. There are no reservations, no contingencies, no fragment of will withheld. Women submit with their whole beings. They see the decrees of fashion as a kind of scriptural injunction and submission as an obligation, a sacred duty. As a result, they do as they are told to do. Fashion thinks for them; they do not think for themselves. They are almost like puppets, swung this way and that, as fashion pulls the strings of their existence.[32]

Furthermore, women submit to fashion not just in the matter of clothing, but in all aspects of their lives. As a nineteenth-century writer put it, fashion is a household goddess

> who presides over all the domestic concerns, and regulates family affairs and expenditures by means of her votaries, the ladies, who alone can comprehend her requirements and interpret aright her oracles and her revelations. Fashion, regardless of expense, convenience, utility, or propriety, imperiously regulates equipage, furniture, balls, parties, education of our children, church attendance, social intercourse, in fine, our whole manner of life.[33]

By contrast, men are said to be aggressive creatures who show independence with respect to fashion. In the late nineteenth century, according to Henry Finck, there were "still a considerable number of shallow-brained young 'society men' who naïvely and minutely accept the slight variations introduced every year" in male fashions. But men generally are no longer ruled by "capricious, cunning Fashion" as are women. Men largely disregard the foolish innovations offered by tailors and "laugh at the silly persons who meekly accept them."[34] In a 1926 editorial, the *New York Times* largely agreed with this assessment, pointing out that women typically accept new styles automatically, while there is "an individuality in fashions for men that defies the regularizing hand."[35]

An interesting explanation of why women are more submissive than men was offered by a correspondent to the *New York Times* in 1930. According to the writer, woman's apparent submission is really a sign of her independence. For women accept change more easily than men. Thus, a woman will wear a straw hat in January if that is the fashion, but a man would not dare wear one until the time prescribed by public opinion.[36] A year later, the editor accepted the notion that women more easily accept change, but drew a different conclusion. Because men fear innovations and approach them warily, they will not as quickly adopt a freakish fashion as will women. Men's reluctance to change helps to keep them from being the slaves of fashion (which is, by definition, change).

As the correspondent's letter indicates, not all observers accept the notion that fashion behavior reveals woman's submissiveness and man's independence. Arnold Bennett insisted that men are as foolish and slavish with respect to fashion as women.[38] A 1911 writer pointed out that women show a good deal more courage in the matter of dress than men, for in order to be well-dressed in the summer, men must be uncomfortable. In fact, virtually every aspect of men's summer attire "is as unsuited to our normal summer temperatures as ingenuity could devise." But the average man will not reject the fashions because "he is pigeon-livered and lacks gall. His mother, his wife or his sister should take him in hand and inspire him with the courage to be comfortable."[39] Again, the voices of dissent are few. In spite of the logic and the evidence they present, most observers have agreed that fashion behavior demonstrates female submissiveness. The man is a creature of independence. The woman, whether by nature or by choice, lives the life of submissiveness.

The Ornamental Sex

The third way that fashion behavior is said to distinguish males from females involves the aesthetic sense and self-adornment. Women have an aesthetic sense that men lack. In fact, men do not understand

FIG. 8. Women as ornamental: a carriage dress and a walking dress from 1855. (*Source:* Godey's Lady's Book, *March, 1855.*)

women's fashion behavior because they lack that aesthetic sense. But all women have it, which is why, said one nineteenth-century editor, they have reigned supreme in the realm of stylishness:

> What does a man know about style? Search all the historians . . . and you shall find no mention of a stylish man! . . . History, common sense, and everyday experience alike prove that woman only understands the esthetics of dress. It is one of the channels in which her intellect has asserted its superiority over man's.[40]

Lest it appear that this editor deviated from the tendency to downgrade female intelligence in the nineteenth century, we should note that his remarks were made in the context of arguing against female suffrage. Female superiority in the realm of aesthetics does not carry over into the more practical affairs of the world. Similarly, another male writer who talked about the fact that "women are so universally gifted with the artistic instinct," also asserted there was a touch of folly in women that "prevents them from producing the finest results of the artistic faculty."[41]

Other writers, both male and female, could talk about woman's innate aesthetic sense without reminding readers of female shortcomings or deficiencies in other areas. Dress will never be neglected, said the editor of *Godey's*, because "love of the beautiful and ornamental is innate in woman's nature."[42] This innate aesthetic sense leads women to both a love of that which is beautiful and a desire to be beautiful herself. As the petals of a blossoming flower express the true nature of the flower, so the well-adorned woman expresses her true—aesthetic—nature. As Pope Pius XII said in 1957, women have an "innate need . . . to emphasize beauty and dignity of the person."[43] He cautioned them, however, to fulfill that need through modest rather than seductive clothes.

Clearly, then, Americans have considered women to be the ornamental sex. By nature, women have a better sense of what is beautiful than do men. This nature leads them to a love of self-adornment so they might be beautiful creatures. Most women, said a 1955 writer, admire other women who have achieved significant things. But they don't want to dress like a suffragette or a scientist. "They prefer to look pretty and to be wooed and won."[44]

The drive for being beautiful, the need for self-adornment, is expressed in varying ways. Many writers see it as an innate characteristic, an aspect of female nature as opposed to male nature. As such, women naturally exhibit a love of fashion, one could even say a hunger for it. A few writers see it in more frivolous terms as the natural activity of those who are not engaged with the truly serious matters of life. All tend to see it as deep-rooted, however. The female love of self-adornment cannot be squelched by changes or occurrences in the larger society. "Democracy has transformed the appearance of men," argued one nineteenth-century writer, but "it has not touched the nature or costume of women. They remain an exclusive and privileged class by all their instincts; with them license and art take refuge."[45] Nearly half a century later, a woman writer said that her sex had not yet conquered the instinct for ornament, and that the instinct consumed so much of women's life that one could wonder if it, rather than other matters, might not be the *"real* 'woman question.' "[46] To the extent that it is in woman's nature to be ornamental, she can hardly expect to be treated as an equal with the rational and practical, albeit less aesthetic, male.

The Superior Sex

As the above suggests, fashion behavior has been said to provide a final answer to the question of which is the superior sex. Aesthetic superiority is nice, but it can hardly compensate for a lack of independence, reason, and practicality. Clearly, according to a number of writers, woman's response to fashion shows her inferiority.

Some male writers do more than hint at the inferiority of women. In fact, some literally harangue women about their deficiencies. In the midst of his long treatise on the cultivation of romantic love and personal beauty, Henry Finck lost no opportunity to remind his female readers of what their fashion behavior said about them. Not one woman in a hundred, he thundered, "had taste or courage enough to revolt" against the bustle, "the latest hideous craze of Fashion." Why do women wear such things? Why would any woman wear a health-destroying corset?

> It is simply the average woman's lack of taste that urges her thus to mutliate her Personal Beauty? Is it the admiration of a few vulgar "mashers" and barber's pets—since educated men detest waspwaists? Or is it simply the proverbial feminine craze for emulating one another and arousing envy by excelling in some extravagance of dress, no matter at what cost? This last suggestion is probably the true solution of the problem. The only satisfaction a woman can get from having a wasp-waist is the envy of other silly women.[47]

Finck goes on to analyze the causes of women's fetish for fashion.[48] None of the five causes is complimentary to females. First, he said, some women like to make a "vulgar display of wealth." Second, some women are deceived by the cunning of the milliners, who "grow fat on fashionable extravagance." Third, some women suffer from the "tyranny of the ugly majority." Most women, he asserted, "are ugly and ungraceful, and resent the contrast which beautiful women, naturally and becomingly attired, would present to their own persons." Such women obviously prefer bustles, corsets, and so forth. Fourth, many women simply suffer because of cowardice. And finally, women are sheepish. It may appear ungallant to compare women with sheep, said Finck, but if women see how they appear to men perhaps they will abandon their sheepishness. As it is, just as a flock of sheep might follow their leader and plunge into the sea, fashionable women "commit aesthetic suicide if their leader sets the example."

In 1925, the *New York Times* reported a similar comparison, though with a different animal.[49] A surgeon said that women, by natural instinct, are more ape-like than men. As a result, they were jeopardizing their health and endangering the future of the race by "trying to look like boys with the aid of barbers' shears, rubber corsets and other contrivances." They could only do such things, said the surgeon, because of their instinct to imitate what other women are doing. Once a craze starts, therefore, it is inevitably spread throughout the female population.

But it is not only males who argue that fashion behavior demonstrates male superiority. Female observers have also consigned their sex to an inferior status. Male wisdom in the matter of dress, said a 1915 writer, has enabled man to "render inestimable service" to the world. Women, on the other hand, have the instinct to make themselves beautiful, but they are ignorant of the true principle of beauty. In particular, they do not see the close relationship between beauty and utility. Women, unfortunately, believe that they can achieve their aim of beauty merely by imitating other women.[50] Women suffer from fashions, said another female writer, but their suffering has no rational basis. Rather, they suffer because they have lacked the good sense to get away from "self-inflicted torment."[51]

In essence, then, the argument is that when one group of people acts with intelligence in order to live well and achieve something, while another group acts senselessly to the detriment of the members of the group, the first group is obviously superior to the second. Since an examination of fashion behavior clearly shows men following the pattern of the first group and women behaving as the second group, it follows that men are the superior sex. As a Cardinal put the matter succinctly to a Diocesan Congress of Catholic Women in 1939, "you can tell the quality of a woman's brain by the kind of hat that covers it," and fashion was "more silly and senseless than ever."⁵² A senseless and silly hat adorning a senseless and silly brain—what more could one say to dramatize the inferiority of women?

FASHION AND THE MAINTENANCE OF SEX ROLES

Pink is for girls and blue is for boys. It somehow seems appropriate but we would have a difficult time defending it upon any rational grounds. Like many other aspects of culture, fashions do not have to be rationally defensible in order to fulfill important functions. The pink and blue distinction is but one of many ways in which fashion has been used to distinguish the sexes and to maintain traditional sex roles. It is not only that fashion *does* maintain the distinction, however, that is of interest and importance. It is also significant that people have typically believed fashion *should* maintain the differences. The strength of this latter belief is underscored by the long and intense conflict over women wearing trousers. We shall discuss this below. First, let us look at the notion that there ought to be congruence between what a man or woman naturally is and what a man or woman wears.

Harmonizing Nature and Appearance

We have learned from our mothers and grandmothers, wrote a correspondent to the *St. Louis Intelligencer* in 1851, that that style of dress "is most becoming to females which most harmonizes with the delicacy and modesty of the female character."⁵³ Most Americans have agreed there ought to be harmony between nature and role, on the one hand, and appearance on the other. Both men and women should dress in a way that is congruent with their respective roles.

At times, the prescriptions for appropriate dress for the sexes have been detailed and rather inflexible. For example, modesty has always been identified as one of the characteristics of females. In order to insure a properly modest appearance, *Harper's Bazaar* offered its readers an outline of the female calf and foot in 1868. The calf was marked to show the proper length for girls' skirts at various ages. At four years of age, the skirt came just below the knee. It descended by degrees at ages eight, ten, twelve, and fourteen and ended at age sixteen just below the top of the high-buttoned shoes. By sixteen, the female leg was no longer to be publicly visible.

Men of course, were not subjected to such detailed prescriptions. Americans have largely agreed with Freud's view of the role of the sexes, namely, that it is man's work to build civilization and woman's work to maintain the home and rear the children. Those who are building civilization require practical clothes. Male dress in America has reflected this role, for whatever may be said about the comfort or utility of male clothes, it is undeniable that the fashions for men have always allowed freedom of movement.

Women, as the creatures who by nature are ordained to reign over the home, do not require clothes that allow great freedom of movement. Whenever women have insisted on a larger role in the social order, there has been controversy over their clothes. The controversy was heated during the latter half of the nineteenth century, when the dress reform movement attempted to provide a more "rational" form of attire for women. It was clear to the reformers that the female fashions perfectly reflected the female role. As Elizabeth Cady Stanton put it in 1857, woman's dress "perfectly describes her condition." For her dress is created to fulfill purposes other than her own comfort and convenience:

> from the bonnet string to the paper shoe, she is the hopeless martyr to the inventions of some Parisian imp of fashion. Her tight waist and long, trailing skirts deprive her of all freedom of breath and motion. No wonder man prescribes her sphere. She needs his aid at every turn. He must help her up stairs and down, in the carriage and out, on the horse, up the hill, over the ditch and fence, and thus teach her the poetry of dependence.[54]

Stanton, of course, did not accept the notion that women are by nature passive, dependent creatures. But she grimly acknowledged that female fashions proclaimed such a nature and reflected such a role. Nearly half a century later, a symposium in *The Arena* argued the same point. As one writer said, female fashions clearly tell women they must stay in the house. Women are expected, presumably for "beauty's sake," to wear clothes that are recognized to be contrary to both physical development and healthy beauty. "Fashion says that the chief use of woman is to exhibit dry goods fantastically arranged on her person."[55] Again and again, the reformers made the point that the role of women restricted them to servility, and that their dress perfectly harmonized with that role.

The apparent victory of the dress reformers in the first part of the twentieth century was only a partial victory in the eyes of later feminists. For by the 1960s and 1970s, feminists were still criticizing female fashions on the very grounds laid down by Elizabeth Cady Stanton, namely, that everything a woman wears "has some object external to herself." For recent feminists that external objective has been the various ways in which men like to keep and use women. Thus, bras were discarded because they were said to have the primary purpose of shaping a woman in accord with male sexual desires. Clothes such as "baby doll" nightwear and revealing or frilly outer garments were scorned because they proclaimed woman as a dependent sex object. Modern feminists, like their sisters in the nineteenth century, see much in female fashion that harmonizes with a nature and a role that they reject.

As the reaction of feminists suggests, fashions do more than merely reflect a particular role; they help to maintain that role. As a 1910 writer put it, in the course of commenting on the absurdity of the hobble skirt, if women want to run for political office they will have to be able to run for a car. If they want to be able to step into a president's chair, they must be able to step into an automobile. "If they want to be legally free, they shouldn't be sartorially shackled."[56] In other words, female fashions were clearly precluding a wider, more practical and involved role for women. In her hobble skirt, the American woman was almost as hampered as was the Chinese woman whose bound feet insured her immobility.

Women who have desired a larger role than the traditional one have frequently advocated a change of fashion. Recognizing the fact that fashions not only reflect, but help maintain a particular role, they have called for styles that will allow the larger role. As a nineteenth-century reformer argued, "until woman is allowed to have ankles, there is no hope for her brains."[57] Another pointed out that "we are ready for a short dress for business women and others, whose out-of-door duties require all the freedom possible."[58] And a St. Louis writer noted in 1893 that the question of clothes has taken precedence over the question of woman's suffrage. That only proved that women were getting down to "elemental facts by leaving the ballot to take care of itself, and giving their attention to the one great disability of the sex, viz., petticoats." Get rid of those petticoats, the writer pleaded, if you want to be thoroughly free. For no woman can be equal to men until she can get around as well as men can. "Stick to petticoats and the ever-present helping masculine hand, or discard the petticoats and be independent."[59]

There is harmony, then, between nature and role and appearance. Fashions reflect and help maintain certain roles, which for many people means they reflect and affirm the nature of males and females. The periodic call by women to reject certain fashions—from the struggle against the corset to the effort to eliminate midiskirts to the call to throw away bras—has therefore typically been a simultaneous plea to accept a new notion or reaffirm an older notion of the meaning of being a woman. Women have attempted to change the accepted definition of their roles by, in part, changing the acceptable clothing they wear.

One of the dramatic changes in role definitions occurred with the flapper costume. Kenneth Yellis, an historian, has contrasted the flapper with her predecessor, the Gibson girl, pointing out that each type reflected a common, though contrary, notion of the female role:

> The Gibson girl was maternal and wifely, while the flapper was boyish and single. The Gibson girl was the embodiment of stability. The flapper's aesthetic ideal was motion, her characteristics were intensity, energy, volatility. While the Gibson girl seems incapable of an immodest thought or deed, the flapper strikes us as brazen and at least capable of sin if not actually guilty of it.[60]

This significance was not lost on contemporaries of the flapper. Depending upon their notion of the proper role of women, they vigorously defended or damned the new styles. We discussed earlier some of the charges of wickedness leveled against the flappers. Defenders of the costume saw instead an era of new freedom for women. A physician pointed out that girls could now do things such as climb trees or jump over ditches, activities that were not possible to an earlier generation. And women were now able to engage in a variety of affairs outside the home. The result, said the doctor, was a happier and healthier group of people, so the flapper costume must be judged to be "the healthiest, most beautiful and most artistic gown woman has ever worn."[61] A female physician who worked for a number of industrial concerns said that women who do not wear corsets are better insurance risks than those who do and that her firms would not hire a woman "who is tightly laced."[62] And a woman who was to introduce the speaker at a "psychic tea" in New York startled her audience by extolling the woman who wore the flapper costume. Such a woman is "doing the very finest thing she can do for society" by shedding all unnecessary clothing. The flapper knows that her brain can only work when her body is free of constricting clothes. The woman exhorted the audience to throw away their corsets so they might learn such wonderful things as the fact that they had nervous systems and a spine to depend upon.[63]

Roles, like fashions, change continually. And there is an ongoing effort to maintain harmony between roles and appearance. People generally agree that the attire of a man or woman should somehow reflect, or at least not contradict, the meaning of being a man or a woman. A good deal of conflict over fashion is the result of the clash between those who want to change the meaning and those who want to maintain the existing meaning.

Clothes as Masculine and Feminine

Since clothing reflects the nature and role of men and women, it follows that particular kinds of clothes become defined as either masculine or feminine. New fashions may vary along different lines, but they must always be in accord with current notions of masculinity and femininity (keeping in mind, as per the preceding discussion, that there is often more than one current notion of masculinity and femininity). There is, of course, nothing intrinsic in any particular style that marks it as masculine or feminine. Rather, the sexual definition of clothes is arbitrary, though no less important for that reason. As Frances Russell observed near the end of the nineteenth century, "anything that women will persistently wear as 'the correct thing' soon comes to be so associated with womanhood in men's minds as to seem the 'womanly' dress."[64]

Once certain kinds of clothes are defined as expressing masculinity or femininity, the definitions tend to remain stable over time. In fact, the question of trousers for women illustrates the intense conflict that can arise when a traditional style of one sex is desired or adopted by the other sex. At best, as the editor of the *New York Times* wrote in 1934, it is "confusing and sometimes startling" to see women outfitted in "gentlemanly" clothing.[65] At the worst, it is immoral or unacceptably rebellious or perverse for those of either sex to want to wear the clothing of the other sex.

The conflict over trousers or slacks for women illustrates the sexual meanings that are firmly attached to clothes. We shall encounter this conflict again when we discuss the Bloomer controversy in some detail. Here we will look at the way in which the battle over woman's right to wear trousers continued off and on for over a century.

In the early part of the nineteenth century, prudish people might not even use the word "trousers" in mixed company.[66] Trousers were, after all, intimately associated with one sex—the male. They also made obvious the difference in the male and female roles. For many female reformers, trousers became a symbol of the freedom the male possessed and they lacked. But every effort of women to wear the bifurcated garment was met with resistance, ranging from hostility and harassment to ridicule. The caustic approach is illustrated by the remarks of the editor of the *New York Times* in 1876, when he called the desire of women to wear trousers a "curious disease" that ought to be investigated by physicians. Continuing with his medical analogy, the editor said that trousers unquestionably make the patient "altogether hideous" and that no woman in her normal state of mind would wear them without suffering a good deal of mental anguish. Why, then, do some women insist upon appearing publicly in men's clothes? "Further investigation will probably show that the disease is simply hysteria, attended by prolonged, and, in most cases, permanent mental hallucination. The patient becomes a prey to the delusion that health, beauty, and happiness are inseparable from trousers."[67] The editor also pointed out that "feeble, delicate, or timid" women are not attacked by the disease, only those women who are "of exceptional masculine strength, and upon those of extraordinary conversational powers." Women who insist upon wearing such obviously male attire as trousers, then, are lacking in both mental health and femininity.

It is interesting to note that, in the midst of such a climate of opinion, women in some utopian communities in the second half of

FIG. 9. An 1855 print dramatizes the sexual meaning of clothes, including the important question of "who wears the pants." *(Source: Courtesy of the New York Historical Society.)*

the nineteenth century adopted trousers with little resistance. From the beginning of the Oneida community, which was founded in 1848, women wore a Bloomer-type costume. The members of the community were accused of the practice of free love and other devious kinds of behavior. In fact, the very existence of the community was considered scandalous by many Americans. The fact that their women wore trousers, therefore, was probably another obstacle in the way of those women in the larger society who advocated change.

By the turn of the century, the inexorable wheel of change had made another move ahead. Trousers were acceptable for female bicycle riders. As we noted in the last chapter, when some women tried to wear the same costume for other purposes, they quickly learned that such behavior was unacceptable. In spite of the opposition, an astute observer at the time might have recognized the bicycle costume as the harbinger of inevitable change. But it was still inconceivable to most observers that trousers on women should become general.

In 1907, Henry Finck raised the question of whether women would ever dress like men. He acknowledged the fact that women in other cultures had bifurcated garments. But as far as America is concerned, he insisted, the answer to the question is "No, with an assurance bordering on mathematical certainty." Finck based his conclusion on the fact that all past efforts had failed. As far as the bicycle costume was concerned, he said, the costume had hastened the end of the craze for cycling. Furthermore, trousers are ugly on women; thus, "every woman with the adorable feminine instinct of showing herself to the best advantage will hasten to get back into her skirts."[68] No, Finck assured his readers, women will never wear men's clothes until that day when the birds stop displaying their beauty in the air and start tunneling through the earth like moles.

The seriousness with which the issue was treated is illustrated by a story out of Kansas in 1910. A woman asked the state's attorney general if she could wear trousers while working in her home! The attorney general assured her that there was no law that prohibited her from wearing men's trousers, especially if she were the head of the house.[69] The following year, the editor of the *New York Times* came to a conclusion similar to that of Finck. The editor acknowledged the fact that trousers on women were not new and even agreed that women should be able to wear them if they wanted. But he was confident that "no large number of them will ever want to wear them," and that the "tailor-made gown" is as close as most women will ever want to get to masculine fashions.[70]

It was scarcely a decade later that Finck, the editor of the *Times*, and numerous other would-be prophets were shown to be wrong. Some female workers in factories wore trousers during the First World War. During the 1920s, trousers finally became acceptable as a female mode of dress. This did not mean either that criticism of trousers on women ceased or that the masculine and feminine meanings of clothes broke down. By 1940, it was still startling when a young woman would purchase some of her clothes in the men's department.[71] In 1941, the *New York Times* had yet another editorial about "pants and the woman." This time, the editor admitted that trousers on women were no doubt here to stay. But he urged women to be cautious in adopting them, for those societies are happiest in which the women do not fear being feminine and the men do not fear being masculine. There is, he concluded, something "mysterious and romantic" about "feminine draperies," and "mystery and romance still have their uses."[72]

Even in the 1970s, a woman could find herself being harassed on the grounds that she looked too masculine. The following exchange took place between President Nixon and reporter Helen Thomas at a public gathering in the White House:

> "Helen, are you still wearing slacks? Do you prefer them actually? . . . Slacks can do something for some people and some it can't. I think you do very well—turn around. . . . Do they cost less than a gown?"
>
> "No," she replied.
>
> "Then change," the President suggested, and everyone in the room laughed.[73]

Fashions, then, are given masculine and feminine meanings. Apart from the type of clothes involved, such as the suit or trousers, various qualities are attributed to the sexes and to the styles that are appropriate to each sex. Throughout the nineteenth and twentieth centuries, feminine clothing means such things as delicacy, softness, and fineness of fabric. In 1976, the *New York Times* reported a "wild outbreak of femininity" in women's fashions. The feminine nature of the new styles was evidenced by "yards of ruffles, petticoats, cotton eyelet and silk taffeta," reminding us of "another, more romantic era."[74] Indeed, notions of femininity in fashions a hundred years earlier were quite similar. In spite of the widespread acceptance and use of trousers in the 1970s, many Americans still preferred to see women in what they regarded as more feminine attire.

CONCLUSION

In essence, fashion reveals the differing qualities of the sexes, shows how the sexes respond differently to the same social phenomenon, and both reflects and maintains sex roles. But there is another facet to this set of beliefs that has often been overlooked. Women are frequently caught in a double bind in the realm of fashion. We have already noted the fact that men sometimes condemn their wives and daughters for wearing the very things they desire or find attractive in other women. We may briefly note one other way in which women face a "damned-if-you-do" and "damned-if-you-don't" situation.

Throughout the history of American fashion, women have been exhorted by men to be strong, courageous, independent, and reject some of the absurdities which have been foisted upon them. Such men also tend to point out that their own sex has set the example by being individualists in fashion. But it really requires little thought to know what would happen to the woman who insisted upon her own idiosyncratic styles no matter what the current fashion might be. A cartoon illustrates the point by showing a man in a hippie-type outfit at a party. A woman, referring to him, says to another person at the party, "You mean he wears *that* and he's nobody?" We may allow idiosyncratic styles on the rich or powerful or famous, but the ordinary person cannot contradict fashion with impunity. In 1919, the editor of the *New York Times* also acknowledged the perils of individuality when he wrote that we might well view "with alarm a sex that disregards all fashion" and insists on dressing purely in accord with individual style and taste. If women are to lead us to a better life, he concluded, they will not go the way of "a mad waging of individual fancies" but will adhere to the simple styles of the war years when they were "uniformly adorable."[75] Similarly, a fashion magazine editor declared in 1926 that a woman who wants to be "smart" will abandon a fashion when it becomes widely accepted. At the same time, said the editor, women should not try to create their own styles. "Whenever a woman departs from the accepted mode the effect is disastrous. She hopes to be artistic. She ends by being arty."[76] Surely any thoughtful woman must cringe before such an onslaught of contradictory advice. What shall she do when she is exhorted to be an individual yet warned against nonconformity? How shall she respond when she is accused of being irrational in fashion matters yet her attempts at reform are labeled as perverse or a further example of irrationality? No matter which way women respond in the realm of fashion, it is evidence to many men of their inferior nature.

Notes

1. Margaret Mead, *Sex and Temperament in Three Primitive Societies* (New York: Dell, 1969), p. 260.
2. Janet Saltzman Chafetz, *Masculine/Feminine or Human?* (Itaska, Ill.: F. E. Peacock, 1974), pp. 27–28.
3. John S. Haller and Robin M. Haller, *The Physician and Sexuality in Victorian America* (Urbana: University of Illinois Press, 1974), p. 50.
4. *Ibid.,* p. 78.
5. See Barbara Welter, "The Cult of True Womanhood, 1820–1860," *The American Quarterly* 18 (Summer, 1966): 151–74.
6. *Godey's Lady's Book* (January, 1851): 65.
7. *Ibid.*
8. *The Ladies' Repository* 11 (July, 1851): 251–52.
9. *The Ladies' Wreath* 4 (June, 1849): 71.
10. *Harper's New Monthly Magazine* 7 (November, 1853): 838–39.
11. John Randolph, in *The Ladies' Repository* 13 (June, 1853): 252.
12. *DeBow's Commercial Review* 17 (August, 1854): 129.

13. Ernest Crawley, *Dress, Drinks, and Drums* (London: Methuen & Co. Ltd., 1931), p. 54.
14. C. A. Bristed, "Dress and Its Critics," *The Nation* 2 (January 4, 1866): 10.
15. "Men's Clothes," *New York Times,* January 27, 1911.
16. Eve Merriam, "Why Do Women Dress Thay Way?" *Reader's Digest* 81 (October, 1962): 113.
17. Nathaniel Ward, "Women's Fashions," in George Mayberry, ed., *A Little Treasury of American Prose* (New York: Scribner's, 1949), p. 21.
18. Edmund P. Banning, *Common Sense on the Mechanical Pathology and Treatment of Chronic Diseases of the Male and Female Systems,* 14th ed. (New York: Wilson & Co., 1852), p. 325.
19. "Fashionable Follies," *New York Times,* November 1, 1868.
20. See Elizabeth Robins Pennell, "For Fashion's Sake," *The North American Review* 224 (September, 1927): 393; Norman Lobsenz, "Mini-Midi-Maxi Madness," *Good Housekeeping* 171 (August, 1970): 129.
21. Frances E. Russell, "Woman's Dress," *The Arena* 3 (February, 1891): 352. See also Julia Cruikshank, "An Economic View of Fashion," *The Arean* 27 (April, 1901): 388.
22. *New York Times,* October 14, 1878.
23. E. Nesbit, "The Slaves of the Spider," *The Living Age* 288 (February 26, 1916): 571–72.
24. *New York Times,* July 29, 1917.
25. Geri Trotta, "Are Women Sheep—or Are Men?" *The New York Times Magazine,* February 6, 1955, p. 40.
26. Prudence Glynn, *In Fashion: Dress in the Twentieth Century* (New York: Oxford University Press, 1978), p. 130.
27. Teresa H. Dean, *How to Be Beautiful: Nature Unmasked, a Book for Every Woman* (Chicago: People's Publishing Co., 1889), p. 75.
28. *Ibid.,* pp. 75–76.
29. *St. Louis Life* 1 (March 15, 1890). See also "The Rational Dress Movement: A Symposium," *The Arean* 9 (February, 1894): 305–26.
30. "The Black Wave," *The New Republic* 27 (July 27, 1921): 234.
31. Elizabeth Smith Miller, "Reflections on Woman's Dress, and the Record of a Personal Experience," *The Arean* 6 (September, 1892): 493.
32. See Elizabeth Robins Pennell, *op. cit.,* p. 392; Elizabeth Hawes, "Fashion Is Spinach," *Reader's Digest* 32 (June, 1938): 49; "The Flat Look," *Time* 64 (August 9, 1954): 29.
33. G. Fitzhugh, "The Domain of Fashion," *DeBow's Commercial Review* 29 (1860): 695–96.
34. Henry T. Finck, *Romantic Love and Personal Beauty* (New York: Macmillan, 1887), p. 391.

134 | FASHION AND SOCIAL LIFE

35. "New Coats of Many Colors," *New York Times,* September 24, 1926.
36. *New York Times,* February 3, 1930.
37. *New York Times,* September 26, 1931.
38. Arnold Bennett, *Things That Have Interested Me,* Second Series (New York: George H. Doran, 1923), pp. 64–5.
39. James C. Bayles, "Courage in Dress," *The Independent* 70 (May 4, 1911): 956–57. Similarly, a correspondent to the *New York Times* (June 29, 1910) asked how men could continually argue that women were slaves to fashion when "they themselves are slaves to the extent of suffering in a sizzling hot day in a stiff, high collar, and a woolen coat?"
40. *St. Louis Globe-Democrat,* February 14, 1880.
41. Eugene Benson, "About Women and Dress," *Southern Magazine* 4 (1869): 604.
42. *Godey's Lady's Book* 70 (March, 1865): 278.
43. *New York Times,* November 9, 1958.
44. Geri Trotta, *op. cit.,* p. 22.
45. Eugene Benson, *op. cit.,* p. 603.
46. Eva Olney Farnsworth, *The Art & Ethics of Dress* (San Francisco: Paul Elder & Company, 1915), p. 3.
47. Henry T. Finck, *op. cit.,* pp. 379–80.
48. *Ibid.,* pp. 387–89.
49. *New York Times,* January 4, 1925.
50. Eva Olney Farnsworth, *op. cit.,* pp. 10 and 41.
51. Agnes Repplier, "The Drolleries of Clothes," *The Independent* 107 (December 3, 1921): 224.
52. *New York Times,* April 27, 1939.
53. *St. Louis Intelligencer,* June 12, 1851.
54. Quoted in Frances E. Russell, "A Brief Survey of the American Dress Reform Movement of the Past, with Views of Representative Women," *The Arena* 6 (August, 1892): 327.
55. "Symposium in Women's Dress," *The Arena* 6 (September, 1892): 500.
56. "The Hobble Is the Latest Freak in Women's Fashion," *New York Times,* June 12, 1910.
57. Quoted in "Rational Dress Movement: Symposium," *The Arena* 9 (February, 1894): 325.
58. "Symposium in Women's Dress," *op. cit.,* p. 496.
59. *St.Louis Life* 7 (May 27, 1893): 4.
60. Kenneth A. Yellis, "Prosperity's Child: Some Thoughts on the Flapper," *The American Quarterly* 21 (Spring, 1969): 44.
61. *New York Times,* June 6, 1921.
62. *New York Times,* September 9, 1921.
63. *New York Times,* April 23, 1922.

64. Frances E. Russell, "Freedom in Dress for Woman," *The Arena* 8 (June, 1893): 70.
65. *New York Times,* August 1, 1934.
66. Jane Dorner, *Fashion* (London: Octopus Books, 1974), p. 67.
67. *New York Times,* May 27, 1876.
68. Henry T. Finck, "Will Women Ever Dress Like Men?" *op. cit.,* pp. 1254–55.
69. *New York Times,* April 29, 1910.
70. *New York Times,* February 18, 1911.
71. Jane Cobb, "Girls Will Be Boys," *The New York Times Magazine,* November 3, 1940, p. 10.
72. *New York Times,* July 5, 1941.
73. Barbara Sinclair Deckard, *The Women's Movement* (New York: Harper & Row, 1975), p. 127.
74. *New York Times,* September 25, 1976.
75. *New York Times,* August 1, 1919.
76. *New York Times,* April 25, 1926.

chapter 4
Fashion and the Nature of Society

While some have inquired about the nature of humans, others have asked about the nature of human societies. What is society? Most who ask the question agree that in the case of society, the whole is greater than the sum of its parts. A society cannot be understood as merely the aggregation of numerous individuals. Or as the French sociologist, Emile Durkheim, put it, a society cannot exist if there are only individuals.

A striking illustration of how a group of individuals becomes a qualitatively unique phenomenon is provided by an experiment of Philip Zimbardo's.[1] He put together a group of mature, emotionally stable, intelligent young men in a simulated prison. By a flip of the coin, half of the men were designated prisoners and half were selected as guards. The guards worked out the rules they would enforce and worked on eight-hour, three-man shifts. The experiment was to take place over an extended period of time, but was terminated after only six days. In that short time, wrote Zimbardo, the young men were transformed by the experience of imprisonment: "human values were suspended, self-concepts were challenged and the ugliest, most base, pathological side of human nature surfaced."[2] One could not have had the faintest notion of the outcome merely by looking at the qualities of the individuals who formed the group.

Some observers of the fashion scene have written as though people acted purely as individuals, as though a person acts the same in social settings as he or she does when alone. But others have recognized that the individual does not exist in a social vacuum. They have seen fashion behavior—rightly, we would argue—as a reflection of the nature of society and not merely as the outcome of the qualities of individuals.

FASHION AND SOCIAL NORMS

All societies and all groups have shared expectations about behavior. Normative behavior is simply prescribed behavior, the behavior expected of each of us by the rest of us. Fashion is a form of normative behavior for there are, and always have been, expectations about proper and improper dress. Those who have derided women for their failure to be nonconformists even when it appeared that the fashions they accepted "uglified" them or created health problems, have ignored the fact that conformity is of the essence of society.

Some people mistake their conformity to a smaller group as an expression of individuality, like the woman who accepted the flapper style early and said to a friend, "Mamie, you simp, why don't you bob your hair like the other girls and show some originality?"[3] The question we all face is not whether to conform, but to which group to conform, and the relative costs and benefits of conformity to various groups.

What, then, are those who have urged women to resist fashions really telling them to do? What would happen to the nonconformist? At the least, the nonconformist would be ill at ease. A woman will "feel very uncomfortable" if she does not "conform to the general standard of beauty," said a nineteenth-century writer.[4] A 1950 study of female college students said that the women would feel "uneasy, uncomfortable, and self-conscious if they did not comply with fashion."[5] Worse yet, the nonconformist could suffer rejection and isolation. A nineteenth-century writer said that he who tries to pursue an idiosyncratic course in fashion "becomes a pariah at once. He is abandoned of society."[6]

Given the costs of nonconformity, it is not surprising that people desire to be fashionable. Perhaps "desire" is too mild. As a 1911 writer put it, being unfashionable is so terrible that a woman will "stretch every nerve to be in fashion."[7] We need only recall the various metaphors applied to fashion to realize the intensity that most writers ascribe to the drive to be fashionable. And why not? Who wants to be a pariah? Who wants to endure the pain of rejection or isolation?

Whether to avoid the costs of nonconformity or to gain the benefits of conformity, most people take care to be in fashion. Even crusaders have sometimes worn the very fashions against which they were protesting. An Anti-Crinoline League was organized in a small Texas town in 1893. One of the organizers wrote to her father about the "horror of hoops" and the numerous accidents that each woman could recall and relate to the hoops.[8] But the pressure to conform was intense, and on balance, the young women ultimately decided accidents and discomfort were preferable to the wrath of society.

The pressure to conform may come in the way of a gentle reminder, as when a woman tells her husband that his selection of light-colored trousers and shirt is inappropriate now that winter has arrived. When gentle reminders are inadequate, people may resort to ridicule or insults. In 1859, the editor of *Godey's* reminded his readers that when little girls go to school they quickly learn the importance of looking attractive, for they hear such things as: " 'What a dowdy she looks like, in that old hat!' 'Miss A.'s trimming cost a dollar a yard.' 'I wouldn't wear such a cheap dress as Miss B. has on.' "[9] Another nineteenth-century writer told of a man who denounced hoops when they were first introduced. But when his wife appeared one evening without the hoops, he looked at her "in mingled perplexity and vexation" and finally told her that she looked as though she had been "dragged through a keyhole," that she was not "decent," and that she should immediately go and put more clothes on.[10] Even total strangers may feel free to rebuke someone for inappropriate dress. In the 1960s, a young woman said that when she appeared in the "military look," "two people insulted me and a little old lady said they needed me in Vietnam."[11] An even more severe form of pressure is intimidation or harassment. In 1830, a man in Massachusetts was derided, had his house windows broken, had rocks thrown at him, was refused communion at church, and finally was physically assaulted on the street. His crime? He wore a beard, and beards were not fashionable then.[12]

Often the pressure has come in a more formal way, ranging from the written or unwritten rules of organization to laws. Religious leaders have often used their authority to gain conformity to "respectable" styles. A Protestant minister in New York ridiculed the 1921 styles in verse:

> *Mary had a little skirt,*
> *The latest style, no doubt.*
> *But every time she got inside,*
> *She was more than half way out.*[13]

A Catholic priest had gone even further in 1920. As the bride was walking down the aisle he halted the ceremony, ordered the lights out, and sent the bride home to put on a more modest outfit.[14]

Various other organizations and authorities have also tried to control dress. In the 1960s, women in tailored or formal pants were not being admitted to some New York restaurants. Some had actually been allowed to dine in lingerie in places that refused to admit them when they wore pants.[15] Many businesses refused to allow female employees to wear miniskirts in the 1960s on the grounds that they interfered with the efficiency of male employees. Dress codes have existed for schools, the Supreme Court, and other organizations.

Finally, norms have sometimes been formalized in laws. Most have regulated female fashions, though sometimes male fashions have been included, and most have been an effort to maintain moral standards. For example:

1. A Richmond, Virginia woman was arrested in 1913 and taken to the police station for wearing a slit skirt.
2. In 1913, the mayor of Portland, Oregon ordered the arrest of any woman wearing an "X-ray" dress in public.
3. A man was arrested for wearing shorts in Great Neck, New York, in July, 1938, because a local ordinance prohibited any "costume which unnecessarily exposes any part of the body."

4. In 1953, a New York City regulation provided a $50 fine for anyone wearing swimsuits, a halter, shorts, sunsuit, playsuit or similar attire in a city park.[16]

SOCIETY VERSUS THE INDIVIDUAL

Some thinkers have gone beyond the notion of society as merely normative. They see society as a transcendent and coercive force in the life of individuals. Durkheim, for instance, argued that society is a phenomenon *sui generis,* so that the thinking, feeling, and acting of a group is quite different from that of the individuals who compose the group. Societies are characterized by "social facts," which are patterns of thinking, feeling, and acting that are "external to the individual and are endowed with a power of coercion over him. Illustrations include maxims of public morality, family and religious observance, rules of professional behavior."[17]

What happens to the needs and desires of individuals if they are dominated or controlled by social facts? In spite of his insistence on the coercive nature of those facts, Durkheim did not, like Freud, see a contradiction between the interests of society and the needs or desires of the individual. In fact, individual well-being hinges upon the solidarity of the society. For Freud, on the other hand, there is an inevitable clash between individual needs and societal development. Life in society is a trade off; individuals give up a measure of happiness (because the sexual and aggressive instincts must be suppressed) in order to gain a measure of security.

The questions of coerciveness of social facts, the extent to which individuals have autonomy, and the possibility of individual well-being in society, are all addressed by those who discuss fashion. For fashion is one of those social facts that is external to the individual. But is it coercive? Does the individual have any scope for action when confronted by fashion? Is there a contradiction between the individual's needs and interests and the demands of the current fashion? Answers differ, but, as we shall see, there is an interesting pattern over time to the answers. Let us look first at those who view fashion as a coercive social fact. Like Durkheim, they see society as dominant over the individual. But, like Freud, they also tend to see a contradiction between the demands of fashion and the desires and needs of the individual.

Fashion as a Coercive Social Fact

Fashion, wrote William Graham Sumner, is a type of group dominance over the individual that is as likely to be harmful as beneficial. Furthermore, one cannot argue with fashion, for its authority "is imperative as to everything which it touches." Those who dissent only hurt themselves. They never affect fashion.[18] In short order, Sumner answers all of our questions. Is fashion coercive? Yes. Is there scope for individual action in the realm of fashion? No. Do the demands of fashion contradict the needs and desires of the individual? They are as likely to as not.

A variety of writers have largely agreed with Sumner. As denoted or connoted by the metaphors of power we discussed in chapter two, fashion is one of the coercive facts of social life. And for many nineteenth-century writers, and some in the early twentieth century, the dominance is complete. An early nineteenth-century writer said that fashion has more influence in civilized society than virtually anything else, "leading men and women by the nose."[19] Fashion compels us to submit, allowing no scope for free action. It is more restrictive than socialism should be, and the fact that we are a democratic people does not mean we are free to choose in the realm of fashion. On the contrary, the spread of democracy only means that the "ravages of Fashion" have now "become well-nigh universal."[20]

Putting the matter into concrete terms, some popular writers have equated the coerciveness of fashion with the work of the designers. That is, it is not some phantom or some ethereal force out there that is imposing itself upon us; it is the designers who decide what the fashion shall be and insist that we accept their decisions. But the designers respond that this is a misreading of the situation. They interpret the times, they say, they do not shape them. Or they sense the will of the public, but they do not mold the public will. Or, like Paul Poiret, they may even claim that they themselves are carried along by the powerful currents of fashion. No one, wrote Poiret, has a choice in the matter, for fashion "controls and rules your decisions . . . like an astral influence upon you without your knowledge."[21]

Both the designer and the consumer must yield before the power of the earthly goddess. Worse yet, they may be yielding to their own detriment. Fashion is not merely coercive; it may be both coercive and deleterious. To be in fashion is both compelling and precarious, for the individual may be thrust into a kind of Freudian nightmare in which every need and desire is thwarted in the course of adapting to fashion's demands. An obviously frustrated writer in 1837 listed many of the ways in which individual needs and desires are contradicted by the coercive social fact of fashion:

> She pinches our feet with tight shoes, or chokes us with a tight neck-handkerchief, or squeezes the breath out of our body by tight lacing. . . . She makes people visit when they would rather stay at home, eat when they are not hungry, and drink when they are not thirsty. She invades our pleasures, and interrupts our business. . . . She ruins health and produces sickness—destroys life, and occasions premature death. She makes foolish parents, invalids of children, and servants of all.[22]

It would seem that humans would attempt to rid themselves of something that has such potential for ill, but individual rebellion against a social fact is, by definition, fruitless. People have tried, of course, and they have inevitably failed. As Mrs. Oliphant noted, all attempts "to guide, control, or modify" the freedom of fashion have been signal failures."[23] The editor of the *New York Times* agreed in an 1879 article: "It is of no use to make war upon it, or to try to keep wholly clear of it, for it is a fact of civilization, and we can no more get out of it than we can get out of history or of society."[24]

A good example of the futility of trying to resist fashion, according to one writer, was the "unending war" against corsets. "It proves conclusively that the corset wins all of the battles."[25] Even businessmen, pointed out another writer, have been unable to stay a fashion trend once it has begun. "Some of the most pathetic as well as greatest losses in the history of American business have been due to efforts to stop the trends."[26] For instance, manufacturers and retailers put forth vigorous efforts to keep the hoop skirt from going out of fashion in the 1870s, but they lost their fight. Similarly, when the hobble skirt became fashionable, fabric manufacturers found their sales were declining and decided to set in motion a new trend that could bring greater profits. An expensive and well-organized campaign began in 1912 to get women to accept a style known as the "pannier skirt," which used considerably more material than the currently fashionable hobble skirt. A number of Parisian designers prepared models, and the promoters arranged for a number of actresses to wear the skirts. Articles describing the skirt and telling of its success appeared in fashion magazines. Manufacturers, wholesalers, and retailers all prepared for the surge of sales, but the outcome was another lost battle. Women showed no interest in the pannier skirts, so "another instance of the futility of trying to change a major trend in consumer demand by the means available to business passed into history."[27]

The pannier skirt is an interesting case. For if the writer used it to illustrate the futility of businessmen trying to alter fashion trends, other writers have used similar types of cases to come to a different conclusion—fashion is not an overwhelmingly coercive social fact after all, for consumers can effectively resist particular styles. Let us look at what these writers have to say about the role of individuals and groups in affecting fashion trends.

Fashion as a Human Enterprise

In one sense, Durkheim and others have been right. The individual is relatively powerless before a social fact like fashion. On the other hand, if fashion is a human enterprise, if it is the outcome of human activity, then collective efforts should be able to affect the trends. The individual may be helpless, but an organized effort should have power. Of course, the nineteenth-century dress reformers were organized, but the bulk of the women to whom they appealed seemed to feel that resistance was futile. Apart from the reformers, nineteenth-century writers stress the coerciveness of fashion. In the twentieth century, however, an increasing number of writers insist that we can control and use fashion to our well-being rather than merely submit to it to our detriment. The developing sense of control was facilitated by the women's rights movement. Increasingly, women viewed themselves as autonomous, rational, competent creatures, rather than the frail, dependent, emotional beings of the nineteenth-century ideal. At the outset of the twentieth century, one woman sounded the note of defiance that would become typical and widespread:

> If the day is past when we allowed ministers to do our spiritual thinking for us and physicians our health thinking, just so surely has the time arrived for us to become responsible for our clothing and no longer allowing the dressmaker to do our thinking for us. To be told what one should and should not wear is an indignity that every mature woman should resent.[28]

The writer went on to point out than an increasing number of women were already speaking out publicly in clubs and elsewhere, defying fashion, and proving thereby "that true worth appeals to the human heart and is respected quite regardless of Dame Fashion's say-so."

Those who spoke out in the first two decades of the century freely acknowledged the foibles of the past and called for a new era. Just because past fashions have always been foolish, wrote a "plain country woman" in 1914, they need not always be so. "There are so many savageries of the past that we are eliminating from our lives, why not let extreme adornment of women's bodies go with them?"[29] Another writer was more forceful: "We refuse to be shackled and bound and boned and tortured longer; we have tasted the delights of Greek drapery and we hate the very name of Catherine de Medici, who invented the corset and the thirteen-inch waist."[30]

Determination, organization, and the spreading sense of control and power combined to make the twentieth-century tale of fashion quite different from that of the nineteenth century. In the world of women's fashions, the relatively docile and quiet consumer of the nineteenth century gave way to the more assertive and articulate consumer of the present century. This is not to say that the nineteenth century was one of total submission and the twentieth century one of total autonomy. But the pervading sense among nineteenth-century writers was that consumers either would not or could not rebel against fashion trends. Twentieth-century writers have considerably more confidence in the efficacy of human action. True, they continue to talk about fashion's power and the way in which the workings of fashion elude human reason. But neither the power nor the nonrationality of fashion can quell their faith in the efficacy of collective action. After all, the twentieth century witnessed the fulfillment of the dreams of the dress reformers. Even if it did require nearly a century of struggle, the discarding of the corset was tangible evidence that the well-being of consumers would not always be sacrificed at the altar

FIG. 10. The flapper costume, a milestone in fashion history. (*Courtesy* Vogue, *Copyright* © *1926, (renewed) 1954 by The Condé Nast Publications Inc.*)

of the earthly goddess. There would still be times when battles would be lost, but the important thing was that people now knew that battles could be won.

Three twentieth-century milestones in fashion history illustrate the above points—the flapper era, the New Look of 1947, and the midi fiasco of 1970. In the 1920s, women's fashions hit a new high in freedom, or a new low in morality and/or femininity, depending upon the observer's point of view. In any case, they were a radical departure from anything before in American history, and they reflected the will of women themselves rather than some mysterious edict. There was, in the words of one writer, "no great and noble exemplar" who led the way into the fashions of the 1920s. Rather, "the voice of the people, the female people, spoke, and the short

FIG. 11. A well-to-do young flapper stepping out of her roadster. (*Source: Library of Congress.*)

skirt was the law, and to the knee legs were revealed for the first time in 3,000 years."[30] The days were past, according to another writer, when fashions would be determined by a few leaders of society. Large numbers of women had entered the labor force, had tasted the freedom of earning their own way, and were determined to have clothing that facilitated their work and careers. The women with pay envelopes were now setting the styles by insisting on fashions that were "simple, smart, becoming, and comfortable to work in." And if a style did not meet those criteria, noted a Fifth Avenue saleslady, it would remain on the racks, for the flapper would simply not buy it.[32]

A number of efforts to impose a particular fashion or alter the flapper styles failed. For instance, in the middle of the 1920s, a manufacturer of veils attempted to make his product popular again. He had photographers take pictures of well-known society women in veils and put them in the newspapers. Articles were written about veils in fashion columns. The veils were well advertised and stocked in department stores, but after six months, the manufacturer gave up the effort as a lost cause. The flappers refused to wear veils.[33] As in the case of the pannier skirt earlier, women refused to be manipulated. They had gained a new sense of power, a new determination to do what they willed, rather than what someone or something else willed for them. A 1929 writer epitomized the self-confidence of the flapper by declaring that the "sheep" now decide rather than follow:

> Ho, Hum! It's good to be a sheep. You do what you please if the fashion pleases you. When the heavy smoke of conference in high places clears away, the sheep are seen placidly browsing in fashion pastures they like. I am glad I am a sheep. I lie down with the lions of fashion but I get up and follow the sheep.[34]

Girls as well as women asserted their right to decide for themselves what was appropriate attire. For example, in 1923 a PTA in Somerset, Pennsylvania asked the school board to forbid rolled stockings and sleeveless dresses in the public schools. A number of girls who opposed the attempt to regulate their dress expressed their feelings in a "short and snappy" verse:

> I can show my shoulders,
> I can show my knees;
> I'm a free-born American,
> And can show what I please.[35]

Clearly, American females no longer regarded themselves as helpless pawns of fashion trends. Fashion designers agreed that styles could no longer be dictated. Worth said that women themselves were the most important factors influencing fashion. Another Paris couturier arrived in New York in 1931 to study the attitudes of American women toward new style trends because, he said, it was the women and not Paris that established new fashions.[36]

Anyone who thought the desires of women had finally and totally dethroned Dame Fashion, however, had a rude awakening when Christian Dior introduced the New Look in Paris in 1947. In contrast to the military look of the war years, the rounded shoulders and wide full skirt of the New Look was a return to femininity in women's fashions. But there was an immediate outcry against the style. The shortage of materials meant that clothing was still a scarce commodity. To come out with a style that required considerably more material was, in the eyes of many people, absurd if not unethical. Moreover, the New Look appeared to be a step backwards to feminists and to many other women as well, for the style did not appear to be congruent with the level of activity desired by most women. Finally, to accept the New Look meant that a woman had to get a completely new wardrobe. Both men and women objected to the financial implications of the style.

Opposition to the New Look was vocal and widespread. A national news magazine commented there had not been such "turmoil, twittering and posturing among American women" since bobbed hair appeared in 1914.[37] Over twelve hundred women in Louisville signed a manifesto against the longer hemlines. A secretary who helped gather the signatures pointed out that many women who buy an expensive dress wear it a few times to special affairs or places and then convert it to a working dress. But that would no longer be practical if the New Look became common: "Can you imaging anybody coming to work in one of those new jobs? They make short women look like a barrel."[38] In Dallas, Texas, thirteen hundred members of the Little Below the Knee Club said they were determined to hold the line on skirt lengths. The founder said she had organized the group because she did not want to discard her entire wardrobe and accept a style that did not look good on her. The members tied up traffic with a parade in downtown Dallas on a Saturday in August. The women wore their grandmother's clothes. Banners asked the onlookers such questions as "Shall it be this?" and exhorted them to "Be sensible."[39]

Throughout the nation, women organized or used existing organizations, to protest the New Look. They were joined by many men in their struggle. Men attended the gatherings of the organizations, and in some cases, formed their own groups. In Georgia, some men formed the League of Broke Husbands in an effort to get at least thirty thousand husbands to "hold that hemline." The governor of Oklahoma spoke out publicly against the lower hemlines, declaring they would bankrupt the nation. Furthermore, he did not care for the looks of the new style, and pointed out that Oklahoma women did not need padded hiplines with the state's plentiful supply of corn, wheat and beef.[40]

Clearly, substantial numbers of Americans intended to be adamant in the face of the New Look. They would not allow it to prevail. But their determination to resist caused little more than a brief hesitation in the onrushing new fashion. In September, 1947, Christian Dior came to America to accept an award from Neiman-Marcus Company for "outstanding service" to the clothing industry. Dior insisted that he knew women well, that short skirts were never very good styles, and that American women, including those protesting the loudest, would soon be wearing the longer dresses. He was right. Acceptance was growing even as he spoke. Many women were attracted by the femininity of the new style and by the shift away from the drabness of wartime fashions. But whatever their reasons, and however much they may have resisted at first, women quickly adopted the New Look *en masse*. It appeared as though the earthly goddess had fully recovered from the apostasy of the 1920s and recaptured the devotion and loyalty of her followers.

But in 1970, the battle lines were drawn again. The "midi," a mid-calf length dress or skirt, was proclaimed the new style. The new style was certainly a radical departure from the miniskirts to which Americans had become accustomed. In fact, it evoked some of the same kinds of outrage and organized resistance that characterized the initial reaction to the New Look. One woman said contemptuously that the midi would be "the year's fashion Edsel." A California woman told her club that the fashion world regards females as a bunch of sheep; "well, let's not let them pull the wool over our legs as well as our eyes." The woman was the head of an organization called Preservation of Our Femininity and Finances. Chapters were organized in New York and London. All members signed a pledge, and worked to get other women to sign one, not to buy or wear a midi regardless of what other women did.[41]

As noted earlier, the outcome of the campaign against the midi was quite different from that against the New Look. The midi proved to be a fiasco. For years afterwards, observers said the midi marked the end of fashion's dominance over women, that never again would fashions be imposed upon women against their will. The year after the midi, hotpants became the rage. For many people, hotpants were "the final crushing rebuke to the midi and to the fashion cartel of designers, manufacturers, and stores that tried to drape long skirts" on women's bodies.[42] If they were the final rebuke, they were not the last word. In a couple of years, long skirts were again the fashion. Nevertheless, those involved in the world of fashion continued to lament the disaster of 1970. For example, in 1972 a New York merchant declared that fashion designers had been thrust into a "Hall of Shame" by women after the midi. "Today's woman," he said, "has had it for the time being with the designer. She feels that he is guilty of trying to foist off on her what she wouldn't be seen dead in."[43] In 1974, another designer said there would be no more Paris or New York dictatorship in the world of fashion, for "the American woman has been liberated from all that. There is no way she is going to be imposed upon."[44]

As the metaphors of fashion remind us, we are dealing with a process that can be devious at times. We would not, therefore, boldly declare that either men or women would never again have a style imposed upon them. Still, it is indisputable that the twentieth century presents a far different picture from the nineteenth century. Fashion is obviously not the coercive social fact that it seemed to be in the nineteenth century. There are limits to what consumers will accept. An interesting study in support of this assertion was published by Jack and Schiffer in 1948.[45] The two researchers compared skirt lengths in *Vogue* and the *Women's Home Companion* with the length of skirts worn by women on the street from 1929 to 1947. The length of the skirt of the woman on the street was obtained by making measurements from photographs of women in a number of popular magazines. The fashion illustrations in *Vogue* and the *Woman's Home Companion* represented the dictated length. To what extent, asked the researchers, did actual photographs of women conform to the dictated styles?

In essence, they found the woman on the street can only be manipulated within certain limits. Within those limits, she tended to conform, but when new styles changed too radically from the old, she resisted. "In other words, the more extreme the 'dictated' hemline, short or long, the greater the nonconformity of the woman on the street."[46]

In sum, from the point of view of the individual, fashion is a coercive social fact. When that individual unites with others in collective action, fashion becomes a human enterprise and efforts to affect trends may be efficacious. To be sure, an individual *can* take a stand and reject the current fashion. But as many observers have pointed out, an individual does not stand against the tide of fashion with impunity. Americans have always idealized the "rugged individualist." We have praised the individual who goes his or her own way in the face of great opposition, but the admiration and the praise have come more in the abstract than in concrete cases. And where an individual is praised for a rugged stand against the onslaught of the majority, the plaudits are more likely to come in retrospect than in the heat of battle. The price of rugged individualism may be high. Most people prefer the comforts of conformity. Society is rarely threatened by individualists.

SOCIETY AS A ZERO-SUM GAME

From chickens to psychologists at a convention, all creatures strive with their fellow creatures for status. In the chicken yard, we call it establishing a pecking order. At a 1972 convention of psychologists, it was illustrated by a jelly bean game. Those who attended one of the sessions of the convention were given bags with different colored jelly beans in each bag. They were then told to give a green jelly bean to a person of their choice, an orange jelly bean to a second choice, a red jelly bean to a third choice, and they could either give a yellow jelly bean to a fourth choice or keep it for themselves. After the jelly beans had been distributed, each person was asked to walk around the room and show the others what he or she had wound up with. The game was intended to show the trauma of social rejection and the gratification of acceptance. And it did so. Some people felt badly because they had not been given jelly beans by others, while some felt the pleasure of full bags. Some had gained a degree of status, even if it was fleeting, and others had lost a degree.[47] It was only a game, but it illustrated the kind of thing that happens regularly in social life.

To some extent, the struggle for status is a zero-sum game. A person often gains status only at the expense of someone else. If someone moves up in the pecking order, someone else necessarily moves down. An individual can move up by a variety of different means in various social settings. For example, one might gain status in a religious group by being defined as one who has advanced spiritually. In some cases, this may involve displacing another individual who was high in the spiritual order. Similar processes occur, though by differing means and with different criteria for advancement, in such settings as trade unions, political parties, and corporations.

Furthermore, the status that any individual has attained may be indicated by a distinctive style of dress. In the Roman Catholic Church, there is a distinctive style of dress for each level of the hierarchy from the Pope down to the parish priest. In a TB hospital observed by Julius Roth, protective clothing such as masks, gowns, and hair coverings was supposed to be worn by hospital personnel whenever they came into contact with the patients. Roth found, however, that the higher the status of the personnel the less likely was the clothing to be worn. Physicians, for instance, rarely wore the clothing, while aides and students wore at least some of it nearly all the time.[48]

We could multiply the examples *ad infinitum*. Clothing is, and always has been, a symbol of status. However the lines of status differentiation may be drawn in a particular society, there is likely to be distinctive styles associated with the different ranks. In America, for example, one tends to lose status as one enters old age. As Max Lerner put it, the elderly in our society are often treated "like the fag end of what was once good material."[49] It is a compliment to tell someone that he or she does not look his or her age. By the same token, however, we expect people to dress in accord with their age. The young, the middle-aged, and the elderly are all expected to remain within the bounds of propriety for their group, as etiquette manuals have reminded us for generations.

A nineteenth-century etiquette guide for women set forth the matter of age-appropriate attire in straightforward terms. Everyone knows, said the writer, that regardless of the financial status of a young woman, "her dress ought always, in form as well as ornaments, to exhibit less of a *recherche* appearance, and should be less showy than that of married ladies."[50] Such things as expensive furs and diamonds are "forbidden" for young women, and those who do not heed the taboo make us believe that they have an "unrestrained love of luxury." Older ladies, on the other hand, should dress like those of a moderate financial status, abstaining from gaudy colors and ostentatious accouterments like feathers, flowers, and jewels. "A lady in her decline, wearing her hair dressed, and having short sleeves, and adorned with necklaces, bracelets, etc., offends as much against propriety as against her interest and dignity."[51]

A twentieth-century authority, Amy Vanderbilt, agreed that each age group should accept certain restrictions of dress. In response to various letters, Ms. Vanderbilt said a very young girl would look "cheap" wearing high heels or dresses that were cut too low. A teenager should not dress as if she were a worldly woman.[52] In the matter of clothing styles, people should act their age.

There are appropriate styles for all of the various kinds of status. People are expected to wear somewhat different styles depending upon their socioeconomic status, their age, their sex, their religious status, their position in an organization, and so forth. It follows that an individual can use style in the ongoing struggle for status. To the extent that society is a zero-sum game of status-striving, individuals will find that clothing styles are an important weapon in the struggle. The significance of fashion for status-striving is clearly seen in the perennial conflict between males and females. We shall explore that conflict and then examine the ways in which both males and females generally try to "make it" in America by using clothing styles as part of their strategies.

In Her Place

Americans have generally agreed that ours is a land of equal opportunity, or at least that it should be. But when it gets down to specifics, there are diverse notions about the meaning of equal opportunity. Among the blue-collar workers he studied, LeMasters found considerable opposition to the woman's movement. When he asked one worker if he would vote for a female candidate for the local school board, he got an "explosive" response: "I wouldn't vote for her if she was built like Marilyn Monroe. The goddamn women are trying to take over this town—they're just like the niggers; give them an inch and they'll take a mile."[53] The man did not dislike women generally, he simply believed that a woman should stay "in her place." A great many men of all sorts, from Freud to blue-collar workers, have agreed that man's place is found in the building of civilization

FIG. 12. The miniskirt was admired, damned, and satirized, depending upon whether one saw it as liberating or as another style to keep woman in her place. (See above and on following page.)

and woman's place is maintaining the home and family, a reasonable conclusion if one accepts the notions about human nature we discussed in the last chapter.

Whatever one may believe about what is right or proper, women clearly have come out on the lower rungs of the status ladder. Just as clearly, they have not been satisfied with their lower position and have struggled to gain equality with men. In that struggle, according to many writers, fashion has played an important role. For female dress styles historically have kept women in subjection to men.

In the nineteenth century, writers argued that a woman who kept in fashion necessarily remained in subjection to men. For one thing, female fashions were visible evidence of the propriety of the

"I tried to hang on to my mother's skirt, but I couldn't reach it."

(*Reprinted from* The Saturday Evening Post © *1966 The Curtis Publishing Company.*)

existing arrangements. The noted reformer, Frances Russell, pointed out that woman's appearance vitiated her claims to equality with men:

> She asks for education, but she usually arrays herself in a style that suggests either the infantile or the idiotic. She seeks for work and good wages, but stands before the world fettered by her clothing and weighted with unnecessary drapery and trimmings. She would engage in political affairs, but seems unable to apply commonsense principles to the clothing of her own body.[54]

As Russell suggested, women's fashions put considerable constraints on mobility and activity. Women simply could not function like men as long as they were wearing fashionable clothes. Even such a simple activity as walking up a flight of stairs posed a challenge to the well-dressed woman. As one writer pointed out, any woman who had ever played a masculine role in a play noticed there was "a distinct loss of ease and freedom of movement" when she returned to her own dress. And any woman who camped out for a month or two in a "mountain costume" found the weight and inconvenience of her "civilized" dress almost unendurable when she had to put it on again.[55]

Lawrence Langner has argued that constricting the movement of women through fashionable clothing has been common in many societies.[56] If Western men allowed themselves such things as trousers, kilts, or knickerbockers, and put their women into binding, heavy dresses and skirts, they were only mimicking the practices of many other peoples throughout history. For instance, cave paintings in Spain that date from around 10,000 B.C. show the men in short trousers and the women in long skirts. The skirts, says Langner, were probably made of a heavy material that impeded the movement of the women. In a number of other societies, the men have worn tunics or kilts, while the women wore long, cumbersome robes. In Venice, upper-class women wore platform shoes that were sometimes so high the woman would have to be supported by a maid on each side of her when she went out walking. As a final example, in central Africa some women may wear nearly fifty pounds of iron ornaments if they are married to wealthy men. American women endured no restrictions upon movement that were not matched by their sisters in other places and other times. Thus, it appears more than accidental that female fashions keep them in subjection to men.

Even apart from problems of movement, to be in fashion, required so much time and energy that the American woman in the nineteenth century was unlikely to have sufficient resources left over for the task of striving with men for equality. It required considerable expenditure "of physical and nervous strength" to wear the "ordinary, distinctive dress of woman."[57] This, too, was not unique to Americans. Nor did it end at the turn of the century. In 1907, an English writer asked how women could possibly be expected to compete with men. Women, she said, were martyrs to clothes. They didn't lack the intellect to compete with men, they lacked the time! "Abolish the tyranny of clothes and see how great we women will become."[58]

Many women continued to see fashion as a male ploy for maintaining dominance over women as late as the 1970s. During the midi controversy, some feminists dismissed the whole affair as simply another attempt to keep women in subjection. For neither the midi nor the mini permitted women the same freedom of movement that men had.[59] As long as fashion makes differing demands on the sexes, with the harsher demands falling on women, men maintain their dominance.

Some writers see the male dominance as a conscious effort. In fact, some nineteenth-century feminists claimed that women's fashions resulted from a male conspiracy. Men tried to create a slave psychology in women in order to keep them in subjection.[60] We doubt there was actually a conspiracy, but there can be no doubt about the fact that men employed a variety of methods to keep women "in their place" and to accept current fashions. In 1878, a St. Louis editor pointed out that many young women would prefer to dress in a healthier and more rational style, but were prevented from doing so by the knowledge that young men would define them as "strongminded" creatures and avoid them.[61] A number of writers pointed out that whatever men said about current fashions, they always expected women to wear them. Indeed, they defined beauty in terms of those fashions. Some men might complain about the wrecked health of wasp-waisted women, but most men defined female beauty in terms of a tiny waist. One nineteenth-century physician speculated that men were attracted to small-waisted women not because of the waist per se, but because the small waist emphasized the largeness of the bosom and the pelvic region. Such a woman would be an excellent childbearer. Unfortunately, the man who married the corseted woman soon found that "what he thought was food for love was only cotton above and hemp below." The man's love was likely to turn into hatred because of the deception.[62]

Even if they know that a certain amount of deception is taking place, men still expect women to be fashionable. That this expectation remains strong is illustrated by the comment of a 1979 writer: "Throughout history, men seem to have hated and feared women who were invulnerable to fashion, who showed little or no interest, apart from the practical, in how they looked."[63] For at least some men, there has been a conscious realization that fashions both proclaimed and maintained their dominance over women, which is why they may have hated or feared women who resisted or rejected fashions. George Fitzhugh, a nineteenth-century writer, told American women they should realize that their subject condition is their glory. If women curtailed their petticoats, he said, they would soon be condemned to the same kind of hard labor as men. If women showed signs of strength and hardihood, men would turn them into beasts of burden. But as long as women are "nervous, fickle, capricious, delicte, diffident and dependent," men will adore and worship them. The weakness of women is actually their strength, and the true art of each woman "is to cultivate and improve that weakness."[64] According to Fitzhugh, fashions did indeed keep women in subjection, and he urged them to accept their subjection and pursue it to their own glory!

If fashion can be used to keep a group in subjection, it can also be used to proclaim a rebellion against subjection. We shall explore the relationship between fashion and social change in more detail in the last chapter. Here we want to point out that women have used fashion in their struggle for equality. For example, on July 4, 1851, a group of women's formulated a "declaration of independence:"

> When in the course of passing events, it becomes necessary for women of one nation to break off the bonds which Fashion has thrown around them . . . When the long trains of their dresses, invariably sweeping the pavements as they move along, evince a design on the part of the Tyranness Fashion to reduce our women under its absolute despotism, it is their right—it is their duty to throw off the long and cumbersome skirts, and to provide shorter ones for their future wear.[65]

The restrictive clothing styles of hundreds of years had to be altered if women were to compete effectively with men. One writer saw the First World War as a watershed in the process. For the first time, women were employed in traditionally male jobs as part of the war effort. Women found the experience of earning their own way exhilarating and determined to maintain what they had gained. When the soldiers returned home, the women decided to compete with men and so minimized the difference in appearance between the sexes. "So the clothes—which had become masculinized at first for comfort—now became even more masculinized."[66] The struggle of women to gain status vis-à-vis men involved the manipulation of fashion for both practical and symbolic reasons. Practically, it was essential for new styles to emerge before women could function effectively in active roles. Symbolically, the new styles would be a continual and unavoidable reminder to the world that a new age had dawned for women.

"Making It" through Fashion

If you were playing a game of word association and you were given the words "used-car salesman," you might respond in terms of the stereotype of such a person—con man, fast talker, or loud clothing, for example. Actually, good used-car salespeople are careful to present themselves in a way that avoids the stereotype. They do not, for example, wear expensive or ostentatious clothing. As one put it, "If you're wearing a $150 sports coat and a $20 tie, you don't sell a car to a ditchdigger."[67] The salesman, by carefully attending to his appearance, was engaging in what Erving Goffman has called "impression management."

We all use impression management, which is simply an effort to control the behavior of others by providing them with the cues that will lead them to define the situation as we wish. As Goffman put it, a man can influence the way others define the situation "by expressing himself in such a way as to give them the kind of impression that will lead them to act voluntarily in accordance with his own plan."[68] For instance, the used-car salesman attempted to convey an impression of himself as a normal, straightforward person who could be trusted in a business transaction. Among other things, he used clothing as a cue to others that they should define him as average and trustworthy, thereby increasing the likelihood that they would purchase a car from him.

In the process of managing the impressions that we give to people, says Goffman, we must attend to setting, appearance, and manner. The setting is the physical environment in which the performance takes place. It includes such things as furnishings and decor. Appearance includes all those things that provide cues to others about our social status. It includes clothing and grooming. Manner refers to stimuli that tells others the interaction role we will play in the situation, that is, whether we intend to be aggressive, mild, sympathetic, or distant, and so forth.

The manipulation of one's dress, then, is an integral part of impression management. In turn, impression management is basic to the American drive to be, or at least to appear to be, successful. Many observers have discussed the importance of success to Americans. "If unfettered consumption is the glowing dream of American culture," wrote one critic, "failure is its darkest nightmare."[69] If one does not succeed, one at least struggles to avoid the appearance of failure, which is one way in which fashionable clothing can be used to manage impressions. A second use of clothing involves the presentation of oneself as a potential success. Finally, people use fashion to display the success they have gained.

EMULATION: AVOIDING THE STIGMA OF FAILURE The emulation of those higher in the social hierarchy by those in lower positions is an effort to gain status or at least to avoid what has been called status degradation. A person experiences status degradation when the opinions of others change so that person comes to be looked upon as a "lower" social type.[70]

The attempt to gain status through fashion is not confined to the lowest rungs of the social ladder. People from both the middle and the lower classes engage in the struggle. In fact, the use of fashion to gain status may occur wherever there are status differences between different groups. An 1870 writer noted that "even the poor blacks are said to be affected by this malady," for the men spend all of their money on fine clothes "to play the gentleman, and the women suffer tortures—like their white prototypes—by squeezing their huge feet . . . into the smallest shoes they can wear."[71] In his study of Sears, Roebuck catalogs from 1905 to 1940, Cohn found that middle-class styles approximated both in appearance and, often, in materials those adopted by the wealthy.[72] In 1895, a "battle of the skirts" occurred in Buffalo, New York. Bicycle girls on the prosperous West Side adopted short skirts, which were then immediately accepted by girls on the East Side. "Whereupon the West Side went back to long skirts. So the East Side went back to long skirts also."[73]

The battle to achieve new status through fashion is based upon a relationship we noted earlier—the quality of the individual is perceived to be reflected in his or her dress. As Ida Tarbell wrote in despair, it is fantastic to think that great numbers of women rely on dress for social advancement; nevertheless, it is true. "They are, or are not, as they are gowned!"[74] If a few writers like Tarbell found the whole affair to be absurd, those engaged in it often found it frustrating. As a nineteenth-century writer said, "it spoils the pleasure of wearing a fine, new article of apparel to see our lowly neighbor wearing a similar one."[75] Some thirty years later, another writer noted that working women would spend their last penny on fashionable clothes, hastening with all possible speed "to join the throng, and "quite unmindful of the disapproving frowns of her wealthy sisters, who will soon have to adopt Puritan simplicity in order to be distinguished from plebeians."[76]

In spite of the absurdity or frustration which some people have found in the matter, fashion continues to be a tool of impression management for those who strive to enhance their status. A 1968 report on poor young men on the Lower East Side of New York City related the way in which expensive, fashionable clothing is a part of their struggle for status. One young man said that the $47 knit he was wearing represented his entire week's earnings as a porter at a housing project. Another expressed the meaning of such clothing succinctly: "They say to the world: 'I've got the bread, man; so treat me with a little respect.' "[77]

Sometimes people use fashion to avoid status degradation rather than to enhance their status. In her study of life during the Great Depression, Caroline Bird talks about the "middle-class horror stories" of the humiliation of failure.[78] In that case, failure meant coming down in the world. Thus, one woman recalled the first time her husband put on overalls to go to work, while others told about the trauma of pawning an engagement ring or going to the relief office. Many of them desperately sought to hold on to some possessions that would continue to identify them as middle class. Even though they had come down, they tried to give the impression of maintaining their status. Clothing, as well as such things as a home or jewelry or servants, was used in the struggle: "In some circles, the fur coat was the last thing to go. Some men insisted on wearing two freshly laundered white shirts a day even when there was not enough to eat."[79] If we wince at such behavior, we must keep in mind the great value that Americans have always placed on success, and the concomitant "nightmare" of failure. On balance, most of us might opt for slight hunger and respect over a full stomach and status degradation.

PRESENTING A PERSON WHO WILL MAKE IT "Young gentlemen," said a judge at a graduation exercise of law students, "nothing insures success in life, professionally and socially, more than dress and address."[80] A good many writers have agreed that the manipulation of one's dress may be an important factor in achieving success. If one creates the impression of being a succeeder, a person who has the ability and drive to make it, one is more likely to attain success. For people will respond by giving opportunities to the individual who convinces them that he or she will use any opportunity fully.

Advice on how to dress in order to present oneself as a potential success has been given for over two centuries in America. In 1912, a magazine reprinted a tract that had been published in 1772 in Philadelphia. The tract was entitled, "Clothes Make Men." It urged the reader to carefully consider the importance of outward appearance, for people are responsive to that appearance:

> How can the world help it, that a great soul hides itself in a mean garment? This world is a stage, and on a stage we only take those for princes who appear in a princely dress. Not every one has patience enough to wait for the last scene, and the unraveling of the play. Let us change the clothes, and we shall find the world very equitable.[81]

One hundred and sixty years later, the same kind of advice was offered to working women: "If you are in a business job, aim to look like one of those clever, high-salaried business women who earn the glamorous salaries the magazines tell about. There are many of them, and one way they earn those salaries is by dressing appropriately all the time."[82]

If we want to succeed, we must present ourselves through our appearance and manner as the kind of person who can succeed. In the late 1930s, the Sears, Roebuck catalog advised readers to prepare for leadership and go up the ladder to success with the proper clothes (which, said the catalog, are the kind of clothes worn by college men).[83] If, as it turns out, we do not succeed, we probably ignored all the advice. Thus, "if at first you don't succeed, change the way you dress" was the title of a 1927 article in the *Ladies' Home Journal*. And then there are the cases of people who both succeed and fail, and who can change some of their failure into even more success through the appropriate dress. For instance, one author tells of a female physician who was quite competent but who was not impressive intellectually because "she was too frumpy in dress."[84] The physician was aware of the problem, and asked the writer to prescribe something for her. In less than two months after the prescription was followed, the physician reported a significant change in the attitudes of people toward her. People had more respect for her and for her opinions. People who had never requested her services before now called upon her for assistance. It was, she said, her "clothes triumph."

In the 1960s, many Americans thought fashion had entered into a new era of "anything goes," which meant what one wore was not particularly pertinent to whether one succeeded. But in the 1970s, there was a resurgence of interest in dressing for success. A variety of writers told Americans they must carefully manage the impressions they give off to others if they wanted to succeed. To package yourself for success, wrote a fashion consultant, means to make sure your appearance tells others that "you are knowledgeable, likable, trustworthy and dependable."[85] The emphasis on new opportunities for women in the 1970s gave rise to a number of articles aimed directly at female job-seekers or workers. One magazine ran a piece on "power dressing." Another reported on how women were being advised to "dress the trip to the top." And a third discussed how "clothes mean business," noting that a woman has to create the right impression by dressing properly in order to maximize the chances for success.[86] Clearly, in the competition for success, the individual who shrugs off fashionable clothes as unimportant will soon discover that he or she is falling behind. As the judge said, proper dress is a form of insurance against the uncertainties of the pursuit of success.

THE DISPLAY OF SUCCESS If fashionable clothes can be used to indicate a potential for success, they can also be used to display the success that has been achieved. For many people, the display of success is natural and proper. The wealthy person is expected to dress like someone with wealth. For social critics, like Thorstein Veblen, the display of success through clothing was a form of the conspicuous consumption they despised. But whether expected, admired, or despised, the successful have always tended to use fashionable clothes to display their achievements. Unlike virtue, success is not its own reward. Particularly if we are talking about monetary success, the ultimate delights are not savored until others acknowledge and admire the success. One of the ways people cue others about their success is the wearing of appropriate clothes.

An individual may communicate success through his or her own mode of dress. In 1978, high-fashion sportswear could be used. Active sportswear was being used for streetwear because, said one writer, of its snob appeal. Other kinds of high-status clothes, such as expensive furs, show that the wearer has taste and affluence. But the sportswear went a step further: "it implies that the wearer is a person of means, taste and energy. And energy has turned into one of the most desirable attributes anyone can have."[87] In other words, people were using the fashion to say to others: "I have made it. Financially, socially, and healthwise, I am a success."

Success can also be indicated through the dress of one's family. If a man is a financial success, said a reporter in 1963, his wife will try to raise the family's status by her dress bills.[88] Parents may display their success through the way they dress their children. A 1960 report told of expensive fashions for two-, three-, and four-year-olds in various New York City shops. Little girls in Central Park could be seen wearing imported tweeds and "nannies." Four-year-olds at parties could be seen in dresses custom-made by well-known designers. Parents might pay as much as $200 for special-occasion dresses. One exclusive shop offered christening dresses for $1,100.[89] In 1960, incidentally, the median family income was $5,620. A $1,100 christening dress represented nearly 20 percent of the annual income of half the families in the nation. Those who are spectacularly successful may display their wealth through extraordinarily expensive attire. Those who are moderately successful may dress themselves and their families in somewhat less expensive, though still costly, clothes. In either case, presumably, the taste of success is made a little sweeter by letting others know that it has been achieved.

CONCLUSIONS

Fashion behavior reflects the nature of society. Moreover, fashion behavior becomes more understandable when we recognize it as social behavior. People respond to fashion in the context of social norms. An individual may not like some new style, but an individual is relatively powerless vis-à-vis society. Furthermore, if we realize that society is a system of competitive behavior, a struggle for status, and that fashion is an important resource in the competition, we can understand why people generally take fashion quite seriously.

Thus, our examination of fashion and the nature of society underscores the conclusions we drew at the end of the last chapter regarding the unrealistic nature of individuality in fashion. The norms that guide fashion behavior allow for some individual variation, but they do not allow for the total rejection advocated by some writers of the past. "If you are not in fashion," wrote Lord Chesterfield to his son in the eighteenth century, "you are nobody." Indeed. For you only become somebody by the consent and agreement of others. But they will not view you favorably if you insult their goddess.

Notes

1. Philip G. Zimbardo, "Pathology of Imprisonment," *Society* 9 (April, 1972): 4–8.
2. *Ibid.*, p. 4.
3. "Styles or Uniforms?" *New York Times,* August 31, 1922.
4. "Dress Reform at the World's Fair," *The Review of Reviews* 7 (April, 1893): 314.
5. W. Godfrey Cobliner, "Feminine Fashion as an Aspect of Group Psychology," *The Journal of Social Psychology* 31 (May, 1950): 285.
6. J. J. Jarvis, "The Generations of Fashions," *Harper's New Monthly Magazine* 9 (November, 1854): 750.
7. Katharine Fullerton Gerould, "Dress and the Woman," *Atlantic* 108 (November, 1911): 623.
8. See L. Moody Simms, Jr., ed. "A Horror of Hoops," *Southwestern Historical Quarterly* 72 (July, 1968): 89.
9. "Our Little Children," *Godey's Lady's Book* 59 (September, 1859): 272.
10. Lucy H. Hooper, "Fig Leaves and French Dresses," *Galaxy* 18 (October, 1874): 508.

11. *New York Times,* August 9, 1966.
12. Richard Corson, *Fashions in Hair* (New York: Hastings House, 1965), p. 403.
13. "Mary's Little Skirt," *New York Times,* June 27, 1921.
14. *New York Times,* June 12, 1920.
15. Enid Nemy, "Dilemma for Restauranteurs," *New York Times,* August 3, 1966.
16. *New York Times,* July 16, 1913; August 20, 1913; July 25, 1938; and July 26, 1953.
17. Nicholas S. Timasheff, *Sociological Theory,* revised edition (New York: Random House, 1957), p. 106.
18. William Graham Sumner, *Folkways* (Boston: Gin, 1940; originally published, 1906), pp. 194–95.
19. "Fashion," *Boston Literary Magazine* 1 (November, 1832): 335–36.
20. Nina Wilcox Putnam, "Fashion and Feminism," *The Forum* 52 (October, 1914):581; "Calling a Halt to Cursing," *The Literary Digest* 87 (November 21, 1925): 32.
21. Paul Poiret, "Who Sets Our Styles?" *The Forum* 80 (August, 1928): 187.
22. "Fashion," *Pennsylvania Freeman* 2 (July 8, 1837): 68.
23. Mrs. Oliphant, *Dress* (Philadelphia: Porter & Coates, 1876), p. 9.
24. "Fashion in America," *New York Times,* March 2, 1879.
25. Teresa H. Dean, *How to Be Beautiful* (Chicago: People's Publishing Co., 1889), p. 70.
26. Richard F. Bach, "Fashion—or What You Will," *American Magazine of Art* 22 (May, 1931): 377.
27. *Ibid.,* p. 379.
28. Marian Gertrude Haines, "Dame Fashion's Thumb," *The Arena* 26 (December, 1901): 626.
29. "The Ideas of a Plain Country Woman," *Ladies' Home Journal* 31 (August, 1914): 26.
30. *New York Times,* December 7, 1913.
31. "Fashion's Effect on Business," *The Literary Digest* 96 (February 25, 1928): 18.
32. Mary Alden Hopkins, "Woman's Rebellion against Fashions," *The New Republic* 31 (August 16, 1922): 332.
33. Franklin S. Clark, "Who Sets Fashions—and How?" *The Review of Reviews* 31 (January, 1930): 53.
34. Marian Hertha Clarke, "The Sheep Decide," *The North American Review* 228 (August, 1929): 237.
35. *New York Times,* August 25, 1923.
36. *New York Times,* December 18, 1929 and October 10, 1931.
37. "Fashion," *Time* 50 (September 15, 1947): 87.

38. *New York Times*, July 25, 1947.
39. *New York Times*, August 18, 1947 and August 24, 1947.
40. "Fashion," *Time* 50 (September 15, 1947): 87; *New York Times*, August 28, 1947.
41. "The Battle of the Hemline," *Newsweek* 75 (March 16, 1970): 70–71.
42. "Fashion '71: Anything Goes," *Newsweek* 76 (March 29, 1971): 68.
43. Isadore Barmash, "Women's Lib Affects Fashion Decisons," *New York Times*, May 7, 1972.
44. "The New Fashions: 'Man as Man and Woman as Woman,'" *U.S. News & World Report*, September 16, 1974, p. 58.
45. Nancy Koplin Jack and Betty Schiffer, "The Limits of Fashion Control," *American Sociological Review* 13 (December, 1948): 730–38.
46. *Ibid.*, p. 738.
47. "The Jelly Bean Game," *Human Behavior*, March/April, 1972, p. 32.
48. Julius A. Roth, "Ritual and Magic in the Control of Contagion," *American Sociological Review* 22 (June, 1957): 310–14.
49. Max Lerner, *America as a Civilization* (New York: Simon & Schuster, 1957), p. 613.
50. Emily Thronwell, *The Lady's Guide to Perfect Gentility* (Philadelphia: Lippincott, 1876), pp. 122–23.
51. *Ibid*, p. 124.
52. Amy Vanderbilt, *Amy Vanderbilt's Everyday Etiquette* (Garden City, N.Y.: Hanover House, 1952), pp. 186–87.
53. E. E. LeMasters, *Blue-Collar Aristocrats* (Madison, Wisc.: University of Wisconsin Press, 1975), p. 182.
54. Frances E. Russell, "Woman's Dress," *The Arena* 3 (February, 1891): 352.
55. Octavia W. Bates, "The Dress of College Women from a College Woman's Outlook," *The Arena* 6 (October, 1892): 625.
56. Lawrence Langner, *The Importance of Wearing Clothes* (New York: Hastings House, 1959), pp. 52–57.
57. Octavia W. Bates, *op. cit.*, p. 625.
58. Annie E. Lane, "The Tyranny of Clothes," *Fortnightly* 87 (January, 1907): 94.
59. See "The Battle of the Hemline," *Newsweek* 75 (March 16, 1970): 70; "Sex and Clothing," *Medical Aspects of Human Sexuality* (September, 1970): 146.
60. Robert E. Riegel, "Women's Clothes and Women's Rights," *The American Quarterly* 15 (Fall, 1963): 391.
61. *St. Louis Evening Post*, February 21, 1878.
62. John S. Haller and Robin M. Haller, *The Physician and Sexuality in Victorian America* (Urbana: University of Illinois Press, 1974), pp. 159–60.

63. Judith Thurman, "How to Get Dressed and Still Be Yourself," *Ms.,* April, 1979, p. 76.
64. George Fitzhugh, *Sociology for the South, or the Failure of Free Society* (Richmond: A. Morris, 1854), p. 214.
65. *New York Tribune,* July 18, 1851.
66. Lee E. Graham, "From the Flapper to the Pin-Up," *The New York Times Magazine,* January 12, 1947, p. 21.
67. B. Davidson, "King of the Iron Merchants," *New York Times,* March 2, 1975.
68. Erving Goffman, *The Presentation of Self in Everyday Life* (Garden City, N.Y.: Anchor Books, 1959), p. 4. See pp. 1–30 for a discussion of the ideas in these two paragraphs.
69. R. P. Cuzzort, *Humanity and Modern Sociological Thought* (New York: Holt, Rinehart and Winston, 1969), p. 263.
70. Robert H. Lauer and Warren H. Handel, *Social Psychology: The Theory and Application of Symbolic Interactionism* (Boston: Houghton Mifflin, 1977), pp. 215–16.
71. "American Dress," *Putnam's Magazine* 5 (April, 1870): 387–88.
72. David L. Cohn, *The Good Old Days* (New York: Simon & Schuster, 1940), p. 308.
73. "Battle of the Skirts," *Outlook* 132 (October 18, 1922): 276.
74. Ida M. Tarbell, "A Woman and Her Raiment," *The American Magazine* 74 (August, 1912): 472.
75. "Fashion," *The Ladies' Repository* 29 (August, 1869): 111.
76. Marian Gertrude Haines, *op. cit.,* p. 624.
77. *New York Times,* October 30, 1968.
78. Caroline Bird, *The Invisible Scar* (New York: David McKay Company, Inc., 1966), pp. 274–75.
79. *Ibid.,* p. 275.
80. Zitella Cocke, "Dress and Address," *New England Magazine* 39 (December, 1908): 483.
81. T. C. Callicot, "Philosophy of Clothes," *The Forum* 97 (March, 1912): 525.
82. Marjorie Kinney, "Individuality, Fashions, and the Clothes We Buy," *Journal of Home Economics* 24 (July, 1932): 609–10.
83. Cohn, *op. cit.,* p. 469.
84. Mary Brooks Picken, *The Secrets of Distinctive Dress* (Scranton, Pa.: International Textbook Press, 1918), pp. 98–99.
85. William Thourlby, "Believe It: Clothes Do Make the Man," *The Kansas City Times,* January 8, 1979.
86. Amy Gross and Nancy Axelrad Comer, "Power Dressing," *Mademoiselle* 83 (September, 1977): 188–89+; "Dress the Trip to the Top," *Newsweek*

90 (September 26, 1977): 76–7; "Clothes That Mean Business," *Woman's Day*, September 1, 1978, pp. 88–91.
87. Judy J. Newmark, "One Step beyond Casual," *St. Louis Post-Dispatch*, August 7, 1978.
88. Bernard Roshco, *The Rag Race* (New York: Funk & Wagnalls 1963), p. 11.
89. *New York Times*, January 31, 1960. See also Florence E. Young, *Clothing the Child* (New York: McGraw-Hill, 1938), p. 69.

chapter 5

Fashion and National Identity

Uncle Sam, dressed in red, white, and blue, has symbolized America since the Civil War when the cartoons of Thomas Nast made him a widely recognized figure. In his distinctive attire, Uncle Sam represents all that for which the nation stands. For many writers, it is not only Uncle Sam and his unique style that symbolize the nation, but also the styles generally worn that express the essence of America. We noted in Chapter 1 that clothing is believed to communicate information about the tastes, principles, character, and mood of a nation. In other words, just as an individual's mode of dress may reveal something about the basic character of that individual, a nation's fashions may indicate important things about the essence of the nation. An individual's personality finds expression in his or her mode of dressing; a nation's identity finds expression in the fashions that are accepted.

The linkage between fashion and national identity has some interesting implications, because fashion gets tied up with such things as patriotism, national values, and national goals. In this chapter we will first discuss the meaning of national identity for Americans, then we will examine the ways in which fashion has intersected with the national identity. Among other things, the linkage has been the basis for a long war of independence. If the war has been bloodless, it has not been painless nor lacking in vigor.

THE MEANING OF AMERICA'S NATIONAL IDENTITY

Who are we? What kind of people are we? What distinguishes us from others? What binds us together and makes us think of ourselves as truly "one" nation? To answer such questions is to construct a national identity. For Americans, that sense of identity developed slowly and painfully. The American Republic, wrote an astute foreign scholar around the turn of the last century, "was created out of several pieces with infinite pains, it was wrested 'by grinding necessities from a reluctant people,' and for a long time afterwards each section pulled in a different direction."[1] In other words, the nation was not forged out of a sense of identity. Rather, the identity was slowly constructed by a people who found themselves joined together in nationhood.

The Struggle for Identity

The problems of constructing a national identity were rooted in the colonial and revolutionary beginnings of the country. Colonial America had none of the qualities essential to nation building. It lacked territorial and cultural unity as well as unity of purpose. There was little sense of anything being distinctively American. An Englishman, traveling through North America shortly before the War for Independence, concluded that any permanent coalition of the colonies seemed nearly impossible "for fire and water are not more heterogeneous than the different colonies."[2]

Although the revolution established colonial independence from England, this independence did not emanate from a common identity that was distinct from that of the mother country. Hans Kohn has argued that the unity of 1776 was mainly a product of enthusiasm for independence, loyalty to George Washington, and hatred for

George III, rather than love of country. The thirteen sovereign states that emerged from the war, notes Kohn, remained separated by mutual antipathies, jealousies, and local loyalties.[3]

The war thus did not create a sense of national identity, nor did the political system foster its development. The federal system, in fact, compounded the problem for it was a constant reminder of the differences within the nation. These differences persisted into the nineteenth century, as Rufus Choate well expressed them: "The affections which we give to country we give to a divided object.... We serve two masters. Our hearts own two loves. We live in two countries at once."[4]

America, then, did not have the usual elements that make up a national identity—a long attachment to a particular territory, common descent, and a shared history, customs, and language. And until the immigration restrictions of the 1920s, the continual influx of foreigners tended to perpetuate the differences of Americans. Nevertheless, the sense of identity did develop. But it was constructed slowly and on a different foundation than that of many nations, for its identity emerged from the context of shared beliefs.

Identity as Shared Beliefs

One way to answer the question of who Americans are, is to say that they are a people that hold certain beliefs in common. Indeed, to be labelled "un-American" means that one has strayed from the shared faith. Americans believe theirs is a nation of liberty, of virtue, of progress, and is therefore a fitting example for all the world to follow. Henry Ward Beecher echoed the feelings of Americans when he proclaimed that the foundation of the nation was "liberty, liberty, nothing less than liberty."[5] In the nineteenth century, liberty was variously described as "our richest inheritance," the "cornerstone of this Republic," the "soul of the nation," and the "bond of the Union."[6] Americans have seen liberty as the vital principle that gives substance and meaning to the nation. The essence of America is not a particular piece of land, but a principle, the principle of liberty. Americans are a free and democratic people. They have a right to exist without dependence on others and with a minimum of restrictions upon their actions.

In addition, they believe that America is a virtuous nation. This notion is rooted both in their religious heritage and in their republican ideals. Throughout their history Americans have argued that virtue is necessary to the maintenance of the Republic (a point not overlooked by the moralists who have expressed outrage over certain female fashions). Virtue is the safeguard of the nation. It will prevent America from going the way of corrupt Europe or heathenistic Africa and Asia.

The notion of virtue is as old as the first settlers who came to the land to establish a new moral order. By the time Tocqueville visited the nation in the early part of the nineteenth century, he found what he called a very distinct pride on the part of Americans. For fifty years, he wrote, Americans had been continually told that

> they are the only religious, enlightened, and free people. They see that democratic institutions flourish among them, whereas they come to grief in the rest of the world; consequently they have an immensely high opinion of themselves and are not far from believing that they form a species apart from the rest of the human race.[7]

Liberty and virtue undergirded a third quality—progress. Americans have traditionally seen the future in terms of an ever closer approximation to the ideal society. As Curti has noted, the developing sense of loyalty to the nation depended strongly on a common faith in the future: "The fundamental and widely held dogma that America was destined to become a nation of great wealth, power, and culture, the home and beacon light of liberty, the Elysium of the common man, prevailed over all competing conceptions of the future."[8] So deeply rooted is the belief in progress that not even such disillusioning events as the Vietnam War and economic crises were able to quell it. In the early 1970s, public opinion polls showed the majority of Americans still believed the nation's future would be better than the past. Like truth, progress may be crushed to earth, but in America it always seems to rise again.

The fourth belief flows quite easily from the other three. For a free, virtuous people who are constructing an ideal society must necessarily be an example for all the world to follow. The belief that America is an exemplary nation was expressed well by Catherine Beecher in her 1841 work on domestic economy. We have, she wrote, "the grand, the responsible privilege" of showing the rest of the world what happens when Christian principles pervade all social institutions. True, she said, our advances so far have been imperfect. Nevertheless,

> already the light is streaming into the dark prison-house of despotic lands, while startled kings and sages, philosophers and statesmen, are watching us with that interest which a career so illustrious, and so involving their own destiny, is calculated to excite. They are studying our institutions, scrutinizing our experience, and watching for our mistakes, that they may learn whether a "social revolution, so irresistible, be advantageous or prejudicial to mankind."[9]

For many Americans, their responsibility has been not merely to be a passive example, but to engage in the mission of sharing American ideals with others. America is the hope of the world. It is its destiny and responsibility to allow the bright light of that hope to illuminate the nations of the world.

These beliefs have formed the basis of American national identity. However, several additional points should be noted. First, these beliefs have persisted over the past two centuries. To be sure, they have been interpreted differently at times by various groups within the body politic. These differences have created conflict and even resulted in civil war, yet, in every instance, commitment to the fundamental principles was affirmed.

Second, American national identity consistently has been fixed in relationship to the rest of the world. Partly because the national past was so tenuous and the sense of identity so fragile, Americans have seemed compelled to contrast themselves favorably to other nations. America is freer, more virtuous, and guided by a higher sense of purpose than the other nations of the world. America is unique.

Finally, despite its essential optimism, American national identity has contained a dark side. Americans have consistently warned each other that their cherished freedom, virtue, and progress cannot be taken for granted. Freedom is precarious. It is continually threatened and requires constant vigilance if it is to be maintained. Virtue is subject to corruption and must also be continually guarded. And of course if liberty and virtue are wrung out of the national life, America would no longer be able to advance nor provide an example for the rest of the world.

Consequently, whether in the political realm or in the realm of fashion, threats to freedom, virtue, or progress, must not be taken lightly. This is why those who wrote about the slavery to fashion, or about the corruption inherent in some styles, or about the fact that a particular style is a throwback to an earlier age or a different people, often used words of intensity to express their feelings. It is not simply that some individuals are being deprived or diverted or hindered in their quest for the American ideal. It is, rather, that the entire nation is in danger of forsaking its sacred calling and stumbling into the graveyard of fallen civilizations. Vigilance must indeed be eternal.

DISTINCTIVE FASHIONS FOR A UNIQUE PEOPLE

Americans, of course, are not the only people to consider themselves unique and even superior to others. Ethnocentrism has characterized human societies throughout history. The ancient Egyptians distinguished between themselves, "men," and others, who were presumably something a little less than human. The ancient Persians, according to the Greek historian Herodotus, held people in progressively lower esteem the farther those people were from Persia. The Persians also required their fledgling physicians to practice medicine first on non-Persians. If the foreigners did not die, the physicians could then treat the Persians. People everywhere tend to think of themselves and of their ways as somehow better or superior than other people and their ways.

A part of the uniqueness of people is a distinctive style of dress. A distinctive style both expresses uniqueness and helps maintain ethnocentric attitudes. The style need not be totally different from that of any other people, but it should have some elements that are peculiar to a particular people. Those who have called for the Americanization of fashion have found the lack of distinctiveness galling. As a unique people, they argue, Americans should have something distinctive about their fashions. But throughout most of our history, this has not been the case. And, as George Stewart has pointed out, the strongest testimony about this lack of distinction is the fact that travelers from other countries have seldom said anything about the American mode of dress. They have discussed American food, drink, religious life, and sometimes even the housing. But little is said about clothing except a rare comment that someone was nicely or poorly dressed or fashionably attired.

> The conclusion is obvious. Travelers, notoriously, write about what is different from their own country. In fact, they have difficulty even in seeing that many things are the same. So, when we find that travelers consistently fail to mention anything at all about American dress, we have very strong evidence that American dress, at any given period, did not differ much from European dress of the same period.[10]

Of course, at the time the American nation was founded, there was a trend toward uniformity of dress among European peoples. By the twentieth century, the varied national costumes had largely disappeared. This fact, however, did not dissuade a number of Americans from calling for distinction in American dress.

The Need for American Fashions

What we need, wrote the editor of the *New York Times* in 1913, are fashions that "rightly express the American genius and spirit."[11] For many writers that necessarily meant Americans would have to design their own styles. Foreigners did not understand them. It is time, wrote the editor of the *Ladies' Home Journal* in 1912, that American women recognize the fact that they can design their own clothes better than the French can "since no Latin race can ever understand an Anglo-Saxon people in clothes or in any other need."[12] Other writers emphasized the fact that the French did not know how to design clothes in terms of the simplicity and practicality that characterized the American way of life.

Foreigners seemed unable to understand Americans. Early in the nineteenth century, a writer contrasted Americans with Europeans in terms not altogether flattering to the former. But the contrast underscored the need for Americans to do their own designing. The love of reason and good taste, as well as patriotism, demanded that people in this "rough-and-tumble country" create their own styles:

> Can we do nothing for ourselves? Why should Paris and London suggest our modes? What have we—a comparative wild people, half of us yet in the woods—to do with London and Paris? We are a different, a peculiar people—have necessities to which people are not subject in those great cities, and our customs should be suited to our conditions. Let us have . . . a maker of modes for ourselves. Let him ask who we are—what are our occupations, our difficulties, our resources, and then determine what are the sorts of dress which we should wear.[13]

Later writers did not make the contrast in terms of the greater wildness of Americans, but they still saw sufficient differences to justify the need for American designers. As the editor of the *Ladies' Home Journal* put the case in 1912, the designs of the French are not suited to modern conditions or to American women. The French design their clothes for the French women. They do not know our women, nor their homes, nor the kinds of lives they lead. Indeed, the French designers are not even sympathetic to American women, whom they treat either with indifference or contempt. But they still attempt to dress our women in order to get their dollars. They greedily pursue their task in blissful ignorance of the differences between their own women and the women of America.[14]

Is it any wonder, the writers demanded, that Americans have continually worn styles that are out of joint with the American way of life? What more could we have expected when we allow the Latins to tell us what to wear? Fashion designers must know the people for whom they design; they must know the way of life of those people. Only Americans fully understand these things. Therefore, only Americans can properly design clothes for other Americans. Foreign fashions may be perfectly appropriate for foreign people, but they have no place in American life.

This line of reasoning was used not only to press for the Americanization of fashion, but also to attack specific new styles. When Bloomers first appeared in the middle of the nineteenth-century, they were attacked by some on the grounds that they were Turkish and were *ipso facto* inappropriate for American women. When the "harem skirt" came out in 1911, the *New York Times* reported that it was an adaptation of Turkish trousers to the hobble skirt. The writer urged women not to submit to the tyranny of the new style. Not only was it ugly, but its origin "should be enough to set women against it. . . . It suggests the customs of a country where women go about with veiled faces and are valued according to their weight."[15] To some critics, the very fact that a fashion was similar to that of women in a foreign country was sufficient reason to reject its adoption by American women. A unique people simply must have distinctive styles.

Dressing the Strong and Virtuous

The task that will confront our designers, said those who urged Americans to nationalize fashion, will be to create clothing that is suitable for a strong, virtuous, and free people. French fashions were not designed merely for a different people; they were created for that segment of the French population that was of dubious reputation, according to some writers. Or they were designed for a people who, as a whole, fell far short of the moral ideals of Americans, according to others. In either case, the French designers were not producing styles that were suitable for a virtuous people.

Where do those injurious fashions that American women wear come from? asked a nineteenth-century reformer. Her angry answer was:

> from licentious Paris and infidel France! Where woman stoops from her high position of virtue and morality, to mingle with the vicious and impure, to pander to the low passions and base desires of compeers in the arts of hell!! Let American and Christian women *blush,* at the character of their Parisian models of fashion![16]

Another nineteenth-century critic of French fashions insisted that the "arbiters" of those fashions had always been "the women of the *demi-monde.* They had nothing to do but spend money, and they welcomed every invention of the mantua-maker with an enthusiasm exactly proportioned to its novelty—and its cost."[17] It makes no sense, therefore, for the "daughters of Puritan ancestors" to imitate the example of "the fashionable courtesan class in the wicked city of Paris."[18] The clothes designed by the French were, in fact, "never intended for decent women in any other city."[19]

Both nineteenth- and early twentieth-century writers played upon this theme of the corruption of the French and the virtue of the Americans. They expressed everything from anger to disgust at the thought that America's virtuous women would accept fashions that were not only worn by, but actually designed for, immoral French women. They called upon all women with Puritan blood coursing through their veins to reject the tainted styles.

In addition to the theme of virtue, a number of twentieth-century writers emphasized the theme of strength and vitality. American women are not only more virtuous than the French, they are also more vigorous. They are more active, free-spirited, and healthier than the French. A 1905 writer insisted that the life style of the American woman necessarily gave her a different figure from that of the French woman. From childhood, the French woman is pressed into a corset that produces long waists and narrow hips. The American girl, on the other hand, "shares her brother's games, is adept at outdoor sports, and develops an expanse of chest that quite unfits her for the confines of the corset affected by the Parisienne."[20] A number of writers agreed that active involvement in sports and other kinds of activity made the American woman more wholesome, healthier, and of a different build than women of other nations. On occasion, said one, an American woman will still indulge in useless decorations or accept some foolish combination of materials that are purely ornamental. But in general "she is proud of her broad shoulders, her fine, strong, chest, and her practical waistline, and her clothes attest these advantages. She cares more about color, comfort, and appropriateness than about French knots and applique and tucks and ruffles."[21]

Even some of the French themselves agreed that the American woman was a peculiarly active creature. A dressmaker who visited this country in 1924 said she came in order to get to know the American women better so she could properly design clothes for them. "There is more life in the American woman," she claimed, "than in any other woman in the world. She is so amusing and gay."[21] One would expect, of course, that someone seeking business would be complimentary to prospective customers. Still, it is significant that the dressmaker pointed out the active and vibrant nature of American women. She faulted them for their tendency to all dress alike and for their passion to appear thin. When you use clothes to "force flesh away," she said, you lose a certain freshness. Nevertheless, the dressmaker conceded, American women are in some ways the best-dressed women in the world and are certainly unique in their active style of life.

Is this the same woman who has been so often condemned for being submissive, slavish, and irrational, if not downright stupid? The contradiction is only apparent. In the first place, any group of people will exhibit contrary qualities at differing times. They may appear strong in some instances and weak in others. They may seem to be acting rationally at one time and quite irrationally at another. Indeed, sometimes the same writer stresses the contrary qualities by saying something like "American women are generally very sensible but they are behaving stupidly in accepting the new styles in shoes." In the second place, one or the other of the qualities may be emphasized depending on the writer's purpose. Those who wish to keep women "in their place" may talk about women's natural submissiveness as illustrated by their response to new styles. Some of the dress reformers tried to get women to act more independently and rationally by chiding them for their dependence and their unreasonable fashion behavior. Like an inept parent who tells a child that he or she is stupid in the hope that the child will be spurred to act intelligently, they tried to use a negative label to motivate women to positive behavior. And those who wanted to Americanize fashion emphasized the strength and virtue of American women and the corruption of French designs and French women. Creating in-group solidarity by means of an external and corrupt enemy is a sound social psychological principle.

In other words, it is not that they disbelieved the things they were saying about women. It is, rather, that they selected from among the contrary qualities that all of us exhibit in order to buttress their case. In point of fact, they believed quite strongly that Americans are a unique people with strength and virtue that are either beyond that of other people, or a stark contrast with the corruption of other people. Furthermore, this means that French fashions are not merely unsuitable. Worse, Americans may be corrupted by continually adopting them. As Mary Fry argued in 1856, we cannot continue to imitate the styles of "one of the most corrupt cities of the old world without a corresponding loss in our morality and native good taste."[23] The controversies over morality that we discussed earlier must be seen in the light of the anxiety over national as well as individual virtue. The controversies were, in part, an effort to preserve national virtue, to avoid the plunge into the corruption of other nations.

If Americans designed their own styles, the nation's strength and virtue would be maintained. There would be no danger of repeating the errors of the French, for American designers would create styles for a different kind of people. Moreover, by affirming strength and virtue through these styles the nation would be able to fulfill its calling to be an example to the rest of the world.

THE WAR FOR INDEPENDENCE À LA MODE

The women of America, wrote the editor of the *New York Evening Post* early in 1913, "are being summoned to a new war of independence." The purpose of the war was summed up in the phrase, "See America's milliners first," a phrase which the editor hoped might become a slogan for people throughout the world. "With America at the head, the nations may press forward to another historic siege of Paris."[24] The war was not really new, of course. But the dominance which France had exerted in fashion since the days of Louis XIV was being challenged with new vigor. Americans were being reminded once again that dress is not merely a personal but a national problem as well. Subservience to foreign influence in fashion, as in any other matter, represents a loss of cherished liberty.

Let Lovers of Liberty Join Hands

For many observers, American submission to French fashions has had a number of undesirable consequences related to freedom. First, and most obvious, it has meant the loss of some of the nation's freedom, a loss which a late nineteenth-century dress reformer called "inexpressibly humiliating."[25] In fact, wrote the reformer, the contemporary movement for rejecting French dominance had to be seen as a "brave stand taken for freedom." After all, our subservience to the French meant that we had sheepishly adopted a whole series of irrational, unhealthy, and unbecoming styles. The only ones who benefitted from this subservience were the French. As a 1922 writer put it, responding to the possibility of longer skirts coming back into vogue, why should the American woman sacrifice her comfort, her good looks, and her freedom simply because "French manufacturers need to sell more yards of cloth?"[26]

Second, subservience to France has meant a betrayal of the American heritage. The nation was conceived in liberty and nurtured by a passion for freedom. Will it now betray that heritage by meekly submitting to every directive from Paris? In the middle of the nineteenth century, a physician who was advocating dress reform in the name of feminine health, wondered if American women could be roused to the independence of character "which is so emphatically their birthright." Independence, he said, is the cardinal feature of the American heart, and that independence was sorely needed if American women were ever going to have a rational form of dress.[27]

Another nineteenth-century writer, Mary Fry, advocated an American Christian costume to replace French styles. To buttress her case she pointed out that the way in which American women were avidly following Paris clearly showed how her generation bore little resemblance to "the good mothers of the memorable '76." We lack the independence of our forebears in the realm of dress. It is plain to any observer, said Ms. Fry, that if the masses of people were as deficient in patriotism as those who submit to French fashions and set the style for the rest of the nation—the so-called society women, "our form of government would crumble to dust almost in a twinkling."[28] According to this nostalgic perspective, in order to fully recapture the spirit of '76 and affirm the great heritage of freedom, Americans needed to create their own unique fashions.

Finally, the observers noted that subservience to French styles means that the nation itself, not merely some individuals, stands in the danger of corruption and decay. Such an outcome cannot be tolerated. Present-day Americans, like their forebears, must seize the sword of rebellion and declare themselves free of the foreign oppressor. As the prominent dress reformer, Frances Russell, put the matter in 1891, "Now let us join hands, all lovers of liberty, in earnest cooperation to free American women from the dominion of foreign fashion. Let us, as intelligent women, with the aid and encouragement of all good men, take this important matter into our own hands and provide ourselves with convenient garments."[29]

Americans have always taken threats to their freedom seriously.

FIG. 13. An "American" costume designed by Mrs. Annie Miller in the late nineteenth century. (*Source: The Review of Reviews,* April, 1893.)

If Parisian dominance in the world of fashion meant a loss of American liberty, appropriate action would have to be taken. Still, a nation does not plunge into war without counting the cost or without being convinced of the justness of the cause. "Rebellion against the oppressor is a noble-sounding action. But can it succeed? Is it worth the cost? Is there really justification for taking such action? Those who called for rebellion had to answer such questions. They had to rouse the public from its torpor and provide just reasons for taking radical action. Their appeal would have to strike a responsive chord in the masses of people, for the entire nation would have to rise up and topple Paris from its position of dominance. Otherwise, the few who did rebel would suffer the fate of all those who have tried to go against the tide of fashion. In sum, those who wanted to nationalize fashion had to construct a strong rationale upon which the rebellion could gain widespread support. The lovers of liberty would be brought to action by being shown the virtues of rebellion.

The Virtues of Rebellion

Those who called for rebellion against Paris appealed to a variety of motives. Negatively they pointed out the detrimental effects on the nation. Subservience to France meant the nation had not developed a national taste or a sense of national quality in fashion. Americans had allowed themselves to be led about like a dumb animal, hardly an appropriate mode of behavior for a free people who are supposed to set an example for the world. They had meekly accepted styles that were unsuited to their peculiar environment and nature. All sorts of undesirable consequences had resulted from the failure to create a distinctively American costume.[30] On the more positive side, writers made a threefold appeal: the vulnerability of Paris; the economic benefits to America; and the virtue of patriotic action.

THE VULNERABILITY OF PARIS By the end of the nineteenth century, a number of the dress reformers were convinced that Paris was vulnerable. Parisian styles were still supreme, but the reformers declared them vulnerable to a firm and united assault by Americans. A concerted effort would free them from slavery to France. As one reformer put it, "There are many evidences that the hour is ripe for a sensible revolt, and that if the movement is guided by wise and judicious minds it will be a success."[31] Two things were important for victory, said the writer. A commission composed of members of the International Council of Women had to decide exactly what kind of changes were needed; to achieve this, an American fashion commission should be formed. And secondly, young women had to be properly educated so they would support the rebellion. "Teach the girls to be American; to be independent; to scorn to copy fashion, manners, or habits that come from decaying civilizations, and which outrage all sentiment of refinement, laws of life, or principles of common sense."[32]

Twentieth-century writers underscored the vulnerability of Paris by pointing out that French fashions really depended upon Americans.

In fact, American women determined what the French would wear rather than vice versa. The French designers had to go about their work with the knowledge that Americans were their most lucrative market. If Americans believed the styles were set in Paris on the basis of French tastes, that was the result of some unfortunate devices employed by the mass media in America and by American businessmen. For the media extolled the French and acquiesced before the prestigious Parisian houses of fashion. Businessmen also perpetuated the myth of French superiority by putting fake labels in dresses, misleading customers into thinking that American-made gowns had come from Paris. Thus, the authority of Paris had been created by people, not by God. And like every other human creation, it could be torn down.[33] After all, no one was advocating that fashion itself be rooted out of human life—that would be impossible. But there was no reason why fashion could not be nationalized. Americans are competent and the French are human and, therefore, vulnerable.

ECONOMIC BENEFITS Nationalization of fashion seemed not only possible but economically beneficial. Both nineteenth- and twentieth-century writers pointed out that French dominance meant a waste of America's substance. Mary Fry argued that the nation's prosperity would be greatly advanced by a national costume. The discovery of gold in California, she said, has great potential for increasing the nation's wealth, but it would do little good to ship millions of dollars of gold to New York if an equivalent sum was being regularly shipped out to Europe to pay for foreign goods. Such a process makes little sense, particularly in view of the fact that we could easily do without those foreign goods.[34] The expendable foreign goods to which she referred, of course, were the materials and accessories used to imitate French fashions.

On the other hand, to substitute American for French fashion would be a great boon to the nation's economy. A 1912 editorial in the *New York Times* pointed out that the current crusade for the Americanization of fashions would greatly benefit our dressmakers, designers, and manufacturers. In fact, if American fashions became dominant, future generations would undoubtedly see the victory in terms of the evolution of business rather than the outcome of some sentimental movement. Drawing on the language of social Darwinism, the editor declared that the struggle between French and American fashions would be decided on the basis of the survival of the fittest. As such, Americans were destined to win. Evolution can be impeded, but not stopped. And American dominance in fashion is part of the evolution of our business and manufacturing enterprises which, in turn, "is only one of many phases in the slow realization of American personality."[35]

People in business and manufacturing, no doubt, were quick to agree there would be great economic benefits from an American victory in the struggle for fashion dominance, benefits which would accrue to workers as well as to businessmen. As a manufacturer in 1912 pointed out, anyone who is unimpressed by the economic power in fashion should note such things as the man who lost a million dollars when close-fitting gowns became fashionable and eliminated the need for petticoats.[36] When Americans control their fashions, capricious changes can be eliminated or beneficial changes encouraged. The whole enterprise can be structured so that businessmen, workers, and consumers alike, experience economic gains.

If such expectations of universal gain appear a bit naïve from our perspective, it must be remembered that they were articulated in the midst of a national struggle for fashion independence. The aim was not so much to provide an accurate assessment of economic outcomes as to rally the populace to support for the cause. It may be overly cynical to say, as did one noted social critic, that the one truly sovereign, universal, and acceptable goal of every American is money. Nevertheless, the promise of financial gain is a powerful motivator, and those who called for an American takeover of fashion did not hesitate to hold out that promise.

PATRIOTISM As one would expect in a nationalistic endeavor, the most common plea has been to the patriotism of Americans. Early in the nineteenth century, a physician delivered a series of lectures on "physical education" to women in Boston. In a lecture on the subject of fashion he called for the development of American styles:

> We talk of our liberty as an invaluable blessing, and boast of our privileges as beyond those of any other nation; yet we are so trammeled by foreign influence, that we dare not adopt a style of garment that has not been designed by the dressmakers of London or Paris. Our ladies are patriotic, and are ever ready to

exhibit their interest in their country's welfare. But what is patriotism but a love of country, and a pride in the cultivation of that country's privileges?[37]

The doctor went on to argue that a woman could do more for her country by rejecting foreign ways and developing American ones, than she could by constructing a monument of brass to the memory of departed heroes. In fact, he lamented, it should make all of our patriots blush to think that the women of the land are borrowing from the ways of those whose impure ways we in America are trying to avoid. On one hand, our men are working to create a government that is untainted by the defects of Europeans; on the other hand, our women are continuing to accept customs and styles from those very same nations. Patriotism weeps.

Wars, and the years surrounding them, are good times to tap into patriotism. The patriotic implications of fashion may be, and have been, raised at any time, of course;[38] it is particularly heinous, however, to be unpatriotic in wartime. Indeed, during both world wars, a number of writers raised the issue of fashion independence and cast it in patriotic terms. American desire to stay out of World War I provided fertile ground for such an issue to take root and grow. In 1914, after the outbreak of war, an American writer called for emancipation from foreign fashion: "If our society leaders would only cultivate patriotism, loyalty to their country—if they would let 'the passion for America cast out the passion for Europe' in matters of dress, at least—we might confidently expect better conditions."[39] Let Paris look to New York. At the very least, the time is long overdue for New York to cease running to Paris for fashion guidance.

The feeling that fashion should be Americanized continued and apparently was widespread. After World War II, the *Woman's Home Companion* polled over 2,000 of its readers about their opinions concerning American and French fashions.[40] The poll, incidentally, was the thirty-fourth in a series and represented an accurate cross section of the 3,500,000 homes in which the magazine was read. The respondents indicated that they liked American clothes. They thought the U.S. designers had done an excellent job during the war in providing women with clothes that were suited to American life. Furthermore, many of the respondents said it was a patriotic duty to support American fashions. As one put it, "Let's set our own fashion pace—we live the American way and should dress the American way." Time and again, the respondents indicated that American fashions were quite sufficient for them. In all, 54 percent said they had no interest in Parisian fashions, 43 percent indicated a moderate interest, and 3 percent said they had a great interest. Finally, among those interested in fashions from Paris, a few suggested their interest lay partly in the fact that the French were our allies and that American interest in French styles might help France along the road to economic recovery.

The combination of the vulnerability of Paris, the economic benefits to be reaped by Americans, and the appeal to patriotism would appear to be a potent force of motivation. Yet the appeals continued for well over a century. The quick and effective rebellion for which many longed always seemed imminent but never quite realized. As it turned out, the war was not the rapier thrust of mass revolt, but a long and fitful struggle. French fashions were less vulnerable than French governments.

The Fitful Course of War

The colonists who settled America could have, in theory, developed their own clothing styles from the beginning. But quite understandably they chose to follow Europe in matters of fashion. With an ocean separating them from all they had ever known, and the need for continuity, stability, and solace, the colonists tried to recreate a society as much like the one they had left behind as conditions would permit. And this extended to fashion. Before fashion plates were available, dolls were dressed in the latest styles, sent from Paris to London, and eventually from London to America. Fashion plates later served the same purpose. Some colonists were also informed by detailed letters from relatives about changing styles. However it came, fashion news was received eagerly and followed avidly.

In the years immediately preceding the Revolutionary War, many colonists began to urge the adoption of American fashions. As early as a decade before the war, women began organizing in some areas to boycott certain products, like ribbons, that came from England. As war drew near, some Bostonians agreed to refrain from purchasing goods on which heavy duties had been imposed. Among other things, they decided to discoutinue wearing black for mourning, substituting

FIG. 14. These early eighteenth-century American costumes were copied from the English. (*Source: Elisabeth McClellan,* Historic Dress in America, *Vol. 1.*)

instead a piece of black material around the hat and arm. Both men and women discarded their imported attire and adopted domestic styles. Leather shoestrings and brown homespun cloth replaced ruffles, silk, and silver buckles.[41]

After the war Americans were urged to continue the boycott of foreign fashions and create a national style of their own. As a 1787 writer pointed out, the fashions of the past had been absurd, a situation which could have been avoided if Americans had consulted their own tastes and interests. "It is the authority of foreign manners which keeps us in subjection, and gives a kind of sanction to follies, which are pardonable in Europe, but inexcusable in America."[42] But the call for independence did not prevail as Americans became more and more dependent upon Paris in matters of fashion.

The call for the nationalization of fashion, however, continued to be uttered into the middle of the twentieth-century. But the nineteenth-century phase of the war remained primarily at the verbal level. It was more of an assault of words than of concrete action. There were some concrete efforts to reject foreign styles, notably the abortive

FIG. 15. American costumes around 1800, also patterned after European styles. (*Source: Elisabeth McClellan,* Historic Dress in America, *Vol. 1.*)

Bloomer style of the 1850s (which we shall discuss in detail in the last chapter). Yet for the most part, the movement for fashion autonomy during the second half of the nineteenth century made little progress. At the turn of the century, Paris was still supreme.

In spite of Parisian domination at the turn of the century, there were signs that the war for independence in fashion was gaining momentum. Although "made in Paris" generally was still the hallmark of good taste, said a 1902 writer, there was a growing tendency in both England and America to reject the directives from Paris and establish a school of "domestic ideals."[43] By 1910 the *New York Times* was telling its readers such things as:

1. do not worry if you like white for, although Paris is putting white into the outmoded category, American women will continue to wear it;
2. the well-dressed woman will wear American shoes for French shoes are ugly whereas, "if there is one thing in the world that

the American floats the flag above and makes the eagle scream and sing 'Old Glory' over, it is her shoes;"

3. designers are quite aware of the desires of their customers, so that the French styles that come over to this country in January and February are "Americanized" in contrast to those that are sent over after the first of March.[44]

Clearly, such fashion news is strikingly different from the reporting of directives that characterized earlier articles.

The hobble skirt of 1910 may have been a major tactical error on the part of Paris. The *New York Times* called it a freak and for the next two years carried various articles on the absurdity and hazards of tight skirts. Voices calling for the Americanization of fashion were heard with greater frequency. Then, in the latter part of 1912, the *New York Times* launched a contest that was to combine "patriotism, sentiment, and business" and produce an American-designed hat and dress. The contest was initiated in the midst of a great deal of discussion of the possibility of American-designed fashions for the nation's women in newspapers, magazines, and trade journals. The time appeared ripe for a successful rebellion, and the *Times* took a concrete step in the direction of victory. Entries came in from all over the country. The response, said the editor, reflected a protest against foreign domination of the outer expression "of an inward and spiritual Americanism, an Americanism which should be distinctive in the garments of our men and women in a real revolt. It will be successful."[45] Success, when it came, would mean the supremacy of American-designed styles in America.

About the same time as the contest was announced, an organization called the Society of American Fashions for American Women was formed.[46] The temporary chairman of the society said he expected America to furnish fashions for the entire world in the near future. "We already have the ability and the resources," he said. What was lacking was recognition. And recognition would come when New York dressmakers stopped putting fake Paris labels in their gowns, when manufacturers started selling their beautiful materials to American rather than French dressmakers, and when dressmakers insisted on buying their materials from American manufacturers rather than rushing off to Paris.

If it is true, as Goethe said, that the struggle rather than the victory pleases us, the rebels against French fashion dominance must have had most satisfying lives. The victory about which they spoke with delicious anticipation in 1912 was still eluding them when the First World War broke out. Perhaps the war would provide the necessary opportunity. As the *New York Times* pointed out in September, 1914, the coming season might be the "psychological one for America to develop whatever talent she has for designing clothes." It was not possible to launch a new style as long as Paris was able to "lay down the law" at the beginning of each season. Surprisingly, the French were still able to provide the world with its dictates for style in the autumn. But what, asked the *Times*, about January?[47] The time, it seemed, was at hand for the Americanization of styles. But again, the speculation was premature. In 1915, Paris continued to dominate the world of fashion and the movement for developing distinctive American styles, reported the *Times*, "died aborning once it was announced that the designers in Paris were keeping on the job."[48]

Nevertheless, there were signs that the iron grip of Paris on fashion was loosening. Obviously, the rapid ascension of America was not taking place, but Paris had been challenged. Many people were discussing the desirability of Americanization. In 1916, there appeared to be a growing independence among the social elites.[49] After the war, opinion was divided as to how much authority Paris retained. But at least it was divided. One designer spoke glowingly about the prospects: "We are making American gowns from American materials and according to American designs for American women. I have made more evening gowns in this year than in any previous, and they are all American."[50]

The division of opinion continued into the 1920s. Some authorities claimed that French styles were still supreme, that the American woman might be independent but she was not so in the realm of fashion. Others continued to insist that America was becoming increasingly independent of France, and that the flapper costume was a symbol to France of America's independence. The flapper, said one writer, was a product of the war, and once she gained a foothold "in the haunts of the haut couture it was impossible to get her out. Fundamentally unFrench, she was an endless source of irritation, a perpetual reminder that there were times when American women insisted on wearing what they chose to wear, regardless of any hints that more intricacy would give better scope for French skill."[51]

If the flapper appeared to give America the upper hand for a time, the return to long skirts in the 1930s seemed to be a victory for Paris. The *New York Times* carried an editorial entitled "Slaves of Paris" in 1931, pointing out that although women had experienced for themselves the meaning of ease in dress, they were now eagerly snatching up the new styles that would make them look like their mothers and grandmothers. Our women had regressed to the point where they would again like whatever Paris decreed. In fact, "if Paris now orders heavy upholstery on a steel frame, they will like that too."[52] A number of writers agreed that Paris was clearly still supreme.

But the evidence was ambiguous. When the long skirts first came out, many women declared they would not wear them. They could not shop, work, or do household chores in long gowns. The French designers responded with horror—their creations were not meant for daytime wear—at work or even at leisure. They were for festive evening occasions. The outcome was a compromise between the original designs and the short skirts of the preceding decade. Both sides seemed to feel victorious, and experts drew contradictory conclusions. Some said Paris would always be supreme; others still claimed that America would become the heart of the fashion world. By 1935, French and American fashions were being shown together at openings, and Hollywood was increasingly important as a style-setter. The war dragged on, with each side able to claim various small victories.

The Second World War again brought speculations about triumph for America in the world of fashion. In 1940, before the U.S. had entered the war, the fall fashion shows in New York were called "epochal" because they "embodied the idea that destiny has moved the fashion capital across the Atlantic."[53] When Paris fell this time, the Americans were cut off from the source of inspiration. American designers now had a unique opportunity to demonstrate their competence and "take up the torch" from the French. Fashion magazines lauded the American efforts. The Americans kept at their work for the duration of the war; there was no fashion news from Paris. The result was the development of a distinctive American style. The Second World War proved to be a watershed in fashion history. This is not to say that Paris was finally and irrevocably dethroned. We have already noted the total acceptance, if somewhat grudging at first, of the New Look decreed by Christian Dior after the war. Like errant children who had abused a time of separation from their mother, Americans seemed to want to regain a place of favor by wholehearted obedience. But the old relationship would never be restored. The prodigal children now had their own styles that were rapidly developing. The New Look was a flare-up in the dying embers of dependence. By the end of the 1950s, Americans had demonstrated their independence in a distinctive style that was recognized throughout the world of fashion.[54]

What was the distinctive American style? It was casual attire that conveyed what one magazine called a look "of youthfulness, of energy, of exuberance, of much time devoted to leisure and to fun, and perhaps even of some irresponsibility."[55] It was an emphasis upon informality, activism, affluence, and freedom. By 1955, according to *Time* magazine, the American look was known throughout the world. It was a look that stressed a "leisure of action:" "From America's lively leisure has evolved a new, home-grown fashion, as different from Paris as apple pie from crepes suzette."[56] For the first time in history, American designers' names became well known.

A distinctive American style did not, as it turned out, mean total American independence. In 1958 American designers seemed to lapse into dullness. One authority called it a "time of pause." Seventh Avenue looked to Paris for guidance. Some observers said that America was still 90 percent dependent on Paris and that even the famous American casual look had to be given final approval by Paris.[57] But Paris, as we have seen, made another tactical mistake in promoting the midi in 1970. In the years following the midi's failure, observers stressed the point that the back of Paris had been broken. Never again would American women accept a style they did not like. By 1972 it was said that Parisian high fashion was increasingly a plaything for the wealthy. The American influence was becoming dominant. A number of U.S. retailers did not bother to attend the showings in Paris.[58] By 1976 it was reported that American designers, "after more than a century of obeisance to Europe's high priests of couture," had won "worldwide respect as creative interpreters of a way of life—and style."[59] The rebellion that had been underway since the end of World War II, said the report, had finally come to fruition in 1976. American designers were not merely known by name; they had become celebrities. And the American casual look was being copied in cities throughout the world. Paris no longer reigned supreme. It was true that the showings continued in Paris, but the French designers were said to offer alternatives if Americans liked them rather than directives regardless of their tastes. As a 1978 writer put it: "The message is do your own thing—the new look from Paris is simply one more thing you might, or might not, want to do."[60]

It has been said that the course of human life runs from the total dependence of childhood, to the independence of adolescence, to the interdependence of adulthood. In some ways, whole societies travel the same course. Colonies have rejected their dependence, declared independence, and established themselves in a new relationship of interdependence with the mother country. It seems to us that the nation has traveled that way in fashion. The long war of independence à la mode may have finally ended in the 1970s. Americans were no longer the serfs of Paris. The dependence of the nineteenth century had been vanquished. What they gained was not a total independence, but a new relationship of interdependence. Paris still has influence. Magazines and newspapers continue to print news of happenings in French couture. But America has also established itself as a creative center of fashions. It did not create a national costume. The bulk of Americans never wanted that anyway. And America did not become a latter-day Paris by creating a new center of haute couture to which all the world would come for fashion guidance. But America did create a distinctive style and did establish the right to choose their own styles. The outcome was somewhat different from that envisioned by many early rebels, but we suspect that they would be satisfied.

CONCLUSION

If some thinkers have regarded patriotism as the last refuge of scoundrels, others, like the nineteenth-century American clergyman, Thomas Starr King, have regarded it as one of the noblest and most sacred affections or treasures of feeling in human nature."[61] Patriotism, said King, is both a privilege and a duty. For a number of Americans who agreed with King, and who also recognized the significance of dress, the nationalization of fashions became an imperative. To some, nationalization meant the development of an American costume. The bulk of Americans never responded favorably to such a notion, however. A uniform costume for all Americans was too rigid and too boring for most people's tastes.

On the other hand, most Americans did respond favorably to the notion that our own designers should create the styles for them and their unique way of life. They believed that fashion should in some way be the badge of their uniqueness as a people, a reflection of their moral superiority, and an indication of their independence. They also responded favorably to the notion that America should become the fashion capital of the world, replacing Paris as the pacesetter for all other nations.

At least some of the goals of the rebels have been realized. Americans have created a distinctive style which reflects their way of life. American designers have commanded respect in the fashion world. Paris no longer can dictate and have its directives obeyed without question. American women have exercised independence and shown a capacity for rejecting some styles.

If all the goals have not been realized, it is, in part, because it is a different world from that in which the rebel cry first arose. What our forebears called a mission, many now call imperialism. It made more sense to talk about a national costume or about America becoming the center of the fashion world when we also talked about carrying our ideals with missionary fervor to the peoples of the world. Or even more than this, perhaps it is no longer necessary to talk of mission when American styles are now copied around the world. The fruits of missionary zeal, however, have been harvested in the form of economic gain rather than political converts. Thus, as with all revolutions, the revolution à la mode took a different course from that envisioned by the first rebels. Still, which of them would not find pleasure in the fact that by the 1970s American buyers were attending American Designer Showings?

Notes

1. M. Ostrogorski, *Democracy and the Organization of Political Parties, II.*, trans. Frederick Clark (New York: Haskell Publ. Ltd., 1970; originally published 1902), p. 581.
2. Rufus Rockwell Wilson, ed., *Burnaby's Travels through North America* (New York: A. Wessels Co., 1904; originally published 1775), pp. 152–53.
3. Hans Kohn, *The Idea of Nationalism* (New York: Macmillan, 1961), pp. 284–86.
4. Rufus Choate, *The Works of Rufus Choate,* ed., Samuel Gilman Brown (Boston: Little, Brown, 1862), p. 419.
5. Quoted in the *Missouri Democrat,* July 10, 1858.
6. For example, see the *Missouri Democrat,* July 11, 1857 and July 19, 1860; Rev. E. E. Adams, *Government and Rebellion* (Philadelphia: Henry B. Ashmead, 1861), p. 4: Rev. Samuel H. Hall, *The Tried Stability of Our Government, a Cause for Thanksgiving* (New York: A. D. F. Randolph, 1861), p. 8.
7. Alexis De Tocqueville, *Democracy in America,* trans. George Lawrence (Garden City, N.Y.: Anchor Books, 1969), p. 374.

8. Merle Curti, *The Roots of American Loyalty* (New York: Columbia University Press, 1946), p. 60.
9. Catherine Beecher, *A Treatise on Domestic Economy* (New York: Schocken Books, 1977; originally published 1841), p. 12. See also Merle Curti, *op. cit.*, p. 63.
10. George R. Stewart, *American Ways of Life* (New York: Russell & Russell, 1954), p. 138.
11. *New York Times,* January 9, 1913.
12. Quoted in the *New York Times,* September 6, 1912.
13. *New York Times,* September 6, 1912.
14. Quoted in "Emancipating Slaves of Fashion," *The Literary Digest* 44 (December 14, 1912): 1154.
15. *New York Times,* February 5, 1911.
16. M. Angeline Merritt, *Dress Reform Practically and Physiologically Considered* (Buffalo: Jewett, Thomas and Co., 1852), p. 59.
17. "Where Fashions Come from," *Every Saturday* 9 (December 3, 1870): 779.
18. Frances E. Russell, "Freedom in Dress for Women," *The Arena* 8 (June, 1893): 74. See also *New York Times,* January 9, 1913.
19. Anne Rittenhouse, "What the Well-Dressed Woman Will Wear," *New York Times,* September 4, 1910.
20. Elizabeth Meredith, "Creating Fashions in Dress," *Cosmopolitan* 39 (October, 1905): 628. See also *New York Times,* January 2, 1943.
21. "Dress and Its Relation to Life," *The Craftsman* 11 (November, 1906): 270.
22. *New York Times,* February 5, 1924.
23. Mary E. Fry, "Let Us Have a National Costume," *The Ladies' Repository* 16 (December, 1856): 735.
24. Quoted in the *New York Times,* January 9, 1913.
25. B. O. Flower, "Parisian Fashionable Folly versus American Common Sense," *The Arena* 8 (June, 1893): 141.
26. *New York Times,* August 22, 1922.
27. Edmund P. Banning, M.D., *Common Sense on the Mechanical Pathology and Treatment of Chronic Diseases of the Male and Female Systems* (New York: Wilson & Co., 1852), pp. 330–32.
28. Mary E. Fry, *op. cit.,* p. 737.
29. Frances E. Russell, "Woman's Dress," *The Arena* 3 (February, 1891): 359.
30. See, for example, Ida M. Tarbell, "A Woman and Her Raiment,' *The American Magazine* 74 (August 12, 1912): 472.
31. B. O. Flower, "Fashion's Slaves," *The Arena* 4 (September, 1891): 425.

32. *Ibid.*, p. 427.
33. See Elizabeth Meredith, *op. cit.*, p. 623; *New York Times*, December 22, 1912; and M. C. C. Crawford, *The Ways of Fashion* (New York: Fairchild Publishing Co., 1941), p. 17.
34. Mary E. Fry, *op. cit.*, p. 735.
35. *New York Times*, December 26, 1912.
36. *New York Times*, December 15, 1912.
37. "Dr. Grigg's Lecture," *The Ladies' Magazine* 5 (January, 1832): 6.
38. See, for example, Charlotte Dean, "The Swing of Styles," *The North American Review* 230 (September, 1930): 362.
39. Margaret Woodward, *op. cit.*, p. 153.
40. "Do You Want Paris Fashions?" *Woman's Home Companion* 72 (October, 1945): 8.
41. Elisabeth McClellan, *Historic Dress in America*, I (New York: Arno Press, 1977; originally published 1904–10), pp. 250–52.
42. "Letter to the Editor," *The American Magazine* 1 (December, 1787): 39.
43. Nancy M. W. Woodrow, "How Fashions Are Set," *Cosmopolitan* 33 (July, 1902): 256.
44. *New York Times*, February 20, 1910; March 13, 1910; and March 27, 1910.
45. *New York Times*, January 9, 1913.
46. *New York Times*, December 17, 1912.
47. *New York Times*, September 27, 1914.
48. *New York Times*, February 21, 1915.
49. *New York Times*, December 17, 1912.
50. *New York Times*, January 5, 1919.
51. Mildred Adams, "Revolt Rumbles in the Fashion World," *The New York Times Magazine*, October 27, 1929, p. 4.
52. *New York Times*, August 1, 1931.
53. Elizabeth Duval, "New York Decrees," *The New York Times Magazine*, September 15, 1940, p. 8.
54. Jane Dorner, *Fashion in the Forties and Fifties* (New York: Arlington House, 1975), pp. 79–82.
55. "America's Own Fashions," *Holiday* 12 (July, 1952): 103.
56. "Fashion: The American Look," *Time* 65 (May 2, 1955): 85. See also Stella Mary Pearce, "The Spirit of the Times—and the Fashion," *The New York Times Magazine*, May 9, 1954, p. 27f.
57. Phyllis Lee Levin, "Paris Sets Pace, but Creative Fashion Talent, Critics Agree, Exists in U.S.," *New York Times*, May 20, 1958.
58. "Medium Fashion," *Newsweek* 80 (August 7, 1972): 68.
59. "American Chic in Fashion," *Time* 107 (March 22, 1976): 62.

60. Judy J. Newmark, "Paris in America?" *St. Louis Post-Dispatch,* November 5, 1978.
61. Thomas Starr King, "The Privilege and Duties of Patriotism," in George Frisbie Hoar, ed., *Book of Patriotism* (Boston: Hall and Locke Company, 1902), p. 53.

chapter 6

The Social Consequences of Fashion

The striking decline in death rates in the modern era has been attributed to four factors: changed diet; increased medical knowledge; the development of personal hygiene; and various public health programs.[1] Personal hygiene cannot be maintained without certain facilities such as clean water and soap, neither of which was readily available until relatively recent times. In addition to soap and water, clothing is an important part of personal hygiene. As Buchanan has summarized the matter, the expansion of the cotton industry in England between 1750 and 1850 significantly contributed to the increase in personal cleanliness. For the abundant and comparatively cheap cotton underclothes and dress materials meant that all except the poorest people could have a number of different sets of clothes, and could change their clothing more frequently "with a consequent reduction in the body vermin which had for so long been a generally accepted but unwholesome feature of life."[2]

Cotton clothing became fashionable, and one of the unanticipated consequences of the fashion was better health. In this chapter, we will explore further the ways in which people have seen fashion bearing upon health. We will also examine a number of other consequences of various fashions. In general, these consequences have not been intended or anticipated by those creating the fashions. But like any innovation, new styles may have consequences far beyond the purposes for which they were introduced.

FASHION AND PHYSICAL AND MENTAL WELL-BEING

"The great demand of the age is for health," wrote a dress reformer in 1862.[3] Full enjoyment of the blessings of life and full performance of one's duties are not possible without perfect health, she insisted. Yet American women were a most sickly lot. "There is scarcely a robust American-born woman to be found. All are complaining of innumerable ailments from which men are comparatively free."[4] What could account for the obvious disparity in the health status of men and women? As far as the reformer was concerned, there was only one reasonable cause—the differing modes of dress of the two sexes.

Thirty years later, another reformer repeated the argument, adding that both physical and mental health are affected by the prevailing styles. Furthermore, she said, if anyone doubts the impact of dress upon health, let the boys and girls change into each other's styles for a single generation. Let the girls have the bodily freedom of boys and let the boys be dressed with typical girls' clothes, "their bodies formed to an unnatural shape, and their minds imbued with the doctrine that beauty of appearance should be the chief aim of life."[5] Both the physical and mental health of boys would be adversely affected. But no man would allow his son to be so tormented. Only America's girls and women are required to wear debilitating styles: "In some heathen countries they kill the girl babies. In America they put them through French fashions."[6]

Fashion may either facilitate or impede physical and mental well-being. As the writers suggest, those styles that impede receive far more attention that those that facilitate. When fashion enhances our well-being, its contribution tends to be overlooked or ignored. When fashion threatens our well-being, the voices of protest are many and loud. Three types of threat have been discussed in popular writings: inadequate protection for the wearer; a hazard or aggravation to those with whom the wearer interacts; and a hazard of some kind to the wearer.

Protection versus Exposure: A Dilemma

Whatever else a particular style may or may not do, it should not prevent the wearer from being adequately protected from the elements. Adequate protection, according to a nineteenth-century writer, would mean that one's dress would be so arranged as to provide an even temperature of body, protecting the body from both heat and cold. This is a fundamental law of dress, yet, along with a few other laws of garmenture, it has been ignored throughout human history.[7] Everyone agrees that protection is one of the basic purposes of dress, yet, oddly enough say some writers, the prevailing styles typically do not provide adequate protection.

What are the consequences of inadequate protection? Various writers, including some physicians, warned the public that colds, influenza, and a number of respiratory ailments were more likely because of certain styles of dress. The high prevalence of tuberculosis among young women was also explained by feminine fashions. Early in the nineteenth century, Mathew Carey wrote that women wore light clothes even on the coldest days of winter until about 1830. As a result, "catarrhs and consumptions were prevalent—doctors' bills increased in families where there were young ladies—and lovely women . . . were hurried to a premature grave."[8] Carey offered the opinion that the change to "a mass of covering" that had occurred about five years before he wrote had produced a "material change" in the looks and health of America's women.

A later nineteenth-century writer agreed that inadequate protection had given rise to many diseases among American women, including the "alarming prevalence of consumption." The latter, she said, was the result of a style of dress totally unadapted to guard the body against cold and against the sudden transitions from heat to cold that occur in the middle and northern states.[9]

The flapper costume of the 1920s was also said to be a culprit in the rate of tuberculosis among young women. In 1927, a physician said the scanty clothing women were wearing caused them to get chilled and weakened their resistance to disease.[10] Another physician, in a letter to the *New York Times,* stressed the entire life style of the flapper as the reason for the increase in tuberculosis, including: "the insane desire to obtain a boyish appearance by intentional undernourishment; insufficient protection of the body, particularly in cold weather; the flimsy dress . . . with next to no underwear; low shoes; compression of the breast by tight brassieres, hindering deep respiration; too much night life; too much cigarette smoking and, in many cases, unsanitary sleeping and living quarters; overheated and badly ventilated workrooms, offices, factories, and stores."[11] The remedies, said the physician, were obvious, and included dress reform.

Thus far, the argument may be summarized simply: exposure means inadequate protection which means disease and possibly even death. As one nineteenth-century physician said, "no part of the body should be allowed to suffer exposure to the atmosphere by being left uncovered; want of attention in this respect has induced a slight cough, or cold, which has terminated in the death of multitudes."[12] But there is a dilemma in all this; namely, that no one, including any physician, can be quite certain about exactly how much exposure is deleterious to health. Was the nineteenth-century physician correct in asserting that none of the body should be exposed to the atmosphere? Were those physicians correct who linked the exposure produced by certain feminine styles with tuberculosis? Was it really true that the development of "ankle agony" among women in 1925 was due to "a combination of the damp weather, fancy footwear, spiderweb stockings, and short skirts"?[13]

If those who argued for the hazardous consequences of certain styles were confident in their denunciations, those who argued for the benefits of the very same styles were no less confident in their praise. In 1913, no less an authority than the U.S. Public Health Service declared the slit skirt and diaphanous gown to be healthy styles. The Assistant Surgeon General said women in the past had worn too many clothes and those dressing in the latest styles would be "less liable to catch cold these chilly days than one who loads down her body with heavy clothing."[14] The flapper costume was also defended by some physicians. A prominent Baltimore doctor said that rather than exposing herself to disease, the modern girl was increasing her resistance. He noted that "savages" got along very well with little clothing. From the health viewpoint, the flapper costume was actually an advantage because "it accustoms the body to the various changes of temperature of our climate."[15]

Thus, for any particular style one might find medical opinion that both damned and praised the mode. One could choose from the contrary positions depending upon one's purpose. Some of the clergy who found the flapper costume immoral, for instance, did not fail to point out that it was unhealthy as well. Unfortunately for the opponents, supporters of the costume had their own medical experts and were able to laud its contribution to good health. The health consequences of exposure have been ambiguous. There is less ambiguity in the implications for health in other aspects of fashion.

The Hazards of Hats

Sometimes a style appears that is said to be hazardous to others, that is, to those who interact with the wearer. This problem is well illustrated by fashionable women's hats in the first decade of the twentieth century. In particular, the large "Merry Widow" style appeared in 1907, and was followed by various other styles, all of which were quite large. The "Merry Widow" hat was oval in shape, large in size, and topped off with plumes or feathers or artificial flowers. Long, pointed pins were used to hold the hats in place.

The hats were considered hazardous in various ways. At a minimum, they produced considerable anger or frustration in public gatherings, for anyone who sat behind a woman wearing such a hat was unable to see. One man was induced to write a letter to the editor of the *New York Times*, asking whether women should be required to remove their hats in church. He had heard all of his life, he wrote, about women's rights, and now he was asserting his right as a man to worship in church "without having both vision and hearing shut out by the length and depth and breadth and height of women's hats." Since the tradition of some churches require women to wear hats in church, he said, smaller hats should be used for Sundays. Otherwise, he predicted one of two outcomes: either men would stop going to church and withdraw their financial support, or public opinion would result in the removal of all hats during church services.[16]

That the man was not expressing an isolated opinion was shown by the fact that a number of cities passed local ordinances restricting the wearing of hats in public meetings. In Boston, for instance, an ordinance was passed that required the removal of women's hats at all public meetings. Some women defied the ordinance at a performance of the Boston symphony on the grounds that people come to a symphony to hear, not to see. The city threatened to take away the license of the theater, the theater manager threatened to ask the women to leave if they did not remove their hats, and the women gave in.[17]

The hats were said to be more than a nuisance. In 1910, a Catholic priest condemned the wearing of the hats during the sermon. He said the women should wear shawls instead: "Besides showing a more meek Christian spirit there is less danger in this style of sticking feathers or daggers in the eyes of the men."[18] The priest was not simply irritated that the hats distracted the congregation from his sermon, there apparently was real danger. In 1911, the city of Rochester, New York, enacted an ordinance forbidding hat pins from extending more than a half inch beyond the hat.[19]

Occasionally, then, a style appears that threatens the well-being of others. An individual's comfort, enjoyment, or physical well-being may be jeopardized by the style that someone else is wearing. But it is more likely that the threat is to the wearer's own well-being. Let us look at the various ways in which fashion can be hazardous to an individual.

Can You Be Both Fashionable and Healthy?

People have done some strange things in the name of fashion. Writers have noted some of the body-deforming practices of other cultures, such as the foot-binding of the Chinese, and the head-shaping of some American Indians, and the various types of mutilation found among some Africans. They have also noted that America has her own tales of horror in the realm of fashion, particularly where fashion has been detrimental to health. Americans cherish good health, yet have willingly adopted a number of unhealthy fashions. Both physical and mental health have been threatened by fashion. Both have also been enhanced by certain fashions, but a good deal more attention has been paid to the unhealthy than to the healthy styles.

FASHIONS THAT INCREASE THE PROBABILITY OF ACCIDENTS

One way that a style may be hazardous to health is by making accidents more likely. Nineteenth-century women's styles all tended to be culpable at this point, for their sheer weight and constricting qualities made mobility a precarious affair. By the 1850s, a fashionable dress could require from twenty to twenty-five yards of cloth. The winter street costume of a fashionable woman could weigh from thirty to forty pounds. By the end of the century, the styles had moderated somewhat, but a description of one outfit still sounds staggering:

> 1. A heavy, closely woven shirt and drawers of cotton, wool, or silk. 2. A thick, stiff corset, heavily boned and composed of at least two layers of thick, closely woven cotton cloth. 3. A thick muslin underwaist and drawers, or a chemise and drawers. 4. A heavy, gathered flannel petticoat that came well below the knee. 5. A cotton, silk, or woolen petticoat at least two yards around. 6. A woolen dress, the shirt lined with silk or percaline, stiffened around the bottom with haircloth, interlined with paper, and at least three yards around. The waist had a heavy cotton lining. This garment alone weighed several pounds. 7. A heavy woolen coat, lined and sometimes interlined. 8. Heavy woolen or cotton stockings. 9. High shoes. 10. Rubbers.[20]

It is understandable that a fashionably dressed woman of the nineteenth century would have difficulties maneuvering, and would be more prone to have accidents. Some of the accidents were minor and some were true horror stories, such as an incident in which a boat sank and all the women drowned because they were physically helpless, or cases where women burned to death when a petticoat caught fire. Many young women could report various kinds of accidents as a result of the hoop skirt, which, interestingly enough, was totally unsuited to the "Wild West" but was in vogue nevertheless. Riding a horse, even sidesaddle, was a perilous undertaking in a hoop skirt. Occasionally, a bold young woman might remove the skirt and ride in her pantaloons.[21]

Twentieth-century fashions have tended to be far safer, but a number of them were perilous in their own right. In particular, the hobble skirt was notorious as a safety hazard. As one woman said, the skirt was a "serious menace to the health and safety" of women, who continually faced the "mortal fear of falling" when crossing streets, getting into trolley cars, or walking up or down stairways.[22] Accessories can also be hazardous. In 1974, a number of Boston physicians reported on the "long-scarf syndrome" which had appeared because of the female fashion of using long, free-flowing scarves wrapped around the neck. They cited two cases of young girls suffering fractures, lacerations, and near strangulation after their scarves were caught in the machinery of a ski tow. The doctors noted that the same fashion had appeared in the 1920s and caused a number of accidents, notably the strangulation death of famed dancer, Isadora Duncan.[23]

FASHIONS THAT PROMOTE UNHEALTHY BEHAVIOR Sometimes a style expresses an aesthetic ideal for the human form. Those who do not possess the ideal form—which may be the great bulk of people—may try to reshape their bodies. As we shall discuss, the corset reflected the ideal of a small waist, and some women even slept in their corsets in their desperate attempt to maintain the wasp-waist figure. In the 1920s, the flapper reflected a different ideal and a number of physicians warned women they were engaging in perilous behavior when they tried to achieve an unrealistic slenderness.

In 1926, a magazine editor, in presenting an article by a noted physician, said that "frantic dieting" had turned into "our national indoor sport." They physician called it "a veritable craze for reduction which has passed the bounds of normality and driven women and young girls to a type of self-mutilation impossible to explain on any other basis than the faddism of the mob."[24] He pointed out that some women were voluntarily regurgitating their food after eating. Some were smoking before meals to cut down on their appetites. Others were going to establishments that had been set up to help women reduce. The resulting under-nutrition and excessive loss of fatty tissue, he said, could lead to various diseases, to problems with pregnancy and childbearing, and even death. The warnings notwithstanding, women continued to employ all sorts of methods to slenderize themselves in order to appear well in their flapper costumes.

FASHIONS THAT CREATE HEALTH PROBLEMS Some fashions create health problems directly. Nineteenth-century styles, in addition to increasing the probability of accidents, directly affected a woman's well-being. In fact, it was virtually impossible to escape detrimental health consequences from many of the fashions of the ninteenth century. Among other things, a number of writers pointed out that the long, trailing skirts of women swept up all sorts of filth whenever a woman ventured out of her home. "What is more disgusting," asked one reformer, than to see a woman "carrying around, with such ostensible quietness, dirty, drabbled, drizzling skirts, which have become such by sweeping the sidewalks and street crossings of their filth!"[25] A physician had a number of women walk around the streets of his city for an hour, and reported finding on each skirt "large colonies of noxious germs, including those of influenza, tuberculosis, typhoid fever and tetanus."[26] Yet another enterprising observer made a count of the items one woman had swept along with her skirts. They included: two cigar ends, nine cigarette ends, a piece of pie, four toothpicks, two hairpins, a pipe stem, three pieces of orange peel, a piece of cat meat, half of a boot sole, and one plug of well-chewed tobacco.[27]

Virtually all writers agreed that the major health hazard to nineteenth-century women was the corset. One newspaper editor said that a corseted woman was dressed in "a prison-house instrument of torture and slow-murderer—this leg-tangling, back-beating, hip-depressing, chest-compressing, arm-imprisoning, breath-stopping, disease-inducing apparatus."[28] One woman described the lacings as "an ingeniously contrived instrument of torture and disease worthy of the agents of the Abolished Inquisition." A corset, she said, totally deformed the female figure: the ribs were crushed; one shoulder was raised higher than the other; the breasts were deformed; the spinal column was "twisted like a cork-screw"; and the neck was pushed out of place like the leaning tower of Pisa. But these were not the worst consequences, for the effect upon the internal organs was devastating. The lungs were denied the room to carry out the functions of respiration and thus became weakened and diseased; the heart, pushed into the space allotted the other vital organs, became diseased and carried "a stream of diseased blood through the suffering system"; the liver and stomach were similarly crowded and ceased to function properly; and the bones which were compressed by the tight lacing grew "rotten and carious, and incapable of supporting the frame." As a result, the victim of the desire for a small waist passed to an early grave.[29]

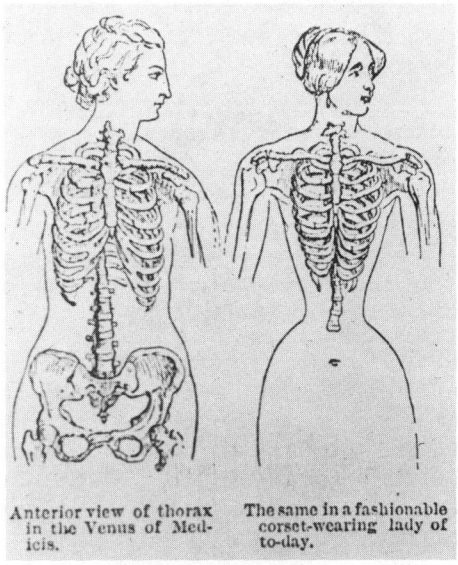

Anterior view of thorax in the Venus of Medicis.

The same in a fashionable corset-wearing lady of to-day.

FIG. 16. A typical illustration of the harm done by the corset, one of a number of fashions that have impaired health. (*Source:* The Arena, *September, 1891.*)

Contemporary physicians agreed with the writer's assessment. In fact, they enlarged upon it. Among the other consequences of tight lacing that physicians mentioned were: headaches, heart palpitations, and coldness in the extremities due to poor circulation; debility of certain muscles which have not been properly used; diseases of the breast, including cancer; various gastrointestinal problems; and nervousness and fatigue.[30] Just how tight were the corsets? In its extreme phase, a young woman was expected to have a sixteen-inch waist by the time she was eighteen to twenty years of age. An occasional woman would boast of a thirteen-inch waist. The force required to achieve this size was considerable. In order to bear the pressure, females had to become accustomed to corsets early in their lives. One early nineteenth-century advertisement advised mothers to have their daughters lie face down on the floor. A mother could then place

FIG. 17. A corset ad in the 1880s implied that women could have both a fashionable figure and their health. (*Source: Claudia B. Kidwell and Margaret C. Cristman,* Suiting Everyone.)

her foot in the small of her daughter's back in order to get the necessary leverage to tighten the laces. In adults the lacing was sometimes so tight that physicians reported the impression of the ribs on the liver in women who had died and upon whom an autopsy had been

FIG. 18. Another nineteenth-century corset ad. According to Dr. Scott, his corset did more than simply allow health; it actually promoted good health! (*Source:* The Fashion Courier, February, 1882.)

performed. One of the common complaints of women who practiced tight lacing was the "chicken-breast," a condition that developed by the continual constriction of the ribs. The woman with a chicken breast suffered from "insufficient respiration, fractured ribs, and injuries to the sternum and clavicle. The lungs, in the parts most compressed, atrophied and collapsed."[31] One of the more terrifying consequences was prolapsus uteri, the falling of the womb down the vagina until it could even project out of the body.[32]

Needless to say, the activity of a corseted woman was severely limited. Nevertheless, many working and working-class women tried to imitate the styles of the middle and upper classes. They did not do so with impunity. Digestive difficulties, chronic vomiting, frequent fainting, and other complaints and ills were common among such women.

Corsets continued to be fashionable into the twentieth century, though the lacing became less tight. More and more, styles appeared that were obviously designed for corsetless women. The noted French designer, Paul Poiret, stressed freedom as his theme and claimed to be woman's liberator from the corset. Not everyone was convinced that the corset could be easily discarded. In 1913, some physical directors argued that women had worn corsets too long to completely discard them. The abdominal muscles, they said, had been weakened by constant support from the corset. If women discard their corsets, therefore, "one by one they will lose their tone and drop, gather flesh, and refuse to do their ordained duty, and the woman will be a shapeless mass and a nervous wreck."[33] But by the 1920s, physicians and others were commenting on the better health that had resulted as women abandoned their corsets.

Next to dresses and corsets, observers concerned with health mentioned shoes most often. Sometimes women's shoes were said to be too open to offer sufficient protection. Sometimes they were said to be wrongly shaped. There has been some question of the consequences of high heels. One writer claimed they throw a woman's spinal column out of line, while another said they caused the ankles to become thickened and lead thereby to ugliness and deformity.[34] In 1979, a podiatrist claimed his patients had a variety of problems as a result of wearing high heels. He said he could see no beneficial aspects at all to them, and they were probably just another male creation designed to keep women in subjection by restricting their mobility.[35]

A variety of other aspects of fashion have been linked with differing physical ailments and problems. For example:

1. in 1911, a physician said the fashionable tight collars of previous years had put pressure on the thyroid gland, which needs to be kept free from such pressure in order to maintain a woman's youth;
2. in 1912, a physician argued that tight skirts were causing knock knees in women, and a newspaper editor agreed, saying we could

become "a nation of knock-kneed, bow-legged, splay-footed, pigeon-toed, bandy-shanked people, a by-word and a reproach of the face of the earth";
3. in 1922, a teacher claimed the head bands that had become popular among girls were so tight they clogged the pores, exerted a harmful pressure, and led to headaches;
4. in 1957, a group of Swedish scientists said tight trousers on men increased heat around the genitals, speeding up the rate of mutations in the genes, and possibly leading to the birth of defective children;
5. in 1977, a physician pointed out that the popular turtleneck sweater could aggravate the problem of acne among youth when the acne had spread to the neck area.[36]

Warnings about the health hazards of fashion have been so frequent and have involved so many different styles that one could reasonably conclude that any new style should be screened by a panel of physicians before being released to the public.

FASHION'S THREAT TO MENTAL WELL-BEING Fashion may have both direct and indirect effects upon mental well-being. For instance, it has been said that the corset was deadening the mental abilities of American women. It has been argued that giving children hand-me-downs instead of new styles, can be emotionally traumatic for those children when they go to school. But the bulk of statements about the relationship between fashion and mental well-being focus on the consequences of the individual's passion to always be in fashion.

Those who avidly rush after every new style create two different kinds of emotional problems. First, women may generate great anxiety in their husbands. A man who constantly faces the pressure of large clothing bills may suffer to the point of mental breakdown and even suicide.[37] Second, men and women (and, of course, most writers mention only women) who must always be in fashion may create for themselves a continuing anxiety. They may live in an unceasing dread of appearing in the wrong styles. They have what we could call the Out-of-Fashion Trauma Syndrome; their emotional state hangs precariously by the thin thread of other's evaluation of their attire.

FIG. 19. Men as well as women have been concerned about the health aspects of clothing styles, as seen in this 1917 ad. (*Source: Claudia B. Kidwell and Margaret C. Cristman,* Suiting Everyone.)

The syndrome includes the frantic rush after every new style, the anxiety of keeping up with the changes, and the careful watch for cues as to how others are evaluating one's dress. The syndrome was discussed from at least the end of the eighteenth century until well into the twentieth century. An eighteenth-century observer, for example, noted it in males as well as females:

> Tell a modern American youth of spirit, that he makes an unfashionable appearance, and that his dress by no means corresponds with the reigning mode, and observe the sudden transition which takes place in his countenance, from the pert smile of self complacency, to the uncourtly grin of Sir Fretful Plagiary. Unaffectedly insensible to every other reproof, this sarcasm rouses his utmost indignation, or overwhelms him with vexatious confusion.[38]

Subsequent writers emphasized the emotional trauma of those who insist upon always being in fashion.[39] The thought of not being considered fashionable, they said, is the "greatest source of anxiety." It is an exceedingly worrisome and perplexing matter, a burden and a bother. It is incompatible with peace of mind, leading not only to anxiety but to that "utter want of hilarity which foreigners, not untruly, attribute to us." It wears one's nerves to a frazzle, and indeed those who have discussed the greater amount of nervousness among women have often failed to take into account the "harassing, nerve-wearing endeavors to keep in the fashion." The Out-of-Fashion Trauma Syndrome, according to a long line of observers, has been an American affliction during most of our history.

FASHIONS THAT ENHANCE WELL-BEING The question we raised earlier, whether one can be both fashionable and healthy, would appear at this point to require a negative answer. But there is another side to the coin. If some new styles have had a deleterious effect on health, others have improved health. If, for example, long skirts and masses of material increased the likelihood of accidents, the short skirts of the twentieth century have meant fewer accidents—a point not overlooked by some observers. We have already pointed out that a number of physicians argued that the styles of the 1920s, which included a greater amount of exposure of the body, were really healthier than those which covered women's bodies with great amounts of material. Generally, observers of the fashion scene see twentieth-century styles in terms of increasingly healthy and comfortable clothes. Particular styles may pose particular hazards, but in general the twentieth-century individual dresses in far healthier styles than did the nineteenth-century individual.

Similarly, fashion may enhance mental well-being. If some people endure mental anguish over fashion, others find that fashion provides them with emotional support or an emotional boost. One woman told about the way in which her sense of being well dressed gave her a sense of inner peace that even religion could not offer.[40] The noted historian of fashion and clothing, James Laver, once told a group of female students that there should be a clinic for women who are unhappy or dissatisfied and Christian Dior should be the resident psychiatrist.[41] Dior himself said that a good dress was the best bargain in the world for a woman, for it will bring her happiness.[42]

Young people have been advised to pay heed to their styles, for those styles are important to their sense of well-being. Stylish clothes can raise morale and "make existence more decorative and more delightful."[43] Even if the monetary cost is high, said a 1912 writer, the benefits may be well worth the cost: "For the depressed and discouraged woman a reasonable extravagance is sometimes as efficacious as a nerve tonic."[44] And the editor of the *New York Times,* commenting in 1919 upon some remarks by the Health Commissioner about the emotional boost that clothes give a woman, said that a stylish mode of dress can be nearly intoxicating. In fact, even physically uncomfortable clothes can act as a tonic to the spirit: "What matter a tottering gait, an organ squeezed dry, and a boreal blast upon the ankles, so long as the spirit soars?"[45]

As these writers assert or suggest, a new set of clothes can be very therapeutic. One fashion consultant told of a woman who had been seeing a psychiatrist and was told by the doctor that her problems were rooted in a bad experience with a boy when she was six years of age. "Psycho-nonsense," was the fashion consultant's response. She advised the woman to get active at something. The woman did so, and then the consultant designed a wardrobe for the woman. Ultimately, the woman reported that her problems had dissolved and she was enjoying a fresh new life. The consultant concluded that in some cases an exterior restyling may bring about a cure of the inner problems. For a woman who feels beautiful on the outside will surely start to feel happy and secure on the inside.[46]

While fashion is obviously not a tonic for every emotional ailment, some professionals have corroborated the therapeutic effect that popular writers extol. One psychoanalyst told of a patient who said she hated everyone when she felt she was shabbily dressed.[47] The statement, he said, should be posted in all clothing stores. "Fashion Therapy" has been used on occasion in treating patients in mental hospitals. The therapy involves a fashion show for the patients and sometimes a designer who creates a dress for each patient (the patient, with help from volunteers, would make the dress herself). In some cases, dramatic improvement is reported. One patient said the therapy was the turning point for her. After one of the classes, she said, "all at once the clouds rolled back, the sun was shining, and I felt like myself again." She was able to leave the hospital shortly thereafter.[48]

Fashion, then, can provide emotional support, an emotional boost, or even therapy. We will see a number of reasons for this later, when we discuss the role of fashion in the presentation of self. First, we must examine some additional consequences of fashion.

THE ECONOMIC CONSEQUENCES OF FASHION

Quite apart from the nativistic concerns discussed in the last chapter, a number of writers have emphasized the role of fashion in the economic life of the nation, business, and individuals and families. With respect to the nation, some have said that fashion is a wasteful process that creates economic woes. But most see it as an integral part of the nation's economy. They have said that we need to keep up our purchases of new styles to maintain prosperity; that a new style can be an economic shot-in-the-arm; that we would all suffer economically if fashion became stagnant; that "when a nation is healthy it can no more remain stationary in the matter of dress than it can in the matter of locomotion or means of communication."[49] The oft-noted relationship between business cycles and skirt lengths also seems to tie in fashion with the economy. If hemlines go down when the economy goes down, more material is needed for dresses at a time when manufacturers need more business.

Of course, longer hemlines cannot themselves pull a nation out of the economic doldrums. But the clothing and textile industry is a significant segment of the economy; in 1929, at the dawn of the Great Depression, the industry's payroll was over 6 percent of the total payroll for all manufacturers. A number of writers, no doubt aware of the sizable economic impact of the fashion industry, either blamed that industry for the depression or called upon it to lift us out of the depression. As one prominent businessman said to the New York Fashion Group in 1934, obsolescence in dress is a necessity if depressions are to be avoided: "To take up the slack, we must create obsolescence. The job of the retailer is to make everybody want something they haven't got. Create new desires, new needs, new ambitions and new habits."[50] A Catholic laywoman told a religious conference that they must pray daily for the revival of business and that they must "go out into the highways and byways and demand long sleeves and long skirts.⁵¹ And the editor of the *New York Times* rebuked those women who insisted on wearing "rational" dress in the face of unemployment in the textile mills.⁵²

When the nation as a whole is healthy, particular businesses may either flourish or collapse. Business people who specialize in some particular aspect of fashion may find themselves quickly wealthy and then quickly impoverished. For example, in 1910 the *New York Times* carried a story about how fortunes could be wrecked by the "fickle caprices of fashion." Pearl buttons had suddenly become fashionable and just as suddenly gone out of fashion. One man who had invested everything in their manufacture was thrust into bankruptcy by the change and reduced to a door-to-door salesman of cheap goods. Nor was he the only victim: "Plants broken up and decaying, men beggared and never landing on their feet again, in a hundred different places tell the story of temptations of dollar-making that were not to be resisted."⁵³

Finally, fashion poses something of an economic dilemma for many individuals. Can an individual be both fashionable and financially sound? Many writers have warned their fellow Americans that fashion can be the financial ruin of an individual and a family. The individual may face the choice of being either fashionable and financially strained or even ruined, or of being unfashionable, financially sound, but socially outcast.

Is the dilemma realistic? Undoubtedly, it is an overstatement, but it does contain a germ of truth. It expresses the fact that there are contradictory demands with which the individual must come to terms. Let us look at the ways in which various writers have explored the dilemma from differing angles.

First, the cost of being fashionable varies from age to age. But it is possible to spend a great deal of money on clothing in any age. And one can spend it on every member of the family. Men's, women's, and children's styles all offer opportunities for extravagance. A 1960 report on fashions for preschool children, for example, noted that one could pay as much as $200 for a dress for a three-year-old in exclusive shops.⁵⁴ The median family income in 1960 was $5620. One $200 dress represented at least 3½ percent and as much as 20 percent or more of the annual income of half the families in the nation.

Second, some people are willing to sacrifice other things in order to be fashionable. A 1916 writer said that children had convinced their mothers that "love, obedience, and affection are swept off the family map if they are dressed in a way to bring forth the taunts and biting sarcasm" of their peers. The result was that other things were sacrificed in order to ensure that the children would be fittingly attired at school.[55] A number of attitude studies have reported that many women would willingly give up other essentials before sacrificing their need for fashionable dress.

Third, some people do spend enormous amounts of money for clothing. The very rich may spend amounts that are staggering to most people. A 1972 report told of a woman who walked into a French house of haute couture and ordered a gown that would "sing." The result was a $10,000 dress, more than many women spend on clothes in their lifetimes. Another wealthy woman ordered a designer's entire collection at a cost of $173,800. The writer of the report estimated that there were about 1000 women in 1972 who spent more than $200,000 per year on clothes and perhaps a dozen who spent $1 million or more.[56]

Such women do not exhaust their financial resources on fashion even with such large purchases. But others have. Early in the nineteenth century, a writer pointed out that the poorer classes were "ruining themselves by a foolish desire of emulating the rich in dress."[57] A line of subsequent writers insisted that the effort to be in fashion could lead not merely the poor, but others as well, to bankruptcy. Since the Great Depression, however, writers no longer speak about the dilemma. Rather, they tell women how they can be fashionable on a low budget. The question of whether one can be both fashionable and financially healthy, which was typically answered in the negative through the second decade of the twentieth century, has since then been largely answered affirmatively.

FASHION AND PERSONAL GROWTH AND FULFILLMENT

"I think, therefore I am." An imaginative twist was given to Descartes' famous dictum by a writer who said it was the outcome of adult reasoning, but that the infant had already arrived at a similar conclusion by reasoning, "I have shoes and a red sash, therefore I am."[58] An infant's sense of individual existence, argued the writer, comes about through the consciousness of adjuncts, attributes, and belongings. "Yes, here I am," the infant appears to say, "I have something which belongs to me." We doubt that infants engage in such a sophisticated line of thought. And we doubt that many women share the feelings of the one who said that women are dresses rather than souls, that her own history was the history of her dresses, and without her clothing she had no existence.[59] Nevertheless, such writers have captured an important insight, namely, that our mode of dress is intimately linked up with our identity, our personal growth, and the fulfillment of our needs and aspirations. We will examine the ways in which fashion has been said to facilitate growth and fulfillment after a brief look at an opposing view.

The Older View—Fashion as an Impediment

From the eighteenth through the early part of the twentieth century, fashion's role in individual development was seen primarily as detrimental. Fashion threatened the individual's psychological as well as financial and physical well-being. The threat was rooted in the time demands made upon the person who was devoted to fashion. Realistically, it did require a considerable amount of time for a woman to be fashionable in the eighteenth and nineteenth centuries. And many writers viewed that expenditure of time as a massive waste of opportunity for self-development.

Americans have always had a strong sense of the importance of the proper use of time. "Time is money" has been a guiding philosophy for children as well as adults, for housewives as well as business people, and for the poor as well as the rich. A long line of Protestant thinkers declared that the waste of time is sin. Thus, the improper use of one's time is immoral as well as unprofitable, and a host of books and magazine articles have been written to help Americans make good use of every minute.

In the context of a sense of urgency about the proper use of time, we can understand the despair of those who saw women committing a good portion of their lives to the pursuit of fashionable dress. Women spend years of their lives, said one observer, in the study and pursuit of fashion, resulting in a waste of their time and a loss of opportunities for moral and mental development.[60] And it is not only the individual, but the society that suffers. For the women who devotedly follow the earthly goddess have many talents that could be put to good use in social improvement. Women could "work a revolution in the manners and fashions of society, that would justly entitle them to the heartfelt gratitude of every republican spirit; and the world would call them, what in truth they would be, the benefactors of their country." Instead of fulfilling that noble task, however, they worship at the shrine of fashion and aspire to no higher distinction than that of personal display.[61] Woman's life, instead of being an ornament to society, is a "giddy round of dress, dancing, and flippant conversation" with hour after hour being consumed in "straining her eyes and wearing her nerves upon intricate patterns of embroidery."[62]

To crown the tragedy, the end result of the pursuit of fashion is remorse in old age. To yield to the temptation of fashion's call in one's youth is to mount up a debt of grief that must be paid in one's later years. As a late eighteenth-century writer put the matter, those who look back and reflect upon the amount of time they have expended on fashion will experience considerable uneasiness. They will say to themselves such things as, "How much more advantageously might we have employed those hours! What a noble opportunity have we slighted for cultivating our minds!"[63] It is, of course, too late then to alter what has been done. The fashionmonger can do little other than reflect with despair upon the years of opportunity that were ignored for the sake of fashion.

May I Present—Me!

There is a decided shift in tone in the twentieth century. Nineteenth-century writers frequently saw fashion subverting individual development. Twentieth-century writers, on the other hand, see some very positive uses of fashion for self-development. They tend to stress the way in which individuals can use fashion to present themselves as they desire in order to achieve their own goals. Roach and Eicher point out that both etiquette manuals and books about the art of dress or selection of appropriate clothes, have a distinctive tone in the twentieth century: "They fall into the prescriptive category as they propose to delineate the *best* ways in which an individual can dress in order to appear handsome, beautiful (or some approximation thereof), and in order to feel socially at ease in various places and on different occasions."[64] We can add that magazine articles can be similarly described.

The college girl who said she wanted to be an individual but not a sore thumb, succinctly expressed the desires of most people. Few of us want to stand out like a sore thumb in a group, but most of us want to be recognized as individuals in our own right. Fashion can facilitate that goal of individuality. It can help each of us to present himself or herself as a distinctive individual. Lilly Dache said that the purpose of fashion was to highlight your assets, hide your faults, and show others clearly and forcefully the kind of person you really are.[65] We might question just how "clear" the picture is if one's faults are concealed and one's assets highlighted. But the main point is valid—fashion does enable the individual to present herself or himself in the particular way that individual desires.

For example, an individual may select a particular style in order to express a mood or the kind of person he or she is, or to recapture a particular experience, or to create a particular feeling. A book of advice for girls, published in 1940, told its readers to choose outfits that express one definite idea about them. The idea expressed must be "YOU," said the writer. It may be the idea that the girl is romantic, or a good athlete, or easy-going, or in love. But each outfit should convey a definite idea about the individual to others.[66] Similarly, a 1978 fashion magazine editor told readers their wardrobes had two sets of meanings. The first set involves cost, practicality, and congruence with the advice of friends and fashion magazines. The second set involves the individual's experiences with each outfit. Some clothes recall good luck. Others help us to feel certain ways. Others were worn on an occasion that was unique in some way. Look over your wardrobe, the editor advised, and make good use of that second set of meanings. Put on that nightgown that is therapeutic for you after a hard day. Of "if the thought of a party or family gathering makes you nervous, wear an outfit you have given the secret label, 'I'm terrific.' "[67]

An interesting illustration of the way in which style interacts with our sense of identity and, therefore, with the self that we present to others, is provided by a nurse who contemplated a switch to a pantsuit uniform which had been approved at her hospital. She promptly went out and purchased one on a Saturday. Sunday, she worried and debated with herself about it. Monday, she canceled the order. She decided that pantsuit uniforms were not professional enough for her. "We all have an image of ourselves which is important and that image just wasn't for me. . . . You may argue that it's not the uniform that makes the nurse and that is true, but it's how I see myself that counts."[68] The style was right for other nurses, but it did not enable her to present the image she wished. Her account shows how a particular style has diverse meanings for people, and how the meaning of a style determines whether it will be useful and desirable to an individual.

I Am Beautiful

As noted, one of the uses of fashion is to present oneself as someone who is attractive or even beautiful. This, incidentally, was one positive function of fashion that was recognized by nineteenth-century writers also. Many of them argued that fashion made people ugly rather than beautiful, but a number recognized the beautifying effect of some fashions, or at least they recognized the ability of certain fashions to conceal unattractiveness. In its own day, said the editor of *Godey's*, every fashion has been considered beautiful and has therefore captured the essence of what is agreeable to people of the time.[69] On the other hand, Mrs. Oliphant pointed out the concealing function of fashions. Whatever else fashion has been, she said, it has always had one principle of humanity in it, namely, that it is virtually always designed to help people who want and need aid— "to cover deficiencies of nature, to conceal the evils wrought by time, and to make those look their best to whom no special charms have been given."[70] Twentieth-century writers make very similar points. All female fashions, some have said, have the one purpose of covering the ugliness of the average woman. Or to put the matter in less crass terms, any woman can engage in fashion therapy on her body, for the same woman can look like three different people in three different outfits. A woman can look younger or older, lighter or heavier, depending upon the styles she wears. She can use particular styles or accessories to draw attention away from what she regards as her flaws. It is true that not all women are beautiful. But every woman can be attractive by properly manipulating her style of dress. She can learn how to shift attention away from her looks to her appearance. Or as a 1911 writer summed the matter up, to all those who feel they lack natural beauty, to those who see themselves as unattractive, "dress should come as an inspiration, a comforter, whispering confident hope of better things." No woman can be responsible for her native attractiveness or lack of attractiveness, but every woman can be responsible for the way in which she appears to the world. And every woman can be attractive by discovering and using those styles that present her as attractive.[71]

There is a good deal of what we would now call sexism in all this. Those afflicted by their appearance, wrote Margaret Gould in 1911, are a sorry lot "for woman should and would be beautiful."[72] Gould told of a woman who regarded herself as unattractive and who heard her minister pray for those who were afflicted in their minds, or bodies, or estates. The woman responded that she would not mind all of the other afflictions put together, if only she did not have to suffer an affliction in her looks. The extent to which women feel constrained to tend to their appearance is illustrated by a 1959 book of advice to wives on the matter of dress. The author, a consultant who had spoken to thousands of women at various functions, said that among the most frequently asked questions she had encountered was what the wife should wear while cleaning house! She answered the question by reminding women they should wear something they would not be ashamed to be seen in by either their husbands or an unexpected visitor and, at the same time, something that would have a positive impact on the children.[73] Traditionally, women have never been free, even while doing menial chores, from the responsibility to look attractive.

But men are not told they must look beautiful. They are not expected to worry about attractiveness while doing household chores. They are not made to feel they are continually on display. In 1955, the editor of the *New York Times* said when a woman was well dressed and about to "step upon the stage" of her social world, she was a "work of art." As such, she would be mortified to see any other woman similarly attired. It would be like Da Vinci suddenly discovering another Mona Lisa. Men, said the editor, do not face the same dilemma. The editor believed they did not face the dilemma because, unlike women, men feel uneasy if they appear in public looking different than their equals.[74] But in our view, if men have not faced the dilemma, it is simply because they have not been expected to always appear

FIG. 20. Styles vary, but in all eras, men and women dress so as to be attractive to each other. *(Source: Library of Congress.)*

as a work of art. The burden of looking beautiful has fallen heavily on the woman in America. Men are expected to look neat and are valued for attractiveness. And in some eras, as we have seen, men have spent quite as much time and energy on dressing as women. Nevertheless, there is a significant difference between being well-groomed and transforming oneself into a beautiful work of art.

At the same time, the sexism in many of the writings should not obscure the important fact that fashionable styles can be used to present oneself to others as an attractive person. Both men and women can learn to use dress to enhance themselves. This is an important function, because most, if not all, people want to be attractive to others. To know that we are attractive is to build our confidence and strengthen our egos. Attractiveness therefore is not a matter of vanity, but an integral part of personal growth and fulfillment.

I Can Lick the World

There is a good deal of evidence that we all have a need for self-esteem. In fact, some have argued that positive self-feelings are a prerequisite for mental health. Self-esteem is related to such things as acceptance of others, social influence, and interpersonal relationships. In essence, the way we feel about ourselves circumscribes the entirety of our lives. Self-esteem is related to all that we think and do and is therefore intimately linked up with the quality of our lives.

If the way we feel about ourselves is crucial to the quality of our lives, then fashion is also crucial. For many writers argue that fashionable styles contribute greatly to the development of positive self-feelings. Men and women, children and adults, all can benefit from the power of fashion. Designer Pierre Cardin told American women that fashion is a stimulant for their character, for it makes a woman "gayer, younger, more sure of her personality." A woman, he said, can both find herself and express herself through fashion and many women are transformed just in the course of trying on a new dress.[75] Lawrence Langner argued that the impact of clothing on behavior clearly shows that if we want to create a nation of self-reliant individuals who will act in accord with their personal and the national well-being, we must insure everyone an adequate income so that everyone can secure those styles that enhance morale and dignity and self-respect.[76] At least some people are convinced that the transforming power of fashion can be used to good effect on female offenders. According to a 1972 report, courses were being given in prisons throughout the nation on "self-esteem through femininity." An integral part of the course was the development of some individual styles in prison garb so the women could express their own individuality.[77]

Young people and children are in a crucial stage of development of their self-feelings. They, too, can be greatly helped by fashion. Both boys and girls are affected by the sense of being well or poorly dressed.[78] Even a five-year-old child can gain a new sense of self-confidence when provided with an outfit that tells the child he or she is competent or brave or strong or attractive.[79]

In other words, fashion builds self-confidence because it can be used to develop feelings and express qualities that underlie self-confidence. If a person wants to feel younger, fashionable clothing can help him or her achieve that aim. In 1930, an officer of an organization of clothing designers said the middle-aged and older men of his day wanted to stay young in order to remain successful in business. Furthermore, he argued, those men knew it was not the mysterious waters of Ponce de Leon that would keep them young, but the cut of their suits.[80] Styles can also be used to give people a sense of power over their environment. A book of advice for boys told them that the proper clothes would send them forth with the feeling they could lick the world, and that others would have the same impression of them.[81] A young woman said when she wore a particular pair of earrings she wasn't "afraid of the devil himself." And an observer agreed that the earrings made a difference in the young woman, giving her "an air of daring somewhat foreign to her otherwise quiet demeanor."[82]

With positive self-feelings, the individual is able to interact with others with great confidence. The individual can more fully participate in social life and can have more positive experiences of interaction. The importance of proper styles is underscored by some observations of playwright Moss Hart in his autobiography. At one point in his life he took a job as a social director at a country club. Although a sport coat and white flannel trousers were as essential to the job, he said, as was a suit of armor to one of King Arthur's knights, Hart had nothing but a blue serge suit. He felt he could not possibly fulfill his functions in such a suit. He lacked the necessary money to buy the proper clothes, however, so he finally secured an advance on his salary from his understanding employer. He wound up buying a number of different outfits and tells of the impact that it had on him:

> I staggered out of the store as a drunk might stagger into the dawn from an all-night bar, wonderfully warm inside and satisfied to the core, my thirst quenched at long last. I well knew that I had bought foolishly and wildly, that I could not afford any of it, that I did not even know how it could be paid for. But for once, none of that seemed to matter in the least, any more than tomorrow's hangover seems to bother a man at the height of a wonderful

jag; and trancelike I moved through the remaining days until we left, thinking of practically nothing but those clothes.[83]

Similarly, a female writer says she could never interact with people with a sense of equality that is important to developing friendships unless she felt properly dressed. No woman, she argued, could ever be fully happy unless she was happy with her clothes. Nothing lifts the spirits like the sense of knowing one's outfit is attractive and stylish.[84]

A variety of studies support the argument that fashionable styles enable us to participate more fully and interact with greater ease and confidence. People of every age are less likely to be self-conscious, and more likely to enter into group activities or relate with confidence to other people, when they feel appropriately and well dressed.[85] Sometimes dramatic changes can be effected in an individual through "fashion therapy." One writer told of a high school boy who was very shy, awkward, and uninterested in either the academic or social aspects of the school. He went to live with an aunt in another city. She sent him to his new school in new and different clothes. A change of schools can be traumatic for an adolescent, but in this case, the aunt recognized that the mother had slighted the boy by providing him only with hand-me-downs in order to save money for college. With his new clothes, he entered into the academic and social life of the school and eventually decided to go into law. The boy's mother was devoted to him, said the writer, "but she didn't understand that, for young people especially, clothing has an important part to play."[86]

Many people do understand the important role of dress in the confidence with which we tackle our roles in life. Articles and books throughout the twentieth century tell young people and adults as well, to attend closely to their mode of dress if they want to confront their life situations with competence and confidence. For example, one college text on clothing begins with a statement about the importance of clothes:

> Being well-dressed for the occasion, and being aware of it, is an advantage physically, psychologically, and socially. It gives a feeling of self-confidence and a sense of well-being, freeing your mind for the enjoyment of friends and intellectual pursuits. The

decisions you make about clothing choices can influence your happiness in day-to-day living during and after college.[87]

The preceding statement is an excellent summary of what a host of both popular and professional observers have said through most of the twentieth century. Fashion is a tool for personal growth and fulfillment because the fashionably dressed individual can confront the world with greater confidence and other positive self-feelings. The earthly goddess has sometimes appeared harsh in her demands, but she can reward her followers by facilitating their passage to a more fulfilling life.

CONCLUSIONS

Virtually every human creation has the potential for being either a constructive or a destructive force. The pen that informs can also be used to slander. The electrical current that illuminates our nights can also be used to thrust an offender into the night of death. Throughout this chapter, we have seen that fashion similarly can be constructive or destructive. It can enhance or detract from the quality of our lives. It can facilitate good health or be detrimental to health. It can put great financial strain upon an individual and family, or merely be another item in the budget. It can be disruptive to family life or make that life more pleasant. It can uglify and divert one from nobler pursuits, or it can be used as a tool for growth and fulfillment.

We have also noted a definite historical trend in the way people perceive the consequences. Until the time of World War I, the bulk of the writers indicate that the negative consequences outweigh the positive ones, especially in the case of women's fashions. After the war, fashion was increasingly seen as that which can enhance the quality of life. We should not fail to note that this shift coincides somewhat with the increasing independence of styles from the dominance of Paris. It also coincides with the passing of constricting and bulky styles for women. Twentieth-century observers have not seen fashion as flawless, of course. But they have seen many positive consequences of which nineteenth-century critics could only dream.

Notes

1. R. A. Buchanan, *Technology and Social Progress* (Oxford: Pergamon Press, 1965), p. 96.
2. *Ibid.*, p. 105.
3. Ellen Beard Harman, *Dress Reform: Physiological and Moral Bearings* (New York: Davies & Kent, 1862), p. 7.
4. *Ibid.*, p. 8.
5. Frances E. Russell, "Freedom in Dress for Woman," *The Arena* 8 (June, 1893): 75.
6. *Ibid.*
7. Ellen Beard Harman, *op. cit.*, p. 6.
8. Mathew Carey, *Philosophy of Common Sense* (Philadelphia: Blanchard, 1838), p. 56.
9. Emily Thornwell, *The Lady's Guide to Perfect Gentility* (Philadelphia: Lippincott, 1876), p. 116.
10. *New York Times,* August 8, 1927.
11. *New York Times,* December 9, 1928.

12. Caleb Ticknor, M.D., "Some Thoughts on Dress," *The Ladies Repository* 12 (February, 1853): 94.
13. *New York Times,* November 2, 1925.
14. *New York Times,* October 22, 1913.
15. *New York Times,* February 5, 1923.
16. *New York Times,* May 23, 1910.
17. *New York Times,* November 19, 1910 and November 20, 1910.
18. *New York Times,* April 26, 1910.
19. *New York Times,* January 13, 1911.
20. Lucy Rathbone and Elizabeth Tarpley, *Fabrics and Dress* (Boston: Houghton Mifflin, 1948), p. 4.
21. Dee Brown, *The Gentle Tamers: Women of the Old Wild West* (Lincoln: University of Nebraska Press, 1958), pp. 134–35.
22. *New York Times,* January 1, 1914.
23. "The Long-Scarf Syndrome—a New Health Hazard," *New England Journal of Medicine* 284 (April 1, 1974): 734.
24. Morris Fishbein, "O Fickle 'Perfect 36'!" *The Delineator* 109 (August, 1926): 2.
25. M. Angeline Merritt, *Dress Reform Practically and Physiologically Considered* (Buffalo: Jewett, Thomas and Co., 1852), p. 82.
26. "The Dangers of Trailing Skirts," *Current Literature* 29 (October, 1900): 433.
27. "Symposium on Women's Dress," *The Arena* 6 (October, 1892): 622.
28. *Springfield Republican,* June 6, 1851.
29. Eliza Cook, "Follies of Fashion," *The Ladies' Repository* 11 (January, 1851): 26–27.
30. See: "The Influence of Fashion," *The Ladies' Magazine and Literary Gazette* 5 (January, 1832): 10; Mathew Carey, *op. cit.*, pp. 65–6; Edmund P. Banning, M.D., *Common Sense on the Mechanical Pathology and Treatment of Chronic Diseases of the Male and Female Systems,* 14th ed. (New York: Wilson & Co., 1852), pp. 321–25; Emily Thornwell, *op. cit.*, pp. 132–37.
31. John S. Haller and Robin M. Haller, *The Physician and Sexuality in Victorian America* (Urbana: University of Illinois Press, 1974), p. 170.
32. *Ibid.*, p. 171.
33. *New York Times,* December 7, 1913.
34. *New York Times,* August 9, 1915; Eva Olney Farnsworth, *The Art & Ethics of Dress* (San Francisco: Paul Elder & Company, 1915), p. 5.
35. Bruce Douglas, "High Heels Deplored as Torture Devices," *Moneysworth,* November, 1979, p. 7.
36. *New York Times,* March 5, 1911; April 30, 1912; September 24, 1922;

December 29, 1957; *St. Louis Post-Dispatch,* January 19, 1880; Leon Goldman, "Turtleneck Shirt and Sweater Acne," *Archives of Dermatology* 113 (January, 1977): 109.
37. Gertrude Lynch, "The Ladies Game," *Everybody's Magazine* 17 (November, 1907): 635.
38. "On Fashion," *The Weekly Magazine* 4 (May 4, 1799): 97.
39. "The Influence of Fashion," *Lowell Offering* 4 (August, 1844): 229; Lucy H. Hooper, "Fig Leaves and French Dresses," *Galaxy* 18 (October, 1874): 504; "The Uglifying Process," *Every Saturday* 9 (January 29, 1870): 77; Marian Gertrude Haines, "Dame Fashion's Thumb," *The Arena* 26 (December, 1901): 624–25.
40. Margaret Woodward, "Sanity in American Fashions," *Country Side Magazine & Suburban Life* 19 (September, 1914): 153.
41. *New York Times,* October 1, 1949.
42. Bernard Roshco, *The Rag Race* (New York: Funk & Wagnalls, 1963), p. 295.
43. Hazel Rawson Cades, *Good Looks For Girls* (New York: Harcourt Brace Jovanovich, Inc., 1932), p. 145; U.S. Department of Agriculture, *Clothing Speaks . . . 4-H Members' Guide* (Washington, D.C.: U.S. Government Printing Office, 1970), p. 30.
44. *New York Times,* March 10, 1912.
45. *New York Times,* December 6, 1919.
46. Lilly Dache and Dorothy Roe Lewis, *Lilly Dache's Glamour Book* (Philadelphia: Lippincott, 1956), pp. 202–204.
47. Bernard Roshco, *op. cit.,* p. 294.
48. Thelma Thompson, "Fashion Therapy," *Journal of Home Economics* 54 (December, 1962): 835–36.
49. "Clothes and Prosperity," *Literary Digest* 101 (June 22, 1929): 59; "The Flat Look," *Time* 64 (August 9, 1954): 29; Enid Campbell Dauncey, "The Functions of Fashion," *Living Age* 269 (June 24, 1911): 792.
50. *New York Times,* October 24, 1934.
51. *New York Times,* May 18, 1931.
52. *New York Times,* February 10, 1932 and August 18, 1933.
53. *New York Times,* July 31, 1910.
54. *New York Times,* January 31, 1960.
55. *New York Times,* September 10, 1916.
56. Fred Sparks, "Rich Dressing, Insatiable Appetite," *St. Louis Post-Dispatch,* September 18, 1972.
57. "Fashion," *Boston Literary Magazine* 1 (November, 1832): 339.
58. "Dress–in a Man's Point of View," *Godey's Lady's Book* 71 (September, 1865): 264.

59. Winifred Kirkland, *The Joys of Being a Woman* (Freeport, New York: Books for Libraries Press, 1968; first published 1918), pp. 87–88.
60. "The Influence of Fashions," *The Ladies' Magazine and Literary Gazette* 5 (January, 1832): 2–3. See also "New Dress Deal," *Saturday Evening Post* 208 (April 11, 1936): 26.
61. "The Influence of Fashion," *Lowell Offering* 4 (August, 1844): 230.
62. Mrs. Sallie J. Elstner, "Fashion," *The Ladies' Repository* 16 (June, 1856): 360. See also "Fashion and the Development of Women," *The Craftsman* 25 (February, 1914): 505.
63. "On Fashion," *The Weekly Magazine* 1 (May 12, 1798): 61.
64. Mary Ellen Roach and Joanne B. Eicher, *The Visible Self: Perspectives on Dress* (Englewood Cliffs: Prentice-Hall, 1973), p. 23.
65. Lilly Dache and Dorothy Roe Lewis, *Lilly Dache's Glamour Book* (Philadelphia: Lippincott, 1956), p. 188. By permission of Harper & Row.
66. Nell Giles, *Susan, Be Smooth!* (Boston: Hale, Cushman & Flint, 1940), p. 19.
67. "Secrets from Our Clothes Closets," *Glamour* 76 (December, 1978): 58.
68. E. Brierley Carroll, "Feelings on a New Mode," *Occupational Health Nursing* 19 (January, 1971): 13.
69. "Editor's Table," *Godey's Lady's Book* 46 (April, 1853): 369.
70. Mrs. Oliphant, *Dress* (Philadelphia: Porter & Coates, 1876), p. 4.
71. Lee Simonson, "Stay, Gentle Stays!" *The New Republic* 70 (April 27, 1932): 296; Edith Head, "Fashion Therapy," *Holiday,* March, 1974, pp. 8–9; Emily Cho, "Looking Terrific," *Family Circle,* September 27, 1978, pp. 103–107; Eleanor Arnett Nash, *Beauty Is Not an Age* (New York: Harper & Brothers, 1953), p. xvii; Grace Margaret Gould, "The Afflicted in Appearance," *Woman's Home Companion* 38 (October, 1911): 38; Christian Dior, "What Fashion Tells You," *Woman's Home Companion* 80 (January, 1953): 17.
72. Grace Margaret Gould, *loc. cit.*
73. Anne Fogarty, *Wife-Dressing* (New York: Julian Messner, Inc., 1959), pp. 143–44.
74. *New York Times,* April 7, 1955.
75. *New York Times,* June 19, 1960.
76. Lawrence Langner, *The Importance of Wearing Clothes* (New York: Hastings House, 1959), p. 155.
77. Joan Cook, "Some Bright Clothes for Women Inmates," *New York Times,* April 18, 1972.
78. Mary S. Ryan, *Psychological Effects of Clothing, Part II,* Cornell University Agricultural Experiment Station, Ithaca, New York, Bulletin 898, July, 1953, p. 26.

79. Florence E. Young, *Clothing the Child* (New York: McGraw-Hill, 1938), p. 67.
80. *New York Times,* July 1, 1930.
81. Nell Giles, *Susan Tells Stephen* (Boston: Hale, Cushman & Flint, 1942), p. 45.
82. Henriette Weber, "Silk Stockings and Sedition," *The North American Review* 225 (January, 1928): 83.
83. Moss Hart, *Act One: An Autobiography* (New York: Random House, 1959), p. 178.
84. Winifred Kirkland, *op. cit.,* pp. 98–99.
85. See, for example, Mary S. Ryan, "Effect on College Girl of Feeling Well Dressed," *Journal of Home Economics* 43 (December, 1951): 799 and Marilyn J. Horn, *The Second Skin: An Interdisciplinary Study of Clothing,* 2nd ed. (Boston: Houghton Mifflin, 1975), pp. 84–87.
86. Frances Frisbie O'Donnell, "The Adolescent and His Clothes," *Parents' Magazine* 6 (April, 1931): 21.
87. Mabel D. Erwin and Lila A. Kinchen, *Clothing for Moderns,* 3rd ed. (New York: Macmillan, 1964), p. 1.

PART  | # A THEORY OF FASHION

chapter 7

Fashion, Ideology, and Change

An Englishman who walked down the streets of London in the 1980s would hardly attract attention merely because he carried an umbrella. But the man who first introduced the umbrella to England was greeted with both rocks and insults when he first appeared publicly with the innovation. One generation's outrage is another generation's convention. But why should an umbrella elicit such a response? For that matter, why have people reacted with such intensity to any number of other new styles, such as pants on women, short skirts, or long hair or purses for men? To answer the quesion, we must explore two final topics: the relationships between social change and fashion, and the role of ideology in fashion. We will then have established the necessary foundation for presenting our theory of fashion.

FASHION AND CHANGE

We have already noted the linkage between social change and fashion. First, the changing styles appear to reflect the spirit of each age. Second, particular kinds of change, such as technological developments, altered values, and wars, are associated with the emergence of particular new styles. But the linkage is more complex. Fashion does more than merely reflect the spirit of the age. According to various observers, fashion helps legitimate the spirit of the age, and it both legitimates and helps perpetuate various kinds of change. Furthermore, fashion can be used to bring about change. In other words, fashion does not merely mirror change, but also creates and helps to seal the changes that have occurred.

The Seal of Fashion

It seems, said a 1929 writer, to be a "human necessity to signalize a change of heart by a change in dress."[1] We would not put the phenomenon into the category of "human necessity," but the writer had a valid insight, for basic social changes are often sealed by a change of fashion. In particular, a new fashion may be used to seal a changed role. We use the word "seal" here to express the twofold function of fashion of both legitimating and perpetuating the change. That is, the new fashion says the changed role has become socially acceptable and that the new role will remain acceptable as long as the fashion (or a subsequent, congruous fashion) continues.

The seal of fashion upon a changed role has been noted by a number of writers with respect to women's fashions. As we indicated in various places, observers have declared certain changes in women's styles to represent a *fait accompli* with respect to a new female role. The role change has occurred and the new fashion means the change is irreversible. As woman's role expanded, women's fashions became increasingly less restrictive. And sometimes women would opt for a style that seemed not merely to confirm a new role but to scorn all tradition. Thus, a 1914 writer said the "transparency" of women's clothes in her day was a "revolutionary sign," a "manifestation of the feminist movement," an indication that woman had become "a law unto herself."[2] A 1972 article noted that a New York men's boutique had as many women as men customers within six months after it had opened. As a result of the liberation movement, said the writer, women were going into what had previously been all-male "strongholds," and were "taking over men's clothes."[3]

It is not only women's styles, of course, that mirror and seal a role change. In a noted study on the disappearance of knickers on boys in America, Bush and London hypothesized that a basic change in a mode of dress indicates a change in a social role and in the self-concepts of the individuals involved.[4] They pointed out that early in the twentieth century prepubescent boys in grammar school typically wore knickers, while adolescent boys—those who had reached puberty—generally wore long pants. This pattern was especially typical for middle-class urban dwellers. By the mid-1930s, the younger boys were increasingly wearing long pants rather than knickers, and by the early 1940s the knickers had disappeared. The authors suggested that the disappearance of the knickers was associated with an altered role for the prepubescent boy. There had been a growing acceptance of the emotional needs of such boys. They were no longer treated in accord with Victorian notions that they were merely small adults who should be seen and not heard until they had passed through their awkward transition to full adulthood. The boys became individuals in their own right, with needs and responsibilities peculiar to their stage of development. And they received a new style of dress that both reflected and sealed their expanded role.

Fashion can act as a seal upon a changed role both because of the way in which clothing functions as a form of nonverbal communication, and because of the impact of dress upon the wearer. With respect to the former, as people who engaged in a new pattern of behavior adopt a new style of dress, the behavior and the clothes become identified with each other. We expect an individual who has adopted the new style to also exhibit the new behavior. The style, in other words, is an ongoing message to observers that the wearer has discarded the old role for the new one. With respect to the impact on the wearer, we have seen that a new style can have a dramatic impact on the attitudes and behavior of an individual. Once a particular style has become associated with a particular pattern of behavior, the individual who adopts the style will likely adopt the behavior as well. An interesting illustration of this phenomenon is the report of a psychologist who headed a school for disturbed adolescent girls. The worst days at the school, said the psychologist, were those of heavy snow, for the girls would have to wear slacks and there would be a number of fights: "When they dress in a way that gives them greater freedom . . . in a somewhat masculine way, they are going to act up. But no girl particularly wants to act up when her hair is well done, when she has had a manicure, when she's made up."[5]

For those who might still be skeptical about the sealing function of fashion, we will note some expressions of concern that certain gains might be lost by the styles that followed those associated with the gains. For instance, a 1929 writer looked at the trend back to longer skirts and smaller waists with considerable apprehension. It might be, the writer speculated, some sort of reversion to the Gibson girl styles and "the question seems to be whether, with the garb of the new freedom out of style, the new freedom itself will still remain."[6]

A similar concern has been voiced by many people at different times. A 1979 writer contrasted "feminism" and "femininity" in the light of women's fashions. Many feminists, she pointed out, thought they were getting rid of femininity in fashion during the 1970s. "Tough Chic" and masculine styles were the haute couture of the feminist vanguard, and some women of a milder ideological commitment followed suit. But, argued the writer, by 1979 the distinction between feminism and femininity was getting blurred. For women had experienced a new sense of equality and security and they wanted to be feminine again. "Women want to be women again but—and this is the point—they don't want to sacrifice feminist victories. It is the classic dilemma of wanting to have your cake and eat it, too."[7] Thus, the question raised in chapter 1 of whether a woman can live a liberated life in a lace blouse continues to perplex some Americans. If we revert back to traditional styles, will we also revert back to traditional roles? Fashion's function as a seal of change is more like a temporary permit than a lifetime guarantee. For fashion changes continually. And the styles that seal a particular change will be superseded by styles that may threaten that change.

Fashion as a Tool of Change

Fashion can be used to create as well as to reflect and seal change. Sometimes, in fact, it is difficult to know which came first, the style or the altered role. Clearly, women have used new styles in an effort to bring about a change in the female role. They have used styles as a tool in addition to accepting styles as a seal. On writer asserted that the "masculinized" styles following World War I were an effort by women to keep what they had gained during the war and to expand their role to one of greater equality. Women minimized the difference in appearance between the sexes in order to "compete with men as a man."[8]

Feminists in the 1960s and 1970s also used dress as a tool of change. Joan Cassell, an anthropologist, did a field study in the early 1970s in which she investigated, among other things, the role of clothing styles among feminists.[9] She found that feminists used "symbolic inversion, where forms are changed or assigned opposite meanings" in order to bring about change. In the case of the feminists she studied, there was an inversion of conventional middle-class demeanor and dress. Lesbian-feminists, the most radical of the various groups, were also the most actively engaged in inversion. They usually wore blue jeans or baggy, workmen's denim overalls, a male t-shirt or workshirt, and no bra. The rest of their appearance reinforced this obvious break with conventional female attire:

> Their hair is not so much styled as *there;* they wear no makeup; steel-rimmed reading glasses or sunglasses are frequent; footgear is comfortable, with a predominance of men's workboots or sneakers; and jewelry is rare, with the exception of political buttons or women's liberation pendants. Associated with this costume is a recognizable deportment and bearing—a freedom of walk, of stance, of language.[10]

The lesbian-feminists used a style of dress in an effort to bring about certain changes they desired.

Lesbian-feminists have not achieved all, perhaps most, of the changes they desired. The fact that one uses fashion as a tool of change does not mean that one always succeeds. Sometimes the effort may be a total failure. Sometimes only small gains may be made where large ones were anticipated. And sometimes changing fashions can help bring about considerable change in a society, as illustrated by the Amana Society in Iowa in the first half of the twentieth century.[11] The Society was formed by German immigrants in the nineteenth century. They were religious refugees who believed in a somewhat spartan, devout way of life. Charles Nordhoff, who visited and wrote about many of the communitarian groups in the nineteenth century, described the dress of the people as plain. Females, he observed, wore "dingy colored stuffs, mostly of the society's own make, cut in the plainest style, and often short gowns, in the German peasant way."[12] They also all wore a black cap, tied under the chin by a ribbon, and a dark-colored shawl draped over the shoulders and "pinned very plainly across the breast." The men were also plainly dressed.

In the first quarter of the twentieth century, there was considerable discontent with the rigid and austere way of life in the community. The people were exposed to the new ideas and the technological developments of a changing American society. Many of them wanted to participate in the larger society. One of the first things to change as people acquired new attitudes was clothing styles, particularly among some of the younger members. At first, the change was minor. A young woman might wear a piece of jewelry or a watch or adopt a lace collar. The religious leaders opposed the new styles and condemned some of them. But the break with tradition in the realm of dress styles facilitated changes in other areas of community life. By 1932, the Society changed its status from that of a communal religious group to a capitalistic corporation in which church and state would be separate for the first time among the people. Fashion was used as a tool of change and ultimately the people created a new social order. They did not cease being religious, but they were radically different from their forebears, for the change to a corporation involved a social as well as an economic transformation.

FASHION AND IDEOLOGY

"Ideology" is a term which has been used in diverse, sometimes contradictory, sometimes ambiguous ways. Here we will use the term simply to refer to a set of normative ideas about some phenomenon. As such, an ideology explains the phenomenon and indicates appropriate attitudes and behavior with respect to that phenomenon and, perhaps, to other phenomena. We have already illustrated our use of ideology in discussing the nature of males and females. The ideology explained the nature of the sexes, indicated the appropriate attitudes and behavior *for* each sex, and also suggested appropriate attitudes and behavior *towards* each sex.

We believe that fashion is invariably tied up with ideologies as well as with change. In some cases, the ideological nature of fashion is obvious. The lesbian-feminists discussed earlier were clearly guided by their ideology in their selection of clothing styles. Various communitarian groups in the nineteenth and twentieth centuries have also expressed something of their ideology through their mode of dress. The early Amana Society believed in simplicity and equality (at least, they believed that all members of each sex were equal to other members of the same sex). The religious ideology of the society stressed obedience to God and to the Elders of the community. And both God and the Elders had declared that self-indulgence, extravagance, or any kind of ornateness were reprehensible. Thus, the plain dress was both consistent with, and an expression of, the value on simplicity. Furthermore, women tended to dress very much alike. Nordhoff, in fact, said there was a "singularly monotonous appearance" to the women of Amana. But that monotony was consistent with, and an expression of, their ideology of equality.

Various other communitarian groups also used a style of dress to express some facet of their ideology. The community formed at Oneida, New York in 1848 was based upon "Bible communism." John Humphrey Noyes, the founder, insisted that Christianity was opposed to any kind of private property. The members of his community owned nothing in the way of any private possession. Even the clothes they wore belonged to the community instead of to the individual. Furthermore, communism meant equality of all members, including equality between the sexes. Women were free to choose their own mode of dress, and since they worked side by side with men at a variety of tasks, they needed a freedom of movement that women in the society at large did not have. In the first summer of the community's existence, the women decided to dress themselves in short gowns and pantaloons, the typical fashion for children. When a very similar costume was advocated in the larger society in 1851, the opposition became fierce. But the Oneida style was congruous with the ideology. As the First Annual Report said: "The women say they are far more free and comfortable in this dress than in long gowns; the men think that it improves their looks; and some insist that it is entirely more modest than the common dress."[14]

The relationship between the ideology and the fashions of a group may not always be as obvious as these examples. The ideology may not so much dictate a particular style as to provide guidelines for evaluating various styles. But every change of fashion must be ideologically acceptable. A new fashion must not appear to flaunt the current ideology about the nature of men or women, or the duties of citizens, or the nature of society. This is not to say that everyone in the society must approve the new style. There are contradictory ideologies in every society. But if a fashion is to be acceptable, it must be perceived to be congruent with the dominant ideology of the society (or of the group in the case of a style that characterizes a minority). The significance of ideology is well illustrated by the nineteenth-century controversy over the Bloomer costume.

A CASE STUDY: THE BLOOMER COSTUME

As we noted earlier, the need for reform in female clothing had been proclaimed since at least the end of the eighteenth century. Both American and foreign observers had warned about the hazards of tight lacings, heavy petticoats, dirty-gathering long skirts, and tight garters. In a speech before the New England Woman's Club, one reformer summed up well the "criminal" nature of women's dress in the nineteenth century:

> . . . when I see women's skirts, the shortest of them, lying (when they sit down) inches deep along the foul floors, which man . . . had inundated with tobacco juice, and from which she sweeps up and carries to her home the germs of stealthy pestilences; when I see a ruddy, romping school-girl, in her first long dress . . . afraid of the stone walls in the blueberry fields, or standing aloof from the game of ball, or turning sadly away from the ladder which her brother is climbing to the cherry tree . . . ; when I read of the sinking steamers at sea, with nearly all the women and children on board, and the accompanying comments, "Every effort was made to assist the women . . . but they could not climb, and we were forced to leave them to their fate;". . . when I consider these things, I feel that I have ceased to deal with blunders in dress and have entered the category of crime.[15]

The effort to find an alternative mode of dress had considerable support on practical, medical, and, some would add, aesthetic

FIG. 21. Mrs. Amelia Jenks Bloomer in the costume that bears her name. *(Source: An anonymous engraving.)*

grounds. In 1851, a costume appeared that seemed to some to provide the desired alternative—the so-called Bloomer costume. The Bloomer was similar to the styles that had been adopted in some of the communitarian groups. But in 1851, it was advocated for the first time as a fashion for the entire society. It was named after the feminist editor, Amelia Bloomer, who adopted it and began publicizing it in her magazine, *The Lily*. Mrs. Bloomer, however, had only followed the lead of a cousin of Elizabeth Cady Stanton, Elizabeth Smith, who had designed the costume for her honeymoon in 1850. Because Mrs. Bloomer promoted the costume through her magazine, her name became irretrievably attached to it.

By later standards, the full trousers gathered at the ankles and the short overskirt would not be considered the ultimate in comfort or practicality. But the Bloomer was undeniably an enormous improvement over the existing styles. By later standards, the costume would also be considered extremely conservative and modest. But when it was offered to the public in 1851, it created an incredible stir. A later generation would accept the Bloomer easily. In the 1850s, the nation seemed to be turned on its head by the costume. Newspaper editors said American society stood "on the eve of a great revolution," a revolution which, they predicted, might eventually be seen as our "second declaration of independence."[16] The rebellion had been set in motion by a small revolutionary vanguard "much after the style of the first drops of an advancing shower" until it seemed likely to encompass the entire nation.[17] It promised to be a "thorough" revolution, declared one editor, for "only those with large feet and badly turned ankles will venture to resist the onward march of destiny, and even they will come up to the march eventually."[18]

The intense interest created by the Bloomer was nationwide. From Maine to Texas, from the Atlantic to the Mississippi, the question of female dress dominated people's conversations, creating "a most furious excitement among old and young ladies, bachelors and married men" and "outstripping interest in all other matters."[19] Newspapers headlined the Bloomer. It seemed there was scarcely a paper in the country which did not have something to say about the new costume.[20] Editors eagerly reported the appearance of a Bloomer in their towns or, if this was not yet the case, encouraged local ladies to don the new dress.[21] In addition, the papers were filled with news of Bloomer activities: Bloomers at church, on picnics, at Fourth of July celebrations; Bloomer balls, theatrical presentations; Bloomer melodies, waltzes, and polkas.[22]

As with every new or proposed fashion, the Bloomer was evaluated. From the beginning of its appearance, there were some negative reactions, but it was vigorously supported by a number of people. Feminists supported it on the grounds of health and practicality. Mrs. Bloomer herself responded to a critical sermon by a Rev. Dr. Talmage with a lengthy defense, arguing there was no reason for women to burden themselves with debilitating clothing while men had styles that gave "freedom of limb and motion." Radical reform in the realm of women's fashions was needed, asserted Mrs. Bloomer, so a woman might become the "free, healthy being God made her instead of the corseted, crippled, dragged-down creature her slavery to clothes had made her."[23]

The new costume also received support from some of the nation's newspaper editors. A Maine editor said he was impressed by the "neatness, elegance and modesty of the dress" and he urged that women adopt it on the grounds of health, good citizenship, and convenience.[24] Many of those who had supported dress reform for health reasons agreed that the Bloomer provided the answer. They said the lack of laces, stays, and whale bones in the Bloomer would result in an immediate improvement in the health of American women. Our women would finally be able to walk around conveniently and pleasantly. And healthier women would be more productive workers and would spend less in medicine and the services of physicians. Consequently, the adoption of the Bloomer would "do more for the national wealth than the mines of California, and more for the national health than all the discoveries of medicine since Galen."[25]

In addition to its impact on health, the Bloomer was promoted on moral grounds by some. A group of women met in Milford, Massachusetts in July, 1851 to consider the propriety of adopting the Bloomer. It was, said the reporter, a gathering of "very intelligent appearing, lady-like women . . . who seemed to feel that they had come together for a very serious and worthy purpose." The women unanimously passed a resolution approving the Bloomer, declaring the existing fashions to be "moral evils," and arguing that the Bloomer would facilitate women's efforts to engage in good works.[26]

A third reason given for supporting the Bloomer involved patriotism. Adopting the costume, said some, was the American thing to do. The *Madison Press* of Iowa pointed out that many women had already begun wearing the Bloomer in June, 1851, and the editor hoped it would not be long before "the peerless beauties of Madison" adopted the new dress. For, he said, the Bloomer reflected "the American standard of taste, economy, utility, and comfort, adopted to the habits and peculiarities of American society."[27] In similar fashion, a St. Louis editor told his readers the Bloomer was "better suited to American wants, American tastes and American independence."[28] And in response to the charge that the trousers in the costume were foreign in origin, a Massachusetts editor said the Bloomer was not "Turkish, nor Persian, but American; the outgrowth of our own wants, the product of our skill, and the sign of our independence."[29] Such arguments provided powerful support for the Bloomer in the context of the desire for the Americanization of fashion that we discussed in chapter 6.

A few people supported the Bloomer simply because they liked the way it looked. The outfit, they decided, was attractive and it enhanced a woman's appearance. In Columbus, Ohio, a judge's wife appeared publicly in her Bloomer in June, 1851, creating "quite a sensation." But it was sensational approval that she generated: ". . . beautiful! becoming! graceful! charming! were whispered from one to another, as with approving smiles they gazed until the dark skirt and white trowsers were lost in the distance."[30]

Finally, a number of people urged that the Bloomer be adopted on the grounds that it was a practical and convenient mode of dress. The current fashion, as many noted, restricted a woman's freedom. How could a woman move freely when she wore twenty pounds of petticoat which "threatened to twist themselves between her limbs and bring her to the ground in a lump?"[31] How could women so cumbersomely dressed manage their households efficiently? It was difficult enough walking up and down stairs, and nearly impossible if one carried anything. According to the noted feminist, Elizabeth Cady Stanton, it was just for this reason that she began wearing the Bloomer. When she saw her cousin, Elizabeth Smith, walking up some stairs "with ease and grace" while holding a lamp in one hand and a baby in the other, she promptly adopted the costume for herself. For she realized that when she ascended stairs while dressed fashionably, she had to pull herself up with difficulty, "lamp and baby out of question. . . . The drapery is quite too much—one might as well work with a ball and chain."[32] We have seen that women could not engage in sports, outside work, or professions in the fashionable dress of the times. Ironically, they could barely function in the home that was supposed to be their domain of concern. In 1865, a woman who still wore the costume responded to the question of why she persisted with it by pointing out that she could do very little work if she dressed in the fashions of the day. She could not even attend to her flower pots or garden: "Any practiced horticulturist will tell you that you would do about as much injury to his tender buds and springing plants, as a flock of sheep, were they allowed to promenade through his favorite grounds."[33]

In spite of such support and the strong arguments in favor of the new costume, the Bloomer effort faded quickly. By the end of 1851, only a few women continued to wear it. With the general rejection of the costume, the struggle for healthy and practical dress would continue for more than another half century before the goal would be realized. Why did this effort at change fail? Why didn't the Bloomer become the fashion? With fairly widespread recognition of the need for a different costume, why was the Bloomer rejected? Why did the opposition swell quickly from a murmur to a roar of outrage?

Just as there were a number of reasons given for adopting the Bloomer, there were diverse reasons given for rejecting it. A favorite explanation of contemporaries for the rapid failure of the costume was that it was "bad fashion," unattractive and inappropriate for the women of the Republic. Opponents referred to it as "the tadpole," as "half-Turkish, half-Yankee, with a little touch of the circus," and as various other things that showed their contempt.[34] They pointed out that the Bloomer was one of those styles that uglified rather than beautified. It might be appropriate for young girls, but it was unbecoming to mature women. It magnified large feet and was unflattering to short women, and one of the functions of fashion is to cover defects in beauty. Consequently, said the editor of the *Boston Post*, the Bloomer will never be accepted. It would have been an immediate success "if all, or the major part, of our fashionable women had tall figures and small feet and a handsome walk." But since most could not be described in such terms, the Bloomer had no chance of success from the start.[35]

Aesthetic considerations have seldom been decisive in any new style. There are always some who say the style is attractive and some who define it as repulsive. A more important consideration in the rejection of the Bloomer is the way in which the opponents defined it as incongruous with the prevailing ideology about women. The contradiction between that ideology and certain reactions to women who wore Bloomers in public was used to create considerable public opinion against the new costume. The Bloomer was attacked as contrary to the female role, and certain reactions to the public appearance of Bloomers buttressed the attack.

Because of the reaction of some men to the costume, women who wore Bloomers in public were suddenly removed from their God-ordained domestic setting and thrust into the light of public scrutiny and debate. Women were causing a sensation in cities throughout the country. An Arkansas editor said the costume was spreading throughout the nation "like wildfire," and that everywhere a Bloomer appeared she created "the most furious excitement."[36] In Milwaukee, it was said that the presence of Bloomers created "a more excited appearance than an election, riot, or holiday."[37] In Washington, D.C., the news that several Bloomers would make an appearance at a band concert produced throngs of people—more than had ever appeared at a band concert before and, for that matter, more than usually attended the inauguration of a President.[38] A New Hampshire newspaper came out one day with the following announcement: "As our paper is going to press, we suspend operations to announce the appearance in our streets this afternoon of a young lady clad in the Turkish costume."[39] And in Bangor, Maine, it was reported that two young ladies in Bloomers had to go home alone after a party "because the young men in attendance had resolved to discountenance the improved style of dress, and not to wait upon anyone who wore it."[40]

Clearly, whenever a Bloomer ventured out she created quite a stir. Crowds sometimes gathered about her and she might be forced to take refuge in a building until the crowd dispersed. Worse, the crowds often became derisive and hostile. In Lowell, Massachusetts, it was reported that several Bloomers "were insulted and hooted at by a parcel of boys and graceless fellows."[41] In New York City, a couple of Bloomers out for a walk soon found themselves accompanied by "a curious crowd of men and boys who indulged in audible criticism of the new costume." The mob increased in size and rudeness until the police finally interfered and broke it up.[42] Public harassment was so common and so severe that a group of women in New York made a passionate, written appeal for help. After pointing out the unhealthy nature of contemporary fashions and the harassment endured by those who adopted the Bloomer costume, the women insisted on their rights:

> We wish now to understand whether we have a civil and political right to wear a decent and healthy dress, and whether we are to be protected in the exercise of this right, or whether the New York public is a mob by majority? . . . We assert, humbly, yet *firmly,* that we wear the improved dress in obedience to conscience

> and the dictates of common sense, and that we are not only willing to live for the principle of freedom, for which our fathers bled and died, but to *die for it also,* if need be. . . . We ask help from our brothers, because we are suffering for freedom, for God, and the right![43]

We should keep in mind, incidentally, that although the public harassment came from men, the issue was not merely one of male versus female. Some observers said the greatest—though not necessarily the most overtly abusive—opposition came from other women.[44]

In the light of such public humiliation, it is not surprising that genteel women relegated their Bloomers to the attics in a few short months or avoided wearing the dress altogether. No woman wanted to create a public sensation or become the butt of public jokes or the object of public ridicule. "The great bugbear in the way of adopting the short dress in the minds of sober-minded, modest women," wrote a correspondent to an Ohio newspaper, "is the dislike of notoriety. To be the subject of newspaper comment and street remark . . . deter most women from the movement. . . . To attempt to storm the fortress of public opinion is not womanly or becoming and savors of fanaticism."[45] Any other position would have been contrary to the prevailing view of the modest, gentle American woman whose place was in her home, not in creating a sensation in the streets. In her 1856 plea for a national costume, Mary Fry argued that reform required something "widely different from notoriety for its accomplishment; we had enough of that in Bloomerism, which was simply a ridiculous affair, and has about died the death of all ridiculous things."[46] Women in the nineteenth century generally agreed that public notoriety had no place in the life of a proper woman. The fact that the wearers were not the ones creating the public stir made no difference. The Bloomer and the notoriety appeared together. The costume was guilty by association.

Some women, of course, did not agree that women, like children, should be seen but not heard. They did not accept the notion that woman's only proper sphere of authority was the home. But many of them decided that the sanctions against wearing the new costume were too severe to justify its continued use. Elizabeth Cady Stanton was one who concluded that the sanctions had sealed the fate of the costume:

Such is the tyranny of custom . . . that to escape constant observation, criticism, ridicule, and persecution, one after another gladly went back to the old slavery, and sacrificed freedom of movement to repose. I have never wondered since that the Chinese women allow their daughters' feet to be encased in iron shoes, nor that the Hindoo widows walk calmly to the funeral pyre.[47]

For many observers, the nature of the public response not only meant that women were thrust into an untoward role, but also that women's responsibility as the keeper of the nation's morals was being compromised. The more enthusiastic the public became about the Bloomer, the harder it was to discount the notion that the enthusiasm hinted of lewdness and indecency. Instead of taming men's passions, the Bloomer seemed to arouse them. For example, male attention often centered more on the Bloomer's exposure of female ankles than on its other, less erotic, benefits. One editor noted that wearers of the dress had quickly gained a great deal of attention from young men and that, overall, "the ladies *had showed well.*"[48] Another editor, when asked whether he was for or against the reform, said that since he did not have much time with the ladies "he wished during those brief opportunities *to see as much of them as he could* with propriety, and therefore he was decidedly a short dress man."[49] And still another editor described his reaction to a Bloomer who dropped into his office in this way: "Our heart accompanied our eyes as they wandered over the enchanting realms of neatly plaited bosom . . . to the full-flowing trousers from their uppermost swell down to the ankle."[50] Clearly, men who had been accustomed to seeing women draped in yards of cloth found the Bloomer to be an erotic change of pace. Unfortunately for the advocates, eroticism in clothing was viewed with moral horror in 1851.

The charge that the Bloomer might be detrimental to the nation's morals was furthered by excesses which were increasingly associated with the dress. In Springfield, Illinois, several young women appeared publicly in their fathers' clothes out of impatience "in not getting their Bloomers done."[51] Worse yet, another lady, wearing the new style, "attracted a throng of anxious spectators," for "a very essential part of the Bloomagainiture, namely, the pantalettes, had been omitted."[52] Public spectacles of this sort did nothing to enhance the reputation of the Bloomer or of those who wore it.

In addition, there appeared to be good evidence that certain unsavory individuals were adopting the costume. The papers carried stories of courtesans dressed in the new attire parading the streets and causing considerable commotion. A story in the *New York Times* is typical of numerous incidents. The paper said two Bloomers paraded Broadway, where they "unblushingly" stopped gentlemen, some of whom were accompanied by their wives, and committed "indecorous acts" which were witnessed by several hundred people, "many of whom appeared to enjoy the scene." The police were called to quiet the disorder and were forced to arrest the two Bloomers.[53]

As a result of the various reactions and incidents, denunciations of the costume on the grounds that it was corrupting the public morals were increasingly made and listened to. Women were reminded of their redemptive role in society and were urged to be above reproach in their dress. A virtuous woman, said one editor, should be graceful to the eye as well as to the heart, so the selection of "a tasteful, proper dress' is not a trivial matter.[54] The Bloomer, according to numerous observers, did not constitute a "proper" dress. Some warned that the costume was the first step on the road to moral degeneracy. Others said those who proposed its adoption in the name of progress were really advocating a progress that "tends to barbarism." Were the citizens of "civilized and Christianized America to go to the heathen, semi-civilized or savage nations for models in dress and manners?"[55] Morality demanded a negative response.

In addition to the immorality of the costume, there was a suspicion among many people that it was "un-American" if not downright seditious. The charge that the dress was "a la Turk" and not vintage America troubled many. Proponents' insistence that the Bloomer was truly American could not overcome the many voices that agreed on the Turkish origin. And if the costume came from Turkey, as one editor put it, it was only fit for Asians. For the dress of Asians is like their character— "intended to excite the dalliance of the hour— no fitting example for the women of America."[56] As the preservers of the Republic, American women could not adopt a mode of dress that would undermine the nation's greatness.

There was another aspect to the charge that the Bloomer would be a destructive force in American society. Opponents of the costume frequently pointed out the close relationship between Bloomers and the women's movement. Indeed, feminists were increasingly active in promoting the new attire. And feminists, most Americans believed, were trying to scrap the traditions of a great society and to create some bizarre new social order that contravened the laws of God and the principles of Americanism. "The Bloomer Costume," one of many songs composed about the dress, illustrates the way in which the Bloomer was linked with the subversive women's movement. The song was first presented to the public in Georgetown, D.C., in June, 1851:

> The "women" advocating, "rights"
>   In Northern State Conventions,
> And basking in the newest lights
>   Flashed from their own dissension.
> Determined that they would man-tain
>   (And this is not a rumor)
> The privilege to swing a cane
>   And—dress like Mrs. Bloomer!
>
> O, dishcloth, pots and pewter spoons,
>   Soapsuds and greasy dishes,
> O! the devil take the one who, first
>   Invented Turkish trousers.
>
> Indeed young ladies we dissent
>   From this strange innovation,
> Lest we, the rude sex, may lament
>   O'er our own degradation.
> When we see women dabling in
>   What our regular trade is;
> I 'spose the men must stay at home
>   A dandling little babies!
>
> O, dishcloth, pots and pewter spoons . . . etc.
>
> The women then would strut about,
>   Nor once consult our wishes;
> While we at home would have to stay
>   —And wash the greasy dishes!
> Or darn the stocking, patch and cook,
>   Else in canal they'd souse us—

> Oh! devil take the one who, first
> Invented Turkish trousers.
> O, dishcloth, pots and pewter spoons . . . etc.[57]

Some contemporaries went beyond such things as caustic lyrics and engaged in vigorous denunciations. They argued that the woman's movement was intimately bound up with all of the radical and infidel tendencies of the day. If a woman accepted a costume advocated by those in the movement, she was contributing to the nation's destruction. A professor William Nevin wrote an article for a woman's magazine in which he advised potential Bloomers that the costume was only one indication of the "wild spirit of socialism or agrarian radicalism which is at present so rife in our land." To the degree that the radicals were successful in "destroying natural distinctions of character and sex between us," he wrote, to the same degree they would succeed "in destroying all moral government and civilization."[58]

Professor Nevin's indictment struck at the heart of the matter, for the fear that the Bloomer would obliterate all distinctions between the sexes was a primary motive of the opponents. An increasing number of people agreed on two points; that the Bloomer broke down the male-female distinction, and that this breakdown contradicted American values and God's laws. Without a doubt, said one writer, a woman unsexed herself when she put on "trousers and a sack." The Bloomer was literally turning "all the women into men."[59] The masculinization of American women was illustrated by one correspondent of the *Boston Transcript* who had observed that when women wore a Bloomer "they can perch their feet about on highback chairs, railings, mantel pieces and window sills without hindrance—in short, they can sprawl their pedal extremities about promiscuously, miscellaneously, masculinally and generally."[60] Women in Bloomers, therefore, were attempting to be equal to men in every respect. And that was an affront to the God who had declared that each sex had certain attributes, certain spheres of action, and even distinct styles of dress. One editor reminded his readers that the Bible stated that the woman who wore "that which pertainth unto a man" was an "abomination to the Lord."[61] How could any man respect such a woman? As the editor of the *New York Tribune* put the matter: "We are sure it would do much to unhinge our reverence for the best of mothers and stifle our affection . . . for the most amiable wives, should we ever see this heathenish caricature of masculinity associated with their sacred persons."[62]

The problem, as contemporary observers saw it, was not merely that women wanted to adopt male attire and mannerisms but that they wanted to share male prerogatives. Bloomerism, it was cautioned, was just the initial stage in the demand for women's rights—demands which would take women out of the home and into politics and public debate. An Ohio editor, who had initially supported the Bloomer reform, came to the conclusion that the women's movement had gotten out of hand. Alarming symptoms of change were beginning to appear. The symptoms were not of great significance by themselves, but when combined, they took on considerable importance. Last night's mail, the editor noted, had furnished two good illustrations of the alarming symptoms. One item reported that the ladies of Pendleton, South Carolina were forming a military organization and would soon apply to the governor "to furnish them with light carbines for use upon horseback—astride, we dare say." The other notice told of Fanny Lee Townsend who had attended a Camp Meeting in Danville. She "talked down the preacher, and finally drew off the biggest part of his congregation, mounted a stump, upset the minister's tenets completely, and swayed the crowd to and fro with her eloquence."[63] Such things were but the prelude, the editor feared; worse would follow if the trend was not reversed.

Women denied the charges and tried to calm the fears. In 1856, a group of reformers passed a series of resolutions, one of which stated: "Resolved, That in addressing Reform in Dress for Woman, our object is not to advocate for her positions of singularity, eccentricity, immodesty, or to get her out of her 'appropriate sphere,' but to enable her to act with that freedom needful to find out what her 'appropriate sphere' is."[64] The resolution was typical of the kind of disclaimers that were made from the first. But they were to no avail. The opponents were more convincing. Furthermore, the opponents played upon some deep-seated fears of Americans. For the nation was undergoing tremendous economic and social change in the years between 1830 and 1860. The peaceful home, guarded over by a virtuous woman, provided an alternative to a society that many saw as "bent on disaster." Woman was the "antidote to a world gone mad with change, acquisitiveness, and individualism."[65] What could it be except disastrous if women donned male apparel, became public brawlers, and dabbled "in the filth and slop of party politics?"[66]

To sum up, the prevailing ideology about women was combined with reactions to the public appearance of women in Bloomers to turn public opinion against the new costume. The combined weight of the mass media and public opinion, buttressed by an ideological evaluation, rendered the reformers ineffective. Even many who had advocated a change in the fashions were unwilling to accept the Bloomer as the answer. One elderly doctor said that frugality, good sense, convenience, and good health all dictated that women's dress should be reformed, but he did not like "the exaggerated and ridiculous caricatures exhibited on the stage and in our shop-windows" known as the Bloomer costume. Sensible women, he declared, would not wear it.[67] But the failure of the Bloomer in the 1850s was not the outcome of women using their good sense. It was, rather, the result of an ideological evaluation, supported by public incidents, that made the wearing of the Bloomer unpatriotic, immoral, and revolutionary.

THE FUNCTION OF IDEOLOGIES IN FASHION CHANGE

Ideology affects social change in a number of ways. Among other things, ideologies are used by the proponents of change to explain and validate the change they advocate and to motivate people to act in bhealf of the change.[68] Opponents of the change will use a counter ideology for the same purposes. In the case of the Bloomer controversy, the ideologies used by proponents and opponents had three functions: to explain and legitimate, to motivate, and to address the real-ideal gap.

First, ideologies were used to interpret the change effort and to either legitimate the new costume (proponents) or legitimate acts of suppression (opponents). Proponents employed an ideology of egalitarianism. Women, they said, had as much right to health, comfort, and extra-domestic activities as men. Opponents, on the other hand, clearly saw that the Bloomer represented a subversion of the natural order of the sexes and that acts of suppression were both inevitable and necessary. As the editor of the *New York Times* summed up the matter, American women were "bent on appropriating more than their fair share of Constitutional privileges," and "anti-masculine agitation must be stayed by some means."[69] If the proponent's ideology explained social reality in a way that legitimated the change, the opponent's ideology explained the change in a way that legitimated suppression.

Second, the ideologies used "glow words" to motivate people. Theodore Abel pointed out a long time ago that an adequate ideology must appeal to some ideal and that the ideology must express the ideal "in terms of current glow words, that is, ideas that carry a strong and prevalent emotional tone."[70] In the Nazi movement in Germany, for example, terms such as "nationalism," "socialism," and "racial superiority" were all emotionally charged words that rallied people to support the movement.

In the case of the Bloomer controversy, the ideology of the proponents employed such terms as freedom and slavery, life and death, health and illness, and Americanism. The ideology of the opponents used terms like un-American, seditious, radical, infidel, and immoral. A number of sermons were preached against the Bloomer. Books were written pro and con. All used glow words, words that would generate emotional responses in people. For example, an 1853 publication of a translation of a Jesuit's work on fashion was brought out because the translator had observed during his ministry that:

> many mothers commit serious faults in the immodest manner in which they dress their female children, following no other rule than the fashion set by persons devoid of the spirit of Christianity . . . it is to be hoped, that mothers and daughters . . . will, after a perusal of these pages, be more afraid of giving scandal than anxious to be dressed (or rather undressed) after the latest style imported from London or Paris.[71]

Those who defined themselves as devout Christians would not lightly shrug off such appeals.

Finally, the ideologies addressed the question of the so-called real-ideal gap. There are ideals in all societies that are only approximated by the reality of life in those societies. Many people accept the gap between the ideal and the real as an inevitable aspect of social life. In addition, they may label those who cannot accept it as fanatics. But others, particularly those who are victims of the gap, may develop an ideology which rejects the validity of such a gap.

Proponents of the Bloomer rejected the real-ideal gap. They argued that the American ideal of freedom had been kept from women, and that the gap between the ideal of freedom and the reality of life for women was intolerable. As one woman wrote in a letter to *Harper's:* "We are emancipating ourselves, among other badges of the slavery of feudalism, from the inconvenient dress of the European female. With man's functions, we have asserted our right to his garb, and especially to that part of it which invests the lower extremities."[72] Other kinds of gaps were also pointed out—the ideal of health versus the reality of a corseted woman's well-being, for example.

The opponents of the Bloomer, however, denied that a gap even existed. Their ideology did not acknowledge any such gap. Rather, they argued that women were not deprived, for it was their nature and their destiny to be subservient to men and to be guardians of home and family life. American women were not the victims of any real-ideal gap, on the contrary, women in America were most privileged. According to George Fitzhugh, American women should realize that subjection is their glory. If women abandoned their petticoats, he said, they would soon be condemned to the same hard labor as men. On the other hand, men worship women as long as the latter are "nervous, fickle, capricious, delicate, diffident and dependent." A woman's weakness is her strength, "and her true art is to cultivate and improve that weakness."[73]

According to the ideology of the opponents, then, an ideology that was shared by far more Americans than was that of the proponents, it is not a case of tolerating an inevitable gap. There simply is no gap. Those who adhere to an ideology that identifies a discontinuity between the ideal and the real, they argued, are blind to the true nature of things. The social order was not flawless, but it was far closer to the ideal than that being proposed by the radical advocates of the Bloomer.

A THEORY OF FASHION

Our case study of the Bloomer controversy has shown that meaning is a crucial element in understanding fashion. If we are to understand how people react to a particular fashion, we must know its meaning to them. Their perception may appear to outsiders to be irrational or somehow off-the-mark or counter-productive or whatever, but it is their perception that is crucial. Furthermore, the Bloomer incident showed that the meaning attributed to any proposed fashion is the outcome of an ideological evaluation. People use ideologies to: 1) understand the proposed fashion and to legitimate its adoption or rejection; 2) provide glow words necessary to motivate others to action; and 3) address the question of the real-ideal gap.

These considerations, along with the materials in previous chapters, have prepared us for a theory of fashion. Such a theory must address the question of the pattern of fashion changes or of why fashion changes in a particular direction. It is pointless, we believe, to ask why fashion changes at all. For it is the nature of human life and human societies to change. As the philosopher, Alfred North Whitehead, once said, our only two alternatives are advance or decay. The pure conservative, the person who wants reality to stay as it is, fights against the essence of the universe. Styles have changed throughout human history. The question is, why have they taken the particular directions that we have observed? Or to put the matter differently, why is one style, out of all of those which are possible, advocated and adopted as dominant?

Previous theories have had either social control or social change as a central theme.[74] Fashion has been viewed either as a mechanism of control or as a process of change. Both themes can be supported with empirical evidence. Blumer reconciled the apparent contradiction by arguing that both are intrinsic elements of fashion, which is "a very adept mechanism for enabling people to adjust in an orderly and unified way to a moving and changing world which is potentially full of anarchic possibilities."[75] In other words, fashion is a form of control in a changing society. Fashion prevents change from becoming chaos by identifying those new directions which are collectively defined as appropriate. If there are no guidelines, there will be chaos and people will suffer anxiety, as a number of popular writers have also pointed out.[76]

Blumer's basic insight is valid. We would extend his argument as follows: Essentially, fashion is a process of collective definition in which a particular alternative in a set of possibilities is selected as appropriate. All phenomena may vary or change in a number of different ways over time. A particular way is selected and becomes the fashion as the result of collective definition. The definition is the outcome of ideological evaluation.

Stated in these general terms, our theory of fashion is broadly applicable. It may be used to analyze fashion in literature or science or architecture as well as in dress and appearance. For dress and appearance, we would add, based upon the materials in previous chapters, that the ideological evaluation will be along two lines: whether the fashion is consistent with values and roles, and whether it is useful for reaffirming or establishing an individual's identity and/or status.

Thus, if a proposed style is defined as having a meaning that is congruent with existing ideology, the style is likely to become the fashion. Such a fashion will be defined as a variation of an accepted theme. Normally, cyclic variations fall into this category. For example, seasonal changes in the length of women's skirts are usually defined as variations on the theme of appropriate feminine attire. They may be disliked initially, but they are congruent with the ideology about the female role.

Some proposed styles may be defined as incongruent with the existing ideology. They will be resisted vigorously. If some group becomes an advocate of the change, there will be a clash of ideologies, a struggle to determine which ideology (and, thereby, which style) will prevail. For example, certain proposed female fashions have generated intense controversy because they were defined as immoral or as in some way inconsistent with the female role.

Does this mean that designers have no impact? No, for designers provide people with alternatives. Furthermore, we have noted that some designers agreed they can only give people what the people want. They tune in to the direction people are moving and provide styles that are consistent with that direction. We believe they are correct in their assessment. Successful designers must be sensitive to trends if they are to remain successful. Their designs must somehow intersect with the needs and interests of people.

Thus, we have incorporated or accommodated the insights expressed in the various theories discussed in the introduction. Each of those theories captures a valid aspect of the fashion process, but none fully explains fashion. As the Bloomer controversy shows, new styles do involve the search for meaning or identity (women searching for their "appropriate role"), the struggle for status (women versus men), and economic considerations (some pointed out the greater economy involved in the Bloomer). New styles do hinge upon who first adopts them (too many unsavory characters and feminists adopted the Bloomer). Erotic meanings are attached to clothes (some men found the Bloomer provocative). And styles must be consistent with the spirit of the times (the Bloomer seemed to violate the era's notions of the proper sphere of women). The insights we gain as we apply the various theories to the Bloomer controversy are all important. And that is the point. They are *all* important. Consequently, our theory, stressing possible alternatives, collective definition, and ideological evaluation along the lines of values, roles, and individual identity and/or status, accounts for all of the data.

CONCLUSION

If our analysis has given us a fuller understanding of the fashion process, it has not robbed the earthly goddess of her fascination. To explain is not necessarily to debunk. Like the scientist whose probings into the nature of the material world become a journey of endless wonder, our venture into the temple of the earthly goddess leaves us captivated. And as Thoreau once said, we may, like all generations, laugh at the fashions of the past, but we shall surely follow religiously the fashions of the present.

Notes

1. Gilbert Seldes, "Dress and Undress," *The Mentor* 17 (November, 1929): 15.
2. "The Ideas of a Plain Country Woman," *Ladies' Home Journal* 31 (August, 1914): 26.
3. *Life* 72 (April 14, 1972): 45. For an example from Africa, see Ali A. Mazrui, "Miniskirts and Political Puritanism," *Africa Report* 13 (October, 1968): 9–12.
4. George Bush and Perry London, "On the Disappearance of Knickers: Hypotheses for the Functional Analysis of the Psychology of Clothing," *The Journal of Social Psychology* 51 (1960): 359–66.
5. Karlyne Anspach, *The Why of Fashion* (Ames, Iowa: The Iowa State University Press, 1967), p. 329.
6. "Woman's Predicament," *Outlook* 153 (October 23, 1929): 300.
7. Marian Christy, "NOW: Feminism vs. Femininity," *St. Louis Post-Dispatch*, November 11, 1979.
8. Lee E. Graham, "From the Flapper to the Pin-Up," *The New York Times Magazine*, January 12, 1947, p. 21.

9. Joan Cassell, "Externalities of Change: Deference and Demeanor in Contemporary Feminism," *Human Organization* 33 (Spring, 1974): 85-94.
10. *Ibid.*, p. 87.
11. Helen Irene Warner, *A Case Study of Change in Dress as an Indicator of Social Change in the Amana Society,*" unpublished M. S. Thesis, Cornell University, September, 1967.
12. Charles Nordhoff, *The Communistic Societies of the United States* (New York: Schocken Books, 1965; first published 1875), pp. 34-35.
13. Fashion has been used as a tool of change in societies other than the United States, of course. See Hilda Kuper, "Costume and Identity," *Comparative Studies in Society and History* 15 (June, 1973): 366.
14. Constance Noyes Robertson, *Oneida Community: An Autobiography,* 1851-1876 (Syracuse, N.Y.: Syracuse University Press, 1970), p. 297.
15. Frances E. Russell, "A Brief Survey of the American Dress Reform Movements of the Past, with Views of Representative Women," *The Arena* 6 (August, 1892): 333.
16. See the Columbus *Daily Ohio State Journal,* May 16, 1851; *New York Tribune,* May 6, 1851; and *Missouri Republican,* June 18, 1851.
17. *New York Tribune,* September 19, 1851.
18. *Trumbell* (Ohio) *Whig,* reprinted in the *New York Tribune,* June 12, 1851.
19. (Little Rock) *Arkansas State Gazette and Democrat,* July 4, 1851; *Cleveland Plain Dealer,* June 11, 1851.
20. This was the assessment of the *Missouri Republican,* July 4, 1851, and our research revealed the same pattern.
21. See the *Bangor Whig and Courier,* May 30, 1851; *Baltimore Sun,* June 13, 1851; *Cleveland Plain Dealer,* June 11, 1851; *Lycoming* (Pa.) *Gazette,* reprinted in *New York Tribune,* May 27, 1851; *Missouri Republican,* June 18, 1851; *Watertown* (N.Y.) *Jeffersonian,* reprinted in *New York Tribune,* June 12, 1851.
22. See the *Baltimore Sun,* May 16, 1851; *Cleveland Plain Dealer,* July 14, 1851; *Lowell* (Mass.) *Courier,* June 20, 1851; *Missouri Republican,* June 30, 1851; *Ohio State Journal,* July 17, 1851; *Springfield Republican,* June 17, 1851; *New York Tribune,* July 18, 1851, August 26, 1851, and August 27, 1851.
23. D. C. Bloomer, *Life and Writings of Amelia Bloomer* (New York: Schocken Books, 1975; first published 1895), p. 78.
24. *Bangor Whig and Courier,* June 18, 1851.
25. *Boston Commonwealth,* reprinted in *New York Tribune,* June 12, 1851.
26. "Bloomer Costume Meeting," *The Practical Christian,* July 19, 1851. See also "Lecture on the Reform Dress," *The Modern Age* 7 (February, 1866): 124.
27. *Madison Press,* reprinted in *New York Tribune,* June 12, 1851.

Fashion, Ideology, and Change | 267

28. *Missouri Republican,* June 22, 1851.
29. *Springfield Republican,* June 12, 1851.
30. *Ohio State Journal,* June 21, 1851.
31. *Cleveland Plain Dealer,* June 3, 1851.
32. Quoted in Alice Felt Tyler, *Freedom's Ferment* (New York: Harper & Row, 1962), pp. 440–41.
33. "Why Do You Wear the Reform Dress?" *The Progressive Age* 6 (March, 1865): 86.
34. *Baltimore Sun,* June 18, 1851.
35. Quoted by the *Arkansas State Gazette and Democrat,* August 22, 1851.
36. *Arkansas State Gazette and Democrat,* July 4, 1851.
37. *Milwaukee Advertiser,* reprinted in *New York Tribune,* May 27, 1851.
38. Washington correspondent of the *Missouri Republican,* June 13, 1851.
39. Reported by the *New York Tribune,* June 12, 1851.
40. *Bangor Whig and Courier,* June 21, 1851.
41. *Springfield Republican,* June 5, 1851.
42. *New York Tribune,* June 26, 1851.
43. Quoted in M. Angeline Merritt, *Dress Reform Practically and Physiologically Considered* (Buffalo: Jewett, Thomas and Co., 1852), pp. 134–36.
44. See the *New York Tribune,* May 20, 1851 and November 8, 1851.
45. "O.S.J.," *Ohio State Journal,* June 28, 1851.
46. Mary E. Fry, "Let Us Have a National Costume," *The Ladies' Repository* 16 (December, 1856): 737.
47. Quoted in Charles Neilson Gattey, *The Bloomer Girls* (London: Femina Books Ltd., 1967), p. 112.
48. *Arkansas Gazette and Democrat,* September 5, 1851; *Belknap* (N.H.) *Gazette,* reprinted in *New York Tribune,* June 12, 1851.
49. This was reprinted in newspapers throughout the country. See, for example, *Cleveland Plain Dealer,* June 19, 1851.
50. *Cleveland Plain Dealer,* June 23, 1851.
51. *Springfield Republican,* June 16, 1851.
52. *Springfield Republican,* July 30, 1851.
53. *New York Times,* October 1, 1851.
54. Quoted in *Arkansas Gazette and Democrat,* July 11, 1851.
55. "J.W.H." to the *Ohio State Journal,* June 24, 1851.
56. *Buffalo Advertiser,* reprinted in *Missouri Republican,* July 4, 1851. Others contended that instead of "a la Turk" the Bloomers were "a la squaw"— introduced by the Sioux Indians. In either case, they were considered "un-American."
57. From the collection in the rare book room, Library of Congress.
58. *The Ladies' Wreath* 6 (September, 1851): 253.
59. *Graham's American Monthly Magazine* 39 (September, 1851): 206.

60. *St. Louis Intelligencer,* June 11, 1851.
61. *Ohio State Journal,* June 24, 1851.
62. *New York Tribune,* June 12, 1851.
63. *Cleveland Plain Dealer,* September 20, 1851.
64. "The Dress Reform," *Practical Christian* 16 (April 5, 1856): 1.
65. Mary P. Ryan, *Womanhood in America* (New York: Franklin Watts, Inc., 1975), p. 146.
66. *The Ladies' Repository* 10 (July, 1850): 220, and 12 (November, 1852): 440.
67. *The Ladies' Repository* 12 (June 3, 1852): 232.
68. Robert H. Lauer, *Perspectives on Social Change,* 2nd ed. (Boston: Allyn & Bacon, 1977), pp. 194–95.
69. *New York Times,* October 18, 1851.
70. Theodore Abel, "The Pattern of a Successful Political Movement," *American Sociological Review* 2 (June, 1937): 350.
71. Jean Baptiste Boone, S. J., *On Fashions* (Baltimore: Murphy & Co., 1853), pp. iii–iv.
72. T. E. Bang, "Woman's Emancipation," *Harper's New Monthly Magazine* 3 (August, 1851): 424.
73. George Fitzhugh, *Sociology for the South, or the Failure of Free Society* (Richmond: A Morris, 1854), p. 214.
74. R. T. Horowitz, "From Elite Fashion to Mass Fashion," *European Journal of Sociology* 16 (no. 2): 286–87.
75. Herbert Blumer, "Fashion: From Class Differentiation to Collective Selection," *The Sociological Quarterly* 10 (Summer, 1969): 290.
76. See Prudence Glynn, *In Fashion: Dress in the Twentieth Century* (New York: Oxford University Press, 1978), p. 85; "The New Fashion is Sans Fashion," *Business Week,* February 6, 1971, p. 25; Gloria Guinness, "Damn Those Young Girls," *Harper's Bazaar* 104 (December, 1971), p. 110.

Index

Accidents, relationship to fashion, 208–09
  hobble skirts, 208
  long scarves, 209
  mid-19th century styles, 208
America, development of fashion in, 189–96. *See also* entries under France, fashion denomination by, National identity
  before Revolution, 189
  early Republic, 190
  early 20th century, 191–92, 193
  flapper costume, 193
  hobble skirt, 192
  long skirts, in 1930s, 194
  New Look, 194–95
  19th century, 190
  in recent times, 195–96
  Revolutionary period, 189–90
  World War I, 193
  World War II, and fall of Paris, 194

Bloomer costume, case history, 246–59
  advantages, 248, 249, 250
  Bloomer, Mrs. Amelia, 247, 248–49
  "The Bloomer Costume," propaganda song, 256–57
  desexing effects of on women, supposed, 257–58
  early reformer, quoted, 246
  and eroticism of, supposed, 254
  and fears of women, 253
  and feminists, 255–56
  interest in, 248, 249, 250
  invention of, 247
  morals, supposed threat to, 254–55
  negative reactions to, 251, 252–53
  Nevin, Prof. William, quoted on, 257
  and patriotism, 249, 255–56
  Stanton, Elizabeth Cady, 250, 253–54
  and women's rights, fear of, 258–59

Change, fashion as tool of, 242–44
  Amana Society, 243–44
  Cassell, Joan, work of, 243
  lesbian-feminists, 243
  Nordhoff, Charles, quoted, 244
  symbolic inversion, 243
Clothing, gender of, 126–30
  discussion, 126
  Finck, Henry, quoted, 129
  Nixon, Pres. R. M., quoted, 130
  Thomas, Helen, quoted, 130
  trousers, example, 126–27, 128, 129–30
  utopian communities, 127–28
Clothing, as medium of communication, 34–36
  Clothing Speaks, 35
  in early 20th century U.S., 35
  Goffman, 34, 36
  Knapp, 34
  meanings of, regulation of in society, 36
  nonverbality of, nature, 34
  and status, 34
Clothing, purposes of, 33–34
  Haweis, Mrs, quoted on, 33
Conformity and clothing, 49–51
  Hamilton Jordan, example of, 51
  incident, in House of Representatives, 50
  occupational roles, 50
  as reassurance about others, 50
  rebellion vs. respectability, 50–51
Congruency, between gender and dress, 122–26
  flapper costume, 125–26
  hobble skirt, example, 124
  and modern feminism, 124
  19th century views on, 122
  petticoats, 124–25
  practicality of women's clothing, 123–24
  Stanton, Elizabeth Cady, quoted, 123
  and women, place of in home, 123
Corsets. *See* Health problems, and fashions
Culture, ideology of, 93–95
  Carey, Mathew, quoted, 95
  determinism, 93
  and metaphors of fashion, 95
  progress, faith in, 93–94
  in 20th century U.S., 94

Cycles, in fashion, 14–16
  and beards, in English men, 16
  skirts, types of, 15
  Reynolds and Darden, research of, 14
  in women's fashions, 14

Deviousness, metaphor for fashion, 92–93
  effects, 93
  Wilde, Oscar, quoted on, 93
Diffusion, as mechanism for spread of fashion, 12–14
  change agents, 13
  compatibility of, 13
  factors in, 12
  Grindering, work of, 13–14
  innovators, 13
  midi skirt, example of, 14
  Rogers, Everett, work of, 12–13
  and sales data in store, 13–14
  strata, social, spread in, 13, 14
  Tarde, Gabriel, 12
  and trickle down theory, 13
Divinity, metaphor for fashion, 82–85
  and Christianity, 84
  and comparison to religion, 83
  nature, 82–83
  in 19th century, 84
  and women, expense by on, 84–85
Double bind, on women, 130–31

Emulation, by fashion, 160–61
  and impression management, 161
  in middle class in Great Depression, 161
  in 19th century, 160
  and status degradation, 160
  Tarbell, Ida, quoted, 160–61
Eroticism, as factor in fashion, 16–18
  Bergler, Edmund, 17
  breasts, covering of, 16
  erogenous zone, shifting of, 16–17
  Kroeber, A. L., 14
  Laver, Jaems, 16, 19, 20
  and men's attention, securing of, 17
  Robinson, 16
  and seduction by women, 16
Ethnocentrism, 176–177
  in ancient times, 176
  and ethnic dress, 176
  Stewart, George, quoted on, 177

Fashion, calls for Americanization of, 177–79
  bloomers, 178
  in early 20th century, 177
  and harem skirt, example of, 178–79
  and supposed conflict with French, 178
Fashion, as coercion, 141–43
  corsets, 142
  and designers, 141
  hobble skirts, 142–43
  hoop skirts, 142
  19th century views on, 142
  pannier skirts, 143
Fashion, economics of, 10–12, 219–21
  and changes of fashion, effects of, 220
  and children, 220–21
  competition in for sales, 11
  and employment, 219
  expense on by rich, 221
  Gregory, Paul, views of, 11
  and novelty, premium on, 11, 12
  Robinson, Dwight, views of, 11–12
  Veblen, Theodore, 10
  and wives, display of, 10–11
  and work, impracticality of for, 10
Fashion, functional explanations for, 2–3
Fashion, in Muncie, Indiana, example in 1935, 1–2
Fashion, nature of, 73–74
  Gardner, Mrs. H. C., quoted on, 73
Fashion, as seal of role change, 240–42
  adolescent girls, example, 241–42
  and feminism, 242
  knickers, in small boys, 241
  nature, 240, 241
  and women's fashions, 240–41
Fashion, and sex roles, 110–11. See also Congruency, between gender and dress
  and appropriate dress, 110
  Crawley, Ernest, quoted, 110
  and gender, 110
Fashion, theory of, 262–64. See also Style
  as antidote to chaos, 262
  application of, 263
  bloomers, 264
  Blumer, quoted, 262–63
  and change, general, 262
  and ideologies, 262
  mechanisms, 262
  resistance to, 263

Fashion, theory of (continued)
  and style, 263
  Whitehead, Alfred North, quoted, 262
Fashion, theories of, critique, 20–23
  coerciveness of fashion, 22–23
  and links with social life, 22
  and fashion as process, 22
  part vs. whole, confusion of, 20–21
  partial failure of all theories, 21
  and sexuality, 21, 22
  trickle across, 21
  trickle up, 21
  types of, 20
  and zeitgeist, 21
Fashion, van Loon, quoted on, on its dissociation with social concerns, 2
Fashion, women's, supposed immorality of, 45–48
  bloomers, 45–46
  early satire about, 45
  in early 20th century U.S., 46–47
  false calves fad, 46
  loose wool shirts, case, 46
  in 1970s, 48
  Roman Catholic Church, reactions of, 47
  short skirts, 47
  slit skirts, 46
Female role, traditional, 107–10
  inferiority, alleged, 108
  and men, restraint of by, 109
  and morality, maintenance, of, 108, 109–10
  and motherhood, 109
  passivity, 107
  and vanity, 109
Force, metaphor for fashion, 75–77
  bangs, example, 76–77
  and conflict of style with self, 76
  defined, 75–76, 77
  Fox, George, quoted, 75
  prevailing style, effects of, 76–77
  as uglifying, 76
France, fashions of, American reactions against, 179–82
  and American vitality, alleged, 180, 181
  and attempts to motivate women, 181
  corruption, fears of, 181–82
  criticisms of, quoted, 179
  Fry, Mary, quoted, 181
  and group qualities, 181

France, fashion domination by, rebellion against, 185-89
  balance of trade, 186
  calls for American dominance, 186-87
  economic benefits, 186-87
  Paris, vulnerability of, 185-86
  patriotism, 187-89
  war hysteria, 188
  after World War II, 188-89

Group membership, and clothing, 59-61
  Amish, example of, 59
  and identification badges, 60
  recent political groups, 60
  and teenagers, 60-61

Hats, supposed hazards of, 206-07
  'Merry Widow' style, 206
  obstructions to vision by, 206, 207
Health problems, and fashions, 209-15
  corsets, compression of organs by, 210, 213, 214
  corsets, discarding of, 214
  corsets, tightness of, 211-12
  high heels, 214
  long skirts, sweeping of surfaces by, 210
  other examples, 214-15

Identity, search for in fashion, 3-6
  and clothes as establishing factor, 4
  conformity vs. self-expression, 3
  Goffman, views of, 4
  and individual types, 5
  Klapp, quoted, 3
  König, views of, 4
  Lakota Indian chief, quoted on, 5-6
  Reed, Julia, work of, 5
  role distance, nature of, 4-5
  and self-display, 4
  Simmel, quoted on, 3
  Stone, study by, 4
  and technical level of society, 3-4
  trickle down theory, 3
Ideology, connection with fashion, 244-46
  in Amana Society, 245
  and 'Bible communism,' 245
  Oneida community, 245

Ideology, and social change, 259-61
  Abel, Theodore, quoted, 260
  and Bloomer case, 259-60
  Fitzhugh, George, quoted, 261
  'glow words,' 260
  and real-ideal gap, 261
Immorality, and clothing, 42-45
  in early U.S., 43
  and female vanity, 42
  Hooper, Lucy, quoted, 43
  and male vanity, 42
  19th century propaganda about, 44
  Penn, William, views on, 43
  and prostitution, alleged link with fashion, 43
  and shoddy, 43
  small town, variety of norms in, 44-45
Impression management, 159-60
  Goffman, Erving, quoted on, 159
  nature, 159
  parts of, 159
  and success, desire for, 160
  used car salespeople, example, 159
Independence, calls for in American fashion, 182-85
  and corruption, fears of, 183
  and French domination, 182-83, 184
  Fry, Mary, quoted on, 183
  Russell, Frances, quoted, 183
Irrationality, metaphor for fashion, 85-91
  capriciousness of, 90
  coherence, desire for, 91
  disfiguring effects, 88
  efficient behavior, 89
  excessive clothing, effects of, 87-88
  Flower, Mrs., quoted on, 90
  'Folly,' verse about, 85-86
  grenadier caps, example, 86
  historic freaks in, 86
  nonutility, 86
  sleeve buttons, example, 86

King, Thomas Starr, quoted, 196

Lincoln, Abraham, quoted, 33
Lord Chesterfield, quoted, 165

Males, attitudes to fashion, 120-22
  and assumed causes of fashion, 120-21

Males, attitudes to fashion *(continued)*
  essential argument, 121–22
  Finck, Henry, quoted, 120, 121
  and women's attitudes to fashion, 121
Meaning and metaphor, relation to question of fashion, 74–75
  metaphor, defined, 74
  metaphors, use of, 74
  and types of imagery, 75
Mental health and fashion, 215–17
  and expense of fashion, 215
  and 'Out-of-Fashion Trauma Syndrome,' 215–16, 217
Morality and clothing, 41–42, 48–49
  enforcement of by fashion, 49
  and juvenile delinquents, behavior modification of, 49
  lust-shame theory, 41
  and nudity, views on, 41
  in nudist colonies, 41
  and repression, 41
  Seton, Dr. Ernest, 41
  1728 tract on, 41
  Shaw, George Bernard, quoted, 41
  and social order, 48
  Tertullian, on self-decoration, 42
  and the young, social control of, 48
Mystery, metaphor for fashion, 91–92
  contrast to irrationality, 91
  nature, 91
  and style, 92
  veils, disappearance of, 92

National identity, and shared beliefs, 173–76
  America as exemplar, Catherine Beecher quoted on, 174–75
  liberty, Henry Ward Beecher quoted on, 173
  progress, Curti quoted on, 174
  de Tocqueville, quoted on, 174
  vigilance, attitudes to, 175–76
  virtue, attitudes to, 174
National identity, struggle for, 172–73
  in colonies, 172
  and Federal system, Rufus Choate quoted on, 173
  in Revolutionary period, 172–73
Nonconformists. *See* Social norms, and fashion

Personal development, and fashion, 221–28
  beauty, proclamation of, 225–28
  Dache, Lilly, views of, 224
  and fashion as impediment, 222
  and fashion as waste of time, 223
  Gould, Margaret, views of, 226
  and infants, 221–22
  and men, 226–27
  nurse, experience of, 224–25
  Oliphant, Mrs., views of, 225
  outfits, to convey messages, 224
  self-presentation with, 223–25
  women, manipulation of appearance by, 225–26
  and work ethic, 222
Personal hygiene, and clothing, 202–03
  and cotton, supply of, 202
  and dress reform in 19th century, 203
Personality, and clothing, 36–40
  conclusions of others, early views on, 39
  Godey's Lady's Book and Magazine, 35, 39
  men, reactions of to women's clothing, 39–40
  neatness, 1879 editorial on, 37
  nun, experience of, 40
  and practicality, concerns about, 38
  and security, feelings of, 38
  shirt, 'clean' message of, 38
  and social meanings, 39
  sloppiness, 1827 view of, 37
  sloppiness, 1936 view of, 37
  women, in 1920s, 40
  women's dresses, views on in 19th century, 37–38
Protection, as function of clothing, 204–06
  and body heat, 204
  and flapper styles, 205
  and 19th century styles, 204
  tuberculosis, incidence of, 204, 205

Reason, perceived conflict of with fashion, 111–15
  Erewhon, Butler, 111
  and gender, 111, 112, 114
  and male vanity, 114
  Russell, Frances, 113
  Ward, Nathaniel, quoted, 112

Reason *(continued)*
  and women's response to fashion, 112, 113
  in World War I, 113
Royalty, metaphor for fashion, 81–82
  'Queen' image, 82

Self-esteem, 228–31
  Cardin, Pierre, quoted, 228
  in children, 228
  in college text, 230–31
  and fashion therapy, 230
  Hart, Moss, experience of, 229–30
  Langner, Lawrence, quoted, 228
  nature, 228
  and self-confidence, 229
  and youth, feelings of, 229
Sex effects on personal nature, 106–07
  gender vs. role, 106–07
  and male chauvinism, 106
  Mead, Margaret, research of, 106
  in New Guinean tribes, 106
  Plato, 106
  tendencies, inherent, 107
Social desirability, and clothing, 51–56
  asking for help, effects of clothing on response, 53
  corporate executives, reactions of to clothing, 55
  dress codes in offices, experiment, 55–56
  and fashion, effects of, 51–52
  Fassett, J. Sloan, political campaign of, 52
  and hiring of employees, 54–55
  Rubin, Lillian, experience of, 53
  in schools, 53, 56
  status degradation, 52–53
  wives of candidates, dresses of, 52
  young executives, work of John Molloy on, 55
Social norms, and fashion, 137–40
  crinoline skirts, example, 138
  harassment of nonconformists, 138–39
  laws, 139–40
  nonconformist, effects on, 137–38
  rebukes to nonconformists, 138
  and religious pressure, 139
  and smaller groups, conformity to, 137
  and women's clothes, 139

Society vs. individual, 140–41
  Durkheim, Emile, views of, 140
  and fashion as coercive force, 140
  Freud, Sigmund, views of, 140
  tradeoff question, 140
Society, nature of, 136–37
  and individuals, Durkheim quoted on, 136
  Zimbardo, Philip, work of with simulated prison, 136–37
State of the nation, and clothing, 61–64
  and cultural trends, supposed effects of, 63–64
  and democracy, 62
  and early 20th century opinions, 61–62
  and female dress, 61
  and individualism, 62
Status, 151–53
  age-appropriate attire, 19th century guide on, 152, 153
  in hospital, clothing as marker of, 152
  jelly bean game, model of, 151
  and old age, 152
  Vanderbilt, Amy, quoted on, 153
  as zero-sum game, 151–52
Status, clothing as indicator, 56–59
  in ancient times, 56
  in early U.S., 57
  and modern technology, 58
  raincoat color, example, 58
  in recent times, 59
  and women, classes of, 57–58
Status, struggle for, and fashion, 6–10
  Barber, Bernard, views of, 8
  in blacks, 8–9
  bra-burning incidents, true meaning of, 9–10
  Cobliner, work of, 8
  in college girls, 8
  conspicuous consumption, 8
  and display of status, 6
  Flugel, J. C. quoted on, 6, 7
  Hoult, work of, 10
  as imitation, 7
  and imitation by lower classes, 7
  Morrison and Holden, work of, 9–10
  Schwartz, work of, 8
  Spencer, views of, 7
  strangers, clothing of, 10
  and timing, in diffusion of style through class, 8

Style, contrasted with fashion, 23–24
defined, 23
Erwin and Kitchen, definition of fashion of, 23
and human behavior, 24
Pucci, Emilio, quoted, 23
Submissiveness, female life of, 115–17
Bennett, Arnold, 117
contrast to men, 116–17
and fashion's demands, 115
and feminists, 116
Finck, Henry, quoted, 116
Miller, Elizabeth, 116
scope, of, 116
and summer wear, 117
as voluntary, 115–16
Success, display of, 163–64
children, dress of, 164
sportswear, 164
Success, dressing for, 162–63
female physician, experience of, 163
in modern times, 163
Sears Roebuck catalog, 162
1772 tract on, 162
and women, 162
Sumner, William Graham, quoted, 141

Trousers. *See* Bloomer costume; Zeitgeist, and fashion
Tyranny, metaphor for fashion, 77–81
Bennett, Arnold, quoted on, 79
and fashionable as slaves, 78–79
Flower, Mrs. B. O., quoted, 78, 81
men, 79, 80
nature of, 78
negative effects of, 80–81
Parsons, Frank, quoted, 78
Poiret, Paul, quoted, 78
Pope, Alexander, quoted, 80
Russell, Frances, quoted, 80
Sister Slaves, 79
top hats, 80

Uncle Sam, as symbol, 171–72
Unhealthy behavior, and fashion, 209
dieting, 209
waistlines, 209

Well-being, and fashion, 217–19
and fashion as therapy, 218
in mind of wearer, 217–18
Women, as ornamental sex, 117–20. *See also* Female role, traditional
alleged artistic capacity of, 117–18, 119
need to attract male, 119
need for self-adornment, 119–20
Women, rebellion against fashion, 143–51
and consumer acceptance, limits of, 150
Dior, Christian, 148, 149
early 20th century views on, 144
and feminism, 143–44
flapper era, 145–46, 147
hemlines, 148
midi skirts, 149–50
New Look, 148–49
rugged individualism, 151
veils, rejection of, 147
Women, repression of by clothing, 153–59
and blue-collar workers, 153–54
clothing, impracticality of, 155–56
and definition of beauty, 157
Fitzhugh, George, quoted, 158
Langner, Lawrence, 156
and male dominance, 156, 157
men, awareness of dominance in, 157–58
motion, restriction of by clothes, 156
Russell, Frances, quoted or claims to equality, 155
World War I, effects of, 158–59

Zeitgeist, and fashion, 18–20
Clerget, 18
dress, effect on with time, 20
and European costume in Chinese Republic, 18
knickers, example, 19
and other arts, 19
trousers, as break with ancient world, 18
zeitgeist as framework, Laver quoted on, 19